LIFE LINES

DON CUPITT

LIFE LINES

SCM PRESS LTD

British Library Cataloguing in Publication Data

Cupitt, Don
    Life lines.
    1. Theology
    I. Title
    230   BR118

    ISBN 0–334–00901–4.

First published 1986
by SCM Press Ltd
26–30 Tottenham Road, London N1

Photoset by Input Typesetting Ltd, London
and printed in Great Britain by
Billing & Sons Ltd, Worcester

Contents

	Prologue	1
1	Genesis	15
2	Mythical Realism	26
3	Doctrinal Realism	34
4	Metaphysical Realism: The Ladder	43
5	Designer Realism	54
6	Obedientiary Realism	69
7	Protestant Ethical Idealism	81
8	Objective Symbolism	92
9	The Crisis	105
10	Aesthetic Expressivism	115
11	Pure Religious Voluntarism	128
12	Militant Religious Humanism	140
13	Slipping Away	153
14	Subversion	165
15	Life Everlasting	178
16	Good Night	192
	Epilogue: The Philosophies of the Religious Life	202
	Glossary and Definitions	215
	Notes	225
	Index of Names	230

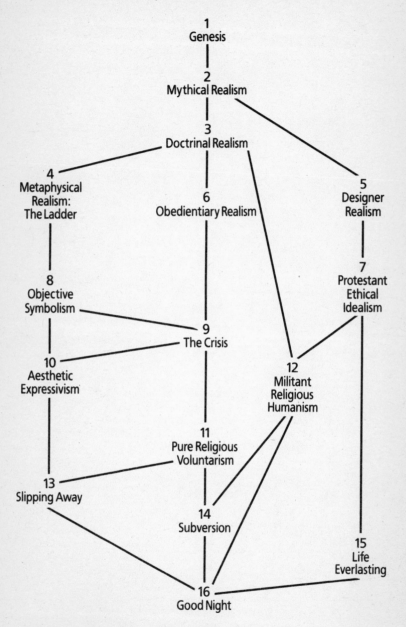

The principal stations and routes of modern and postmodern forms and philosophies of the religious life.

Prologue

Philosophers have written a good deal lately about ethics and the philosophy of life, but it has to be said that among the general public the old questions about the purpose of it all, the meaning of life and human destiny, have fallen into considerable disrepute. In the last generation of Modernism, the age of Camus and Sartre, the questions were still being taken seriously. Admittedly, the answers given were bleak, but at least they were answers to what were still seen as being real questions, and indeed the most important questions of all; whereas in our own increasingly postmodern times the questions themselves seem to have lost so much weight that they are greeted with ridicule. One bright spark has made a fortune by suggesting that the Answer to the Ultimate Question of Life, the Universe and Everything is 42. Just that: 42. The answer mocks the question, and if we want to know why, then we should ask ourselves what could in fact have counted for us as being a satisfactory answer. We soon realize that we already know all the answers: they have been given long ago, and they have all become clichés.[1] We wonder how people could ever have thought them deep.

The post-modern age is a Silver Age, a time when people are so knowing that they are convinced that all possibilities are already exhausted. They have heard it all before. It is a museum and university culture, a culture of commentary in which everything we can produce is secondary, derived, ironical and indirect, and nothing remains that is new, deep, primal and direct. The commentary, and the mockery of seriousness, may take many forms, gentle, teasing, malicious, ribald, boisterous, surreal or black, but always the effect is to eliminate depth. Reality becomes a beginningless, endless, shimmering interplay of signs on a flat surface. A temper of mind appears which is as uncomprehending of the seriousness of old-time atheism as it is of old-time faith.

Although I shall therefore be compelled to assert that it has an ironical and fictional character, this book is nevertheless undeniably some kind of solemn work on the meaning of life. It is based on the presumption that even post-moderns may at times succumb to deep thoughts, and feel the need to frame a view of life and a policy for life. They want to know how to live, what sort of sense may be made of life and what lessons can be learnt from it; and I am supposing that these questions may still be asked even after the old ultimates have been dispersed or de-centred. Thus, even if the self has now been deconstructed, it is still my past life that I remember and not yours. Morality, after its full secularization, can no longer be assumed to be unitary, superhuman and objective. But even though morality now looks more improvised, fragmentary and changeable than it did, moral questions remain as practically urgent as ever. The idea of God is no longer as clear and unquestionable as it once seemed to many people to be; but the various spiritual values, goals or ideals that it so powerfully unified remain available to us as options for guiding our lives.

Because of these various changes, then, religion has become something rather different from what it was. It is less centred and unidirectional, more human and pluralistic. The change is obviously comparable with the social change from absolute monarchy to democracy. In a monarchy sovereignty is centred, in a democracy it is dispersed: but although in a democracy sovereignty is more dispersed and politics more pluralistic, nevertheless there still is sovereignty and there still is political life. The de-centring of sovereignty does not mean its abolition: and so it is with religion.

So if, undeterred by all the mockery, you remain one of those who persist in thinking that the old questions about the meaning of life, however badly framed they were, had something important behind them, then the answer offered here is that there is indeed such a thing as the religious life, that it has a variety of different possible shapes or courses, and that there is something important to be learnt from a consideration of the map of life as a whole.

There is not just one linear track running through three or four stations, as used to be thought in the past, but there are at any rate a large number of stations and a web of lines connecting them. I have set them out (in a necessarily simplified form) after the Contents page as a kind of Metro map of the spirit. The idea is that after the book has explained the map, you may be able to find on it the life-route you have yourself followed so far.

The adjective 'religious' which we have already used does not imply any narrowing of concern, and we are traversing as broad a territory as that traversed by philosophers like Hegel or Nietzsche. The religious life is not just one distinct and specialized region that can be defined in a single theological system and rationalized in just one philosophy of religion. In fact, most of the theology and philosophy of religion so far written is unsatisfactory, because it is insufficiently pluralistic. The religious life is not one, but the whole range of possible forms of consciousness and ways of life, where each is lived with a certain depth of commitment, and brought into representation – articulated and made aware of itself – through a certain stock of symbols and practices. Religious language is so extraordinarily flexible that through it the whole of our growing and developing sense of ourselves and our life can come forth into representation, stage after stage. It does not fix us in one system, but precipitates us into a process, a course of personal growth. Its very flexibility and the stresses to which it subjects us generate continual spiritual movement. So, live with as much commitment to life as you can, broadly within the framework of our Western and Christian tradition, and you will find yourself passing along a route shown somewhere on the map. And the route you take as a whole is the meaning of your life.

I said, 'the Western and Christian tradition', and that does imply a certain limitation. Unfortunately, it seems that we are not quite ready yet to attempt a fully global Metro map of the spirit. We do not yet have a sufficiently deep inside knowledge of all the varied possibilities that are available, for example, within Buddhism. When we have explored them more fully, we will probably be in a position to extend the map substantially. Meanwhile there is much to be discovered, rediscovered and assembled within the Western tradition.

Each station on the map or stage in the religious life represents a more or less coherent and autonomous religious philosophy and policy for life that we may perhaps remain in for a lengthy period. Hegel's dialectical method would require us to examine each station in detail and show how it runs into contradictions or strains that eventually force a movement to the next point along the line. However, this is the post-modern age, and we cannot do that. We argue in and around each position, but we cannot pretend that there is some built-in arrow of logical necessity that forces the movement to go in one direction rather than another. My lines indicate only common or probable routes, and I am not pretending to legislate. We have to avoid (or at least, attempt to avoid) any suggestion of coercing the reader to run along one track rather than another.

This book therefore differs from most earlier ones like it – with the distinguished exception of that by William James – in being less prescriptive and unilinear than they were. However, before we can begin we need to place what we are doing in its historical context by saying something about the traditional conception of the philosophy of the religious life, about why it was lost, and how it can now be restored in this somewhat different form.

In the Western tradition the classical scheme of stages of the spiritual life was laid down by Plato in the *Republic*, the *Symposium* and elsewhere. It underwent various transformations, but proved very durable and continued to serve as the basis for Christian mysticism until the seventeenth century. Plato's metaphor of an ascent or journey through a series of stages remained popular. Thus Bonaventure (1221–1274) wrote an *Itinerarium Mentis ad Deum*, John of the Cross (1542–1591) described *The Ascent of Mount Carmel*, and Bellarmine (1542–1621), Galileo's Jesuit friend, produced his *De Ascensione Mentis in Deum;* and whatever their differences in detail they were all describing what was essentially the same journey and all shared deep assumptions ultimately traceable to Plato.

Just these assumptions, however, separate them decisively from us. Andrew Louth makes the point well in his book on *The Origins of the Christian Mystical Tradition*, when he discusses the meaning of the Greek word *nous*, the equivalent of the Latin *mens* in the book-titles mentioned in the last paragraph. *Nous* is commonly translated 'mind' or 'intellect', but the notions of mind and thought were quite different in the old tradition from what they are today:

The most fundamental reason for this is a cultural one: the Greeks were pre-Cartesian, we are all post-Cartesian. We say, 'I think, therefore I am', that is, thinking is an *activity* I engage in and there must therefore be an 'I' to engage in it: the Greeks would say, 'I think, therefore there is that which I think – *to noeta*'. What I think is something going on in my head; what the Greek thinks, *to noeta*, are the objects of thought that (for example, for Plato) exist in a higher, more real world.[3]

The older tradition was intensely realistic, in a way that we cannot now recapture. If there was knowledge, then there was an object known; if there was understanding, then there were real intelligible essences out there which were being understood. The very notion of mind or intellect was highly intentional or object-centred; so much so that philosophy typically did not start from thought or mind and then try to work its way towards Being, but started with Being. You began with Being – and Being made itself understood by you. As Aristotle puts it, only in God is there fully autonomous thinking. For the rest of us thought is not autonomous, but rather is evoked by its object. Human thought was not separated from Being, because to be thinking at all was already to be participating in the universal intelligibility of Being in all beings, the immanent Logos.

Of course other philosophical traditions were known to exist, and of course the mystics spoke much of symbolism falling away, of a journey into unknowing, and of the divine darkness and silence. Such language may at first seem to bring them close to us; but it does not bring them anything like so close as we might think. For even while they invoked the metaphors of darkness and silence, they did so against the background of a realistic metaphysical conviction (Being comes first, thought is necessarily a response to Being) that we have lost. Their darkness was created by an excess of dazzling light, but ours is real darkness. For them there was necessarily something Real there, even though because it was infinite and simple it presented nothing that the finite mind could grasp. So it dazzled, and you had simply to rest in it without understanding, in wordless love. But it was certainly *there*: whereas for us this is no longer the case.

In that older tradition reason did not just *happen* to possess the capacity to pierce the veil of sense and reach towards the underlying eternal Reality. On the contrary, that was the way it necessarily worked. If we had reason, then its proper and highest Object was necessarily real. In complete contrast, René Descartes introduced a new way of thinking in which the individual human mind was to become increasingly conscious of itself as an autonomous centre of constructive thinking activity, like Aristotle's God. It is fully present to itself and thinks itself before it knows of any independent reality to think about. It has to generate its own objects of knowledge by pure thought, perhaps also utilizing the materials given in sense-experience. And because knowledge is now seen as being not object-centred but subject-centred, it needs to be justified. The intelligibility of Being and the adequacy of knowledge to its object can no longer be taken as axiomatic; they wait to be proved. Philosophy no longer starts from ontology, the doctrine of objective Being, but from epistemology, the doctrine of knowledge, how we construct it and how we are to justify it. That our knowledge is *of* something cannot be assumed, but needs to be established.

More recently, there have been moves to displace the individual human mind and the theory of knowledge and instead centre philosophy upon language and the social production of both knowledge and reality. But this second revolution only pushes the older tradition still further back into the past. And whether philosophy begins with the subject and knowledge, or in the newer manner with language and society, or in the latest postmodern style with just communication, all these starting-points are by the older standards atheistic because they no longer begin with objective absolute Being.

One post-Cartesian thinker, Baruch Spinoza, did produce a philosophy which was still cast in the old style of an ascent of the soul towards absolute Being, while yet being thoroughly revised to take account of the new naturalistic and critical ways of thinking. This, however, was very exceptional. In Descartes himself, and in such more typical post-Cartesians as the British empiricists, what we find is that philosophy's new starting-point has eliminated the old conception of the religious life. Philosophy is no longer a way of life in the old sense at all, but has become simply an attempt to vindicate the objectivity of human knowledge. Enthralled by the success of the new natural philosophy, the post-Cartesians made the scientific views of the world, of knowledge and of the observer central to their new metaphysics. The world was a machine, a great system of inert material bodies moving about in space and time according to the mathematical laws that govern all motion, and manifesting themselves to us through our sense-experience. The self was somehow distinct from this mechanical universe. It was an ideal observer of its own experience and a constructor of theories. Its aim was to build an accurate inner model or map that would replicate the structure of the external world. The chief task of the spiritual life was therefore now merely to create a good copy in the thought-world of what was out there in the physical world.

The consequence of this was that for the Enlightenment the knowledge through which human beings would gain liberation was of a quite new character. A secular and epistemological ambition had replaced the old religious and ontological quest. In the old scheme philosophy *was* the spiritual life. Commitment to philosophy committed you to passing through a series of spiritual transformations on your way to the absolute knowledge of and union with absolute Being for which you had been created. But in the new scheme all this had been replaced by the expansion of scientific knowledge, seen as the construction in thought of a mathematically exact representation of the way things are in nature. The human person had in the process become a mere spectator of the world, of his own experience, and even of his own life as a body moving in the world of bodies. The old idea of the spiritual life had become unthinkable – and it was accordingly lost. The philosophy of life ceased to exist as a topic.

The new model of the self was decidedly odd, for surely we do not merely observe our lives, but lead them; and the actual living of life must surely be prior to whatever capacity we have for stepping back and watching ourselves do it. Nevertheless, the picture of the human subject as a disengaged observer of his or her own experience seemed to be the best model to work with so long as the hegemony of classical physics lasted, and so long as the chief task of philosophy was to explain and justify scientific knowledge.

However, as many thinkers have complained, the dominance of natural science and of empirical, factual knowledge had catastrophic effects on the way the other great areas of human concern were treated. Since science had now become the paradigm case of well-founded knowledge, the other areas were all looked at and assessed from the standpoint of science. Thus religion came to be seen not as a way of life, but as a putative knowledge-system which either did or did not correctly represent the natural and supernatural facts it claimed to describe. The dynamics of the religious life were forgotten. Similarly, morality became a matter of holding and acting upon a system of true moral beliefs, the chief question being whether there are or are not objective things (like a moral order, or moral standards, relations or essences) such as might justify our moral convictions. Even art had to copy nature, and the first question in the philosophy of art was whether things like beauty were subjective and existed only in the eye of the beholder, or were genuinely objective.

There was therefore a strong tendency to push morality and religion on to the defensive by challenging them to decide whether they did or did not claim to meet the scientific criteria for knowledge. If they *did*, then you ended with utilitarianism in ethics and Designer-Realism (station 5, on the map) in religion. Both of these are open to criticism, but if the other option was taken and it was said that morality and religion do *not* claim to deliver scientific-type knowledge, then people felt bound to conclude that our beliefs in these areas are mere groundless resolutions of the will, or expressions of feeling. In British terms, this result is prescriptivism or emotivism; in Continental terms, some form of existentialism or moral nihilism. And all these outcomes for the philosophy of religion and morality are rightly felt to be disappointingly reductive.

We have been airing ideas that are rooted in eighteenth-century thought but which are still alive, at least in the English-speaking world. I have suggested that we got into this mess because of the long dominance of conceptions of the self, knowledge and the world that go back to Descartes. He developed these conceptions as part of his apologia for science. The self was distanced from physical nature and made into a pure observer of the world, its own experience and even itself. Knowledge was the building in thought of a replica of the external physical world. Truth lay in the accuracy of the copying. Belief had to have an objective counterpart independent of consciousness, if it was to be worth anything. And this whole complex of ideas left no room for the classical conception of the task of philosophy, which had asked what it is to lead a life, and what it is to gain blessedness or wisdom at the end of the course of one's life.

When the older philosophy of the spiritual life was lost, the tendency in both morality and religion was, then, to replace the concrete process of life with some kind of theoretical system. Thus, eighteenth-century moral philosophy cherished the idea that just as Newton had (more or less) explained all events in the physical world in terms of a small set of definitions and laws, so everything in the moral world might correspondingly come to be explained in terms of a small set of self-evident and interconnected principles. There were a number of such systems on the market, and no single one of them could claim any special privileged status for itself. Any of them might turn out to fail; and in practice all of them did.

In the case of religion, a formidable doctrinal orthodoxy which did claim a privileged status was already in place. It was not altogether unhappy about the decline of the older conception of the religious life, because it had long eyed the mystics with some suspicion. Their spiritual mobility always tended to relativize any particular doctrinal system, so that they were liable to be seen as subversives who undermined ecclesiastical authority. The power-structure always felt more secure if it could succeed in fixating the soul in passive obedience, and so inhibit the proper development of the religious life. It seldom hesitated to persecute its own mystics, saints and thinkers. The mystics, for their part, had done what they could to avert hostility. Rather as even the most subversive writers once sought the protection of aristocratic patronage in dedicating their books, so spiritual writers used to preface their works with a disclaimer in which they loyally submitted everything they said to the judgment of the church. By this device they hoped to shield themselves against attack; but often they hoped in vain. Frankly, the church suspected the religious life, and was secretly glad to see it banished in the post-Cartesian generations. It was a threat. Static and authoritarian religion is much easier to teach and to enforce.

The revival of interest in the idea of a developing spiritual life therefore stems not from the church but from the Romantic Movement, and in particular from two slightly-heterodox Lutheran laymen, Hegel and Kierkegaard. Hegel's profound insight into the history of Western philosophy enabled him to grasp and to demonstrate the idea of a long unfolding series of distinct and historically-conditioned forms of consciousness, or ways of constructing oneself and one's world view. He thus introduced an historical dimension that the older conception of the spiritual journey had lacked, with an accompanying suggestion that the individual in his or her own development must recapitulate the thought-history of the race. It is a powerful idea, and will play some part in this present work because (as I should openly confess) the spiritual task of any English-speaking person at the time of writing is so largely the task of getting his own thinking up-to-date and learning to live truthfully in his own time. As for Kierkegaard, he also used the idea of a progressive movement through a series of autonomous and coherent world-views. But he made a rather more restricted use of it in the service of his apologia for Christianity, working it out with great brilliance and showing in detail what it is for an individual to be converted from one form of consciousness and way of life to another.

So far, so good. However, both thinkers arranged the various stages that they recognized along single ascending linear scales in the traditional Platonic manner, trying to show that there is just one arrow and it points ever upwards. Hegel's historicizing and dialectical version of the standard Enlightenment ideology led him to postulate our ultimate liberation by the attainment of absolute knowledge, which consisted in an astounding and highly optimistic totalizing vision of the ultimate unification of every aspect of thought and reality. Kierkegaard more modestly set an existentialist and privatized version of Lutheran Christian faith at the summit of his scheme. As a result they are now both somewhat dated, not only because they were not to know how greatly Marx, Darwin, Nietzsche, Freud and others were subsequently to reshape the intellectual landscape, but also because by later standards they were not fully self-critical. They were too keen to pass off their personal visions as universal truths, and too heavy-handed in drawing their arrows. For some time past we have lived in a fully post-modern era in which every legitimating myth of progress – whether the Enlightenment one, or Hegel's, or Marx's, or even that of the artistic *avant-garde* – has broken down. These myths have broken down in the usual 'demythologizing' way, by being at last recognized as just human fictions. No such legitimating myth has a privileged status, or is in any way objectively guaranteed and compulsory. On the contrary, it is always surrounded by other options with which it is in conversation; and it needs to be so, for every totalizing vision that seeks to bring all of human reality under the dominion of a single system of thought must if it prevails be, precisely, totalitarian. Both Hegel and Kierkegaard were right to see that an interesting philosophy of life needs to be edifying rather than descriptive. It must open new possibilities of spiritual life and growth. But if it is unilinear with a heavy arrow, then it will look like an attempt to coerce. Our problem in post-modern times is to be edifying without that paranoiac urge to totalize, to bully, and to produce a dominating system. A Metro map with many stations and routes, and no dominating arrow, is part of the answer; but we also need to acknowledge the inevitably historically-conditioned and artificial character of every Metro map, including our own.

The scheme I present is therefore a fiction and a hybrid concoction, its sources being partly traditional, partly autobiographical, partly derived from the history of ideas, and in part no doubt persuasive, angled and polemical. Inevitably, it involves a good many value-judgments. For example, I have been unable to assign special stations on the map to the many semi-realist theologies that are being promoted in the academic world today. Often they shelter under the authority of a well-known philosopher such as Hegel, Whitehead, Heidegger or Maréchal, though usually they do him some violence in their interpretation of him. My problem, however, is that I have not been able to see any of them as expressing a new distinct and substantial spirituality fit to be ranked with those that have got on to the map. They seem best regarded as attempts to provide a rationale for something else that is already on the map, such as Objective Symbolism (8) or Protestant Ethical Idealism (7). For similar reasons I have not found separate places for charismatic and evangelical forms of belief. Although large-scale and undoubtedly of great interest to social psychologists, these movements are from our point of view merely variant (and, given the state of the objective culture in which they are found, encapsulated) forms of Mythical Realism (2) and Doctrinal Realism (3). They are not of sufficient interest to merit separate investigation, whereas in Subversion (14) we examine a spirituality which is highly interesting, even though there may not be one person alive who has the qualities needed to be an exponent of it. Call me perverse if you like, but my criteria are not statistical. They are qualitative.

The use of qualitative criteria and a broadly postmodern point of view accounts for the fact that after station (9) even the most attenuated forms of objective theism are left behind. Morality still goes on and justice still matters to us, after we have ceased to think of Justice as being 'literally' a blindfolded woman with a pair of scales and a sword, and even after we have ceased to think (in Platonic fashion) of Justice as an objective metaphysical essence; and the same is true of religion and belief in God. To some this is obvious; to others it remains a scandal. In our scheme we stress the importance of the Crisis (9), because only after it can the religious possibilities of the present time be at last seen clearly. For a religious writer today addresses, and is himself a member of, a generation of people who have been described as 'orphans, atheists and nomads': 'orphans', because we have broken away from the patriarchal, hierarchizing and oedipalizing forms of the past; 'atheists', in the sense that we have no old-style realistic beliefs at all, for everything of that kind is simply gone; and 'nomads', in the sense that we cannot now be bound in quite the old way to any particular territory and its customs. On the contrary, we are transgressors, who are impelled to violate frontiers. To persuade such a generation of people that religion has any place at all in their lives is not easy. We try to do it by showing that the movement of the religious life is the movement of life itself, expressed in symbolic representation; but we must neither underestimate the difficulties nor claim too much. We cannot pretend to compel, but only to offer an imaginative fiction which may or may not succeed in making religion a live option again.

In order to present and argue our way around a range of possibilities we shall need from now on to be somewhat masked. This is not easy to accept; but the movement away from Anglo-Saxon philosophy to a more Continental and post-modern idiom requires a move away from direct communication, whether of the scientific or the confessional type, to a more indirect style. This will enable the sheer variety of options now available to us to stand out more clearly, and the series of personal stations I have described in recent books will therefore not figure as such in the account we are to give. Pursuing consistency, I have 'decentred' and dispersed my own views.

So the religious life is here presented as a complex movement on several fronts through a whole series of distinct religious philosophies, different self-understandings, life-views and life-policies, and different conceptions of the very nature of religion and religious belief. The series moves (roughly) from birth to death, and the three main tracks (very roughly) correspond to the Catholic and mystical, the orthodox Protestant and existentialist, and the liberal Protestant and ethical strands in the Christian tradition. We begin with a primal condition of thought in which our attempt to establish a primitive metaphysics is intertwined with innocently egoistic fantasies. (Do we ever really get beyond this?) Next, five forms of theological realism are distinguished, followed by two of semi-realism. In the past few years we have become much more refined in our perception of the nuances here, and the distinctions could have been much further elaborated. Indeed, every major theology now seems to incorporate a distinctive standpoint on the realism/anti-realism issue; but it has here been necessary to confine this account to the principal options.

The transition to non-realism belongs historically to the great period of theological crisis (1780–1845). For many, it is still a personal Crisis (9); but not for all. Then we move to the various possible modern and post-modern forms of Christian existence. Because the objective culture (Georg Simmel's term, by the way) has been secular and non-religious since the period of the theological crisis and the French Revolution, all these newer forms of religious existence are in varying degrees either world-combatting or world-renouncing. Only at the very end do we glimpse new possibilities of acceptance and affirmation.

There is a complication. The various spiritualities here described are a procession of ideal types, rather more self-consistent than actual people are. Observation suggests that nowadays many people are anthologists who gather a personal collection of themes drawn from several of the types here described. In Mythical Realism (2) we briefly indicate why this procedure, although seemingly inconsistent, may in practice turn out to work very well.

Although it is more complicated than older schemes, our map still broadly follows the traditional Way of Purgation, seen now as a long process of demythologizing. Reflection and our life-experience progressively deprive us of our illusions, and our outlook becomes less mythical and more ethical. The first result of this is the peak of the active life in our long middle years, during which faith is seen as commitment to an action-guiding symbol-system. Our self-expression through this system enables us to invest our life with meaning, affirm it to the full and strive to realize religious values in, or in spite of, the world. The process of purgation continues, however, mercifully and relentlessly, and eventually leads us from the active life to the contemplative. If we have assimilated its teaching, then we can call the night good. The whole scheme is one of progressive gain by progressive loss, and truth lies not in any single position held but in the movement as a whole.

1

GENESIS

In the past the religious quest has sometimes been motivated by a desire to achieve mastery over oneself by breaking one's own rebellious will. The self became like the Laocöon sculpture, and in the confusion of the struggle it was hard to make out who was trying to defeat whom, and who was being the more injured by the two-edged weapons used. This intropunitive ascetical psychology is even yet not extinct, but we differ from people of earlier periods in that for us its true character has been exposed and we are obliged to recognize it as pathological. Many traditional ascetical practices have therefore been discredited, and the religious quest now takes the form of the sustained pursuit of intellectual and moral integrity, authenticity or sincerity in the way we lead our lives. And we are suggesting that anyone who sets out from the first to pursue the religious life consistently in this spirit will find herself passing through a series of stages. Each stage represents one particular mode of understanding of the very nature of religious truth, and approximately corresponds to a stage in the human life-cycle.

At the very beginning of life narcissistic fantasy predominates in our construction of reality – reasonably enough, given the way things are for us then. We are dominated by our own feelings and needs and our condition of utter dependence; and objective reality, which for us largely consists of the mother's breast, arms and face, does indeed obligingly revolve around us and our desires. But life as it passes acts upon us as a continual persuasion to become less and less egoistic. The world which once revolved around us eventually passes us by, and means less and less to us as we mean less and less to it. Although our love of life continues unabated as long as life lasts, it is perforce slowly purged of egoism. If we can reach a state in which we still love and affirm life to the full, but do so in a way which is no longer at all anxious, demanding, clinging or selfish, then we shall have achieved the special synthesis of Yes and No, life and death, attachment and detachment that religious people call eternal life. It is supernatural in the sense that, early in life at least, it looks to be a biological impossibility. However, culture is capable of transforming nature, and our cultural life can become something more than the biological life-impulse that drives it. Even erotic love can become unselfish, and if that is possible then it must be possible for our love of life in general to become so.

Before we can set out the sequence, however, we need to describe how it manages to get going at all. How has the human and cultural managed to emerge from its background in nature? During the past fifty years study of animal behaviour has shown us forerunners of human social organization, curiosity, play, inventiveness, symbolic communication, ritual behaviour and even subjective consciousness within the animal kingdom. This has done a good deal to persuade us that we can understand in broad outline the transition from nature to culture, and the emergence of humanity.

However, the scientific type of understanding here involved needs to be treated with some caution and scepticism. It is a very recent cultural product, developed by systematically concentrating on the objective pole of our experience where we step forward, disregard our own subjectivity, and give all our attention to the structure of the objective world. Doing this, we have built our sciences and have carried them so far that nowadays everyone is in possession of a highly elaborated narrative scientific cosmogony that runs from the Big Bang to the beginning of history. However, this great myth shows only that scientists are just as prone to realism, the objectifying habit of mind that turns theories into things, as are religious believers. The 'initial singularity' postulated by standard-model cosmology is a part of physics rather than of nature. It is a meta-theory, a high-level physical theory whose function is to connect up a large number of lower-level theories. It already does this rather well, and there are those who claim that we are on the brink of a grand unified theory of nature. Maybe, and maybe not. Certainly the completion of physics would be a considerable intellectual event; but it would not *ipso facto* be the attainment of old-style absolute knowledge. We would merely have found that one particular method of inquiry had been pushed as far as it can, and the considerable energy that has been put into it would be available for redeployment into one or more of the indefinitely large number of other methods and lines of inquiry that are open to us. That is all.

Similarly, 'evolution' should not be reified. K. R. Popper once called it 'a metaphysical research hypothesis', but I would prefer to describe it as a body of theory that inculcates the specifically biological way of thinking about living organisms. A good deal of biology has been reduced to physics and chemistry, but evolutionary theory still defines something distinctively biological. Once you have grasped current evolutionary theory you are in possession of an extremely powerful tool for interpreting the living world. It can be used to generate thousands of useful detailed hypotheses that give illuminating answers to questions about how and why organisms are as they are and live as they do. Its truth lies in its interpretative power and its imaginative productivity, and in these respects it has no rival worth considering. Biologists are right to defend it strenuously, not because they are dogmatic about some vast narrative about past events which we will never be in a position to view *in toto*, but because it is a very powerful theoretical tool, and because to understand it is to understand their subject.

These two examples, by reminding us that 'the Big Bang' and 'Evolution' are theories of different kinds, developed within distinct communities for different purposes, show us why we should be dubious about large-scale stories of cosmic evolution that have been put together by amalgamating disparate bits of theory from various sciences. It would be better to confine ourselves to the recognition that the various sciences, in their different ways, project back historical narratives about the shaping of their own subject-matters. These stories are popular versions of theories. They may help us, each in its own province, to explain astronomical objects, geological formations, botanical structures and so on. But it is unwise and unnecessary to claim more than that.

In any case, my own conviction is that an objective-pole,

scientific explanation of the emergence of human beings and of
the origin of thought is unlikely ever to be complete. It has to
explain its own possibility, for we need some story about how we
ever came to be able to take an objective-pole view of our own
experience in the first place. How did we first become capable of
language and theory? The scientific type of explanation must, in
being formulated, already presuppose the very capacities it is
trying to explain; and in both human and communal life subjective-pole thinking evidently came first. At first, there was only a
flux of physiological states, emotions and experiences, out of
which the I, the Thou and a world-hypothesis emerged. This first
emergence of human thought from nature is a difficult event to
investigate by the methods of archaeology and physical and social
anthropology, but a subjective-pole inquiry may yield something,
for it has been recapitulated in each one of us. We have some sort
of access to it.

What events, then, must have taken place before we could
become capable of understanding a story? How did we acquire
the minimal conceptions of the self, others and the world which
are presupposed by even the most primal form of religion? At
least six steps seem to be involved:

(i) *Thou.* The infant (who for convenience we will refer to as 'he')
must have assembled his intermittent and fragmented experience
of his mother's breast, arms, face, hands and voice into the
conception of a distinct person over against him, with moods of
her own, and whose favour and disfavour matters ultimately to
him. Since she is not around for much of the time, he must
eventually frame some kind of world-hypothesis which postulates
her identity and continuity between her appearances. This may
be connected with faith in the power of the Word – i.e., how
reliably she appears when he yells. In that case there is a connection
between the power of language and our sense of reality. If you
belong to a generation of people who suspect that they may suffer
from attacks of unreality because they were left to cry you may
have sought to give your own children confidence in reality – or,
which comes to the same thing, in their own power – by running
to them every time they cried at night during the first two years
or so. Perhaps it works, and perhaps not. At any rate, the
recognition of the mother as a continuing identical person is
clearly an extraordinary intellectual feat.

(ii) *I*. At about the same time (I have no views about which came earlier, important though the question seems, because I cannot tell), the infant must also have assembled his own varied organs, succeeding physiological states and changing feelings into a relatively unified subjectivity, an I.

The emergence of the I is difficult to grasp, because we are not even sure with what it is contrasted. Is it formed by contrast with the maternal Thou; is it contrasted with the not-me, the environing world that begins where my body stops, at my skin surface; or do I recognize the I transcendentally as the presupposed unifying subject of my own changing physiological and emotional states? There are difficulties with each of these theories, and I shall propose a fourth which connects the origin of I with the origin of story.

(iii) *We*. Even more astonishing is the emergence of the recognition that Thou and I, mother and me, are beings of fundamentally the same kind. We are, after all, very disparate: as a baby I was dwarfish, powerless and as-yet-incapable of speech, and the evidence through which we recognize ourselves as persons from the inside – at the subjective pole – is very different from the evidence on the basis of which we recognize someone else as a person, from the outside. For the mother to be more than a fantasy-object, I must have succeeded both in distinguishing the objective from the subjective poles of experience and in bridging the gap between them, as the chief metaphysical postulate within the subjective pole, the self, establishes its community with the most important reality at the opposite pole, the mother. Presumably it is the milk that makes this feat possible: it is a sign not only of my dependence but also of our continuity of being. Shakespeare expresses this in the phrase 'the milk of human kindness', where he uses the word 'kindness' in its etymological sense of kinship or of-a-kind-ness.

(iv) *Communication*. Community rests on communication, minimally through body-contact, the gift of milk, cries, gestures and facial expressions. To recognize selfhood – perhaps the order runs: first obscurely in myself, then clearly in the mother, and finally with reflexively enhanced clarity in myself *vis-à-vis* the mother – presupposes a grasp of the concept of communication. We communicate, therefore we are.

Could all this be fully explained in behaviouristic and objective-pole terms? Striking evidence of the capacities of primates continues to be adduced, and it may be that we shall one day feel justified in attributing the capacity to generate true, syntactically-structured language to the pygmy chimpanzee, a self-image and subjective consciousness to the chimpanzee, and so on. Even the capacity to generate stories may, for all we know at present, exist in animals. Its forerunner might be found in the simulation of possible future sequences of events, as when young carnivores at play practise hunting.

At present we must be agnostic: but it is already clear that the Chomskyans who seek to defend the uniqueness of the human by drawing a sharp line between animal performances (which are behaviouristically explicable and do not include true syntactically-structured language) and human performances (which are *not* behaviouristically explicable, because true language is not so) are making a tactical mistake. Chomsky's own early polemics against crude behaviouristic analyses of language may be leading his followers to paint themselves into a corner. I would prefer to keep open the possibility that objective-pole scientific theorizing may establish full continuity between the animal and the human, and that refined behaviouristic accounts of all human performances may, in principle, be possible. By the same token, we may find ourselves compelled to attribute to some animals subjective-pole experience and the primitive metaphysical capacities employed in framing the I, the Thou, the We and the concept of communication.

If this happens, then we will have at last fully accepted the Darwinian idea of continuity between the animal and the human. I suggested earlier that although much that happens in the living world can be fully described in terms of physics and chemistry, biologists may still legitimately claim to possess their own distinctive way of thinking, and have no need to defend that claim by positing in reality any sharp line between the living and the non-living. Similarly, the various human sciences can legitimately defend the distinctiveness and autonomy of their own ways of thinking without needing to posit in reality a cut-off point between the animal and the human. To seek an ontological ground for an interdisciplinary frontier is objectifying thinking. And if the outcome of all this is that we end by granting ever-greater legal protection and even quasi-human status to the anthropoid apes, I for one will be glad to see the day.

So we are not claiming that symbolic communication (of some particular degree of complexity) is uniquely human. We are asserting only that an objective-pole scientific theory, however complete at its own level, is insufficient to account for the primitive metaphysics of I, thou, we and communication. We must presuppose subjective-pole thinking, and an interplay between it and objective-pole thinking, in order to describe the first emergence of these things – and it is only after these things have become well established that the pure objective-pole thinking of science can get under way.

(v) *The extra-human.* We must now raise the question of the origin of the extra-human environment. Again, there are various ways it could begin. It could be simply the not-me, of which I become aware as soon as I have established the boundaries of my own body. Perhaps coupled with this, it could be that which stays around when mother is absent. The infant's own excreta produced by him, which were once part of his body and are now extra-human, may suggest the idea that the extra-human environing world has been made from a superperson's body – an idea common in mythology.

However that may be, at some stage the infant moves from the idea that the mother is omnipotent and herself determines all the conditions under which he lives to the idea that he, she and others are denizens of a world, in common subjection to a set of environing conditions within which they live and on which they all depend.

Since personal categories are primitive, it is natural that these powers and limitations that frame our life should at first be envisaged in quasi-personal terms. Darwin thought that even animals might be animists. In *The Descent of Man* he relates how he once saw a dog bark aggressively each time it saw an open parasol that lay on the ground being shifted by the wind, as if it had concluded that the movement must be caused by an unseen living agent. At any rate it is obvious that we do, and at first must, attempt to extend our human forms of interpretation and communication to the extra-human realm, in order to come to grips with it.

(vi) *Story.* We are approaching the brink of religious thought.

Religion at least involves a set of stories, symbols and practices through which we frame our conceptions of ourselves as being both persons with individual stories, and members of a community defined by its common story. It is through stories that we situate ourselves in existence as a community with a shared theory of the world and shared standards, allegiances and expectations of each other. And through stories we seek to represent to ourselves and so to familiarize the surrounding extra-human conditions and powers that frame our life. In all the environment animals stand out as being the most readily familiarized or domesticated, and accordingly they make good images of the gods. Our success in familiarizing them encourages us to hope that we can also tame the rest of all that is wild.

Growing out of what we have called the primitive metaphysics, religion is then a social phenomenon; not just a philosophy of nature, but an attempt practically and socially to establish a scheme of life. We need to order our common life in the world, to make ourselves at home in the world, and to find a significant plot in the story of our life.

What then are the sources of time and story? Time can only be recognized where some continuous process is varied or interrupted. The notion of a temporal sequence, a broken flow of discrete units, is doubtless of physiological origin. There are sequences of breaths, heartbeats, paces, draughts of liquid and mouthfuls of solid. At the other end, the flow of urine and especially of our primary creative product, the faeces, is intermittent; and notice how readily we view a mass-production machine, such as a sausage-machine, as *excreting* its products. The broken flow of the products generates the vivid sense of time (and bondage to it) that so irritates critics of industrial production.

The primary case of an organic unity, of a coherent whole emerging through a synthesis of parts, is the synthesis into a single enduring person of our own very diverse organs, states and feelings. The Trickster myth of the Winnebago Indians is one of many stories describing the unification of the human body. Story will then involve a synthesis of parts, a reconciliation of conflict or some similar drama, though which a subject passes or from which he emerges. A primal example of such a sequence might be: waking, discomfort, distress, crying, the arrival of the mother, feeding at the breast, satiation, burping and blissful sleep. To make it a story, such a sequence of events must be recognized as being unified in or undergone by a subject: that is, these things are united by the fact that they all happened successively to *me*, I am the one who has passed through this adventure. Narrative requires subjectivity, and stories are the means by which a person recognizes his own unity-through-time. Every person has a story, for a person is necessarily one who finds himself as the subject of the story of what is happening to him. I am a person insofar as I am a *dramatis persona*.

More than one story is involved here, and symbolic stories which are more than simple recitations of events have multiple interpretations. Consider for example how the infant at play generates and enacts simple stories of being lost and hidden, and then found again. What is he re-enacting when he plays hide-and-seek or peek-a-boo? It could be his own coming into the world from the hiddenness of the womb, it could be his pleasure in seeing his mother again after waking and calling for her, it could be the primal terror of being lost and abandoned, and then being found again, and it could be sheer intellectual pleasure in playing with the contrast between the flickering realm of seeming, where things cease to be as soon as we shut our eyes, and the stable world of our world-hypothesis which postulates a trustworthy continuity of things. The simple drama of losing and finding, being hidden and then discovered, has many applications. And as soon as the child has language we hasten to equip him with many more symbolic stories, for it seems that the wider the range of basic stories he has to draw on the greater will be his subsequent ability to cope with life. The stories are both interpretative and generative resources. We have the mysterious power to call up the relevant one from our stock and use it to make our interaction with life intelligible to ourselves.

How do we find the right story? It seems to me that we fantasize continually, at very high speed, both scanning our story-stock and generating new stories. When we find one that fits, we lock on to it. If it transpires that the story is after all unsuitable – 'we have the wrong end of the stick' – then we try again.

The stories need to be as diverse as the challenges that life presents, and a culture's story-stock may be as untidy and chaotic as life itself. Provided that you have in your tool-kit a tool to hand that will meet every emergency, it matters not a whit whether the tools are of some standard design and fit neatly together in the box. Mythological thinking is commonly very diverse and unsystematic, especially in palaeolithic societies, and we ourselves, when we read Grimm, Hans Andersen, Lewis Carroll and Beatrix Potter to our children at bedtime, never suppose that all this material would be in any way improved by being translated into a systematic body of doctrine. What really needs explaining is not why myths are so diverse but why the theologians – and even certain poets – should have felt there was a need to systematize them. More of this later.

We have been reviewing various transformations that the productive life-energy undergoes. At successively higher levels of representation it becomes physiological states, experience, the subjective and objective poles within experience, symbolic communication and story. The passage through these levels of representation generates the primitive and minimal metaphysics of I, thou, we, communication and the world.

In this light we may see stories of the emergence of the subject – such as the Winnebago story of the Trickster unifying his own recalcitrant body – as stories about stories that reveal the nature of story. They show that it is through story that we become primally aware of ourselves as subjects persisting through time, agents who make things happen and patients to whom things happen. To lead a life is to become oneself through a temporally extended dialectic of activity and passivity, freedom and necessity. Religion is a way of symbolizing and facilitating this process.

We have not yet asked about the nature of the productive life-energy itself. It has been given a great many names. For the Buddha it is *tanha*, craving, for Spinoza *conatus*, for Hegel *Geist*, for Schopenhauer the Will, for Nietzsche the will-to-power, for Freud *libido*, for Bergson the *Elan Vital*. In some philosophies it is viewed optimistically, and in others pessimistically. Some wish to give a materialist account of it, some a vitalist biological account, and some take an idealist view of it.

I reject all these overbeliefs and say that the productive life-energy itself is neither machine nor *Geist*, neither good nor evil, neither mental nor material, because it is primal, and is prior to the levels of representation at which those distinctions arise and on which alone those terms have meaning. For the same reason it has nothing to do with physics. There is simply nothing to be said about it – except that it manifests itself in its various levels of representation. It is its expressions: like the self and others and the world, it appears only within the sphere of representation.

2

MYTHICAL REALISM

The productive life-energy, passing through a series of levels of representation, manifests itself successively as our physiological states, our experience, the differentiation of experience into its subjective and objective poles, symbolic communication and story. Through these transformations the primitive metaphysics arises: I, thou, we, our communication, our world – these items being not primal absolutely but our primal constructions, decidedly hazy at first though they are.

The self emerges spinning stories, the first of them being its paradoxical story of its own synthesis, and story remains the basic form of understanding. *Persona dramatis persona est*: story gives us our basic conception of ourselves as leading our lives, persisting through time and yet gradually becoming ourselves, by dialogue with other persons, by making things happen and having things happen to us, and throughout endeavouring to make a coherent and satisfactory whole of our lives. So when in early fiction a new character arrived on the scene, he would identify himself by recounting his life-history. 'That's the story of my life!'; and when we have heard his story, we know who he is.

Communities also require stories through which they can identify themselves, and the community's stock of symbolic stories, communicated to the child, gives him his cultural identity. There is no generalized human identity over and above particular cultural traditions, for I awake to my selfhood *vis-à-vis* a mother, who represents and communicates to me the universal human only as mediated by the particular cultural tradition into which I have been born.

My people's corpus of stories, through which I have gained my cultural-personal identity, shapes the earliest form of religious consciousness, mythical realism.

The 'realism' here is pre-theoretical; that is, it is not backed by any theory and is therefore not self-conscious. It simply fills the imaginative world and suffuses all experience, having no rival. It is received from tradition, and is taken entirely for granted. It does not need to be, and is not aware of being, instilled, maintained and enforced by any coercive structures of authority, and is therefore content to be haphazard and quite unsystematic.

We should not suppose that at this stage of consciousness people live in a dream-world. On the contrary, every society has always possessed a large body of perfectly sound practical knowledge interwoven with its craft skills. The bare necessity to survive teaches people the ways of animals and plants, and the skills of cookery, house-building, weapon-making, hunting and so forth. Where the correct exercise of these skills is perceived as being especially vital to society as a whole, they will tend to be ritualized and invested with religious solemnity so as to stress their importance and protect them against change. But the secular skills are not developed into a systematic theory of nature that can challenge the great sacralizing religious narratives and symbols. The secular realm is at first no more systematically organized than is the religious realm, and it is by definition the religious realm that includes all the potent stories and symbols that have created us and our world – that is, it is by these stories and symbols that our form of social life as persons has been first constituted, and is now ordered and infused with significance.

To us who are trained in later ways of thinking the disorderly, fractured and dreamlike character of mythology is disturbing and puzzling. But incoherence of belief causes most people no trouble at all. Among the population in modern Britain there are widely diffused at least six different notions of the hereafter, drawn from as many incompatible systems of thought. They include the Christian eschatology of judgment, heaven and hell; various forms of the Indian doctrine of rebirth or reincarnation; the belief in ghosts that still lingers from the old pre-Christian religion of Northern Europe; the memorializing of all the dead without distinction on public monuments as venerated forebears, with a background in civil religion and even Chinese-style ancestor worship; the Spiritualist and Gnostic belief in spirits who may communicate with us from the other side or the astral plane through mediums; and simple 'sleep', as a euphemism for the naturalistic idea of extinction.

To say that many people appear to hold several of these theories at once without noticing their mutual incompatibility would be misleading. They are not 'theories', and their seeming incompatibility is of no consequence. The position is rather that on a particular occasion in life people unreflectively and spontaneously invoke those images and stories from their varied stock that they find most immediately helpful and fitting in shaping their language and practice. In the past the church possessed the power to make its own eschatology dominant, but now that that is no longer the case most people have had to be content to do without any guiding orthodoxy and change to an older, more eclectic and pre-'rational' way of thinking. The change has not been so very great in fact, because the church's teaching was itself complex and equipped the faithful with a wide range of symbols and practices.

Using Jung's formula, 'symbols attract and transmute libido', we might describe what happens as follows. The productive life-energy in us continually seeks self-expression in representation. A culture is a large repertory of channels through which it can find expression in our thought, speech and action, each channel being a practice guided and shaped by a story and symbols. On any given occasion the productive life-energy will simply select that channel through which it can pass most readily and effectively. Now, any encounter with death is a major challenge and threat, and the life-energy must seek out some story-channel through which it can assimilate, interpret, transmute and triumph over this threat, and so continue to affirm itself. But the process of life continually confronts us with reminders of death, and does so in a great variety of ways and contexts. All the better, then, for us to be equipped with a varied stock of symbols and stories. We do not need to systematize them, and we certainly do not need to do any conscious seeking-out of the right one for the right occasion. Libido itself does all that at the unconscious level far more quickly and efficiently than we could do it after reflection. The right, the best, symbols, stories and practices come to mind quickly, spontaneously and with an air at once fresh and inevitable. The religious authority of a myth is its power promptly to evoke and channel our life-expression.

Hence the vivid, new-washed immediacy of mythical realism. It is pictorial. Its colours are primary and brilliant – white, gold, sapphire-blue, blood-red and emerald grass-green – and much of its imagery is familial but encoded, as in fairy-tales. God the Father enthroned in the sky surrounded by grave-faced angels making music, all things bright and beautiful, invisible protective presences surrounding us, scriptural tales of magical deliverances. Even though today we no longer communicate these images very enthusiastically to our children, and they have long ceased to be represented with any conviction in art and popular stories, nevertheless, they survive. Children seek them out, pick them up and store them away, instinctively recognizing their significance.

How do they do this? Mythical thinking readily postulates the existence of other families analogous to our own in other cosmic regions: there is a royal family at the head of society, there are animal families, and there is a family and social life of dwarves beneath the hills, and of mermen and the like at the bottom of the seas and lakes. But all these families have basically the same structure as our own and are therefore not religiously potent, whereas the sacred family on earth, and still more that in heaven, are strangely transformed and anomalous; and this strangeness is the sign of their religious potency. The earthly Holy Family comprises the shadowy, elderly figure of Joseph, the young virgin Mother and Jesus. It is in fact the family as seen from the point of view of the earliest childhood. Father is somewhat redundant: mother and child are absorbed in each other and Joseph, if present at all, merely hovers benignly in the background as an admiring spectator of the mother's perfect *rapport* with her Son-Lord. This is the way things really ought to be, we say to ourselves. The child has the mother all to himself, with not the faintest hint of protest from the father.

Oddly overlapping with this earthly ideal family, however, the heavenly Family is still more anomalous. God the Father sits with his now adult and co-equally divine Son at his right hand surrounded by their court. The mother seems at first to be absent: but no, although a merely human figure now, and their creature, she is raised up to be crowned by them and co-opted into their society, as the Spirit hovers above. She may henceforth be called

Queen of Heaven and the Mother of God, but exalted though her titles are there is an impassable line between the Father and the Son on the one hand and her on the other. They have their dignity eternally and in their own right, whereas she has hers by their grace as a reward for her merits.

The earthly Holy Family represents a primal perception of the way things are and should be that we never wholly give up, and for which the mother is the central source of life and love and object of veneration. But it is over-ruled by the triumph in heaven of the patriarchal principle. The narratives that link the two pictures must be concerned with guiding the progress of the soul from infancy to a fully adult integration into the Christian social order.

It is very noticeable that the various heavenly beings of different ranks who are objects of devotion are not, at the mythical stage of religious consciousness, strongly individual personalities. Whether the beings round my bed are angels or evangelists, I cannot clearly distinguish one of them from another. They are more like pictures. Hence the importance of iconography, and indeed the possibility of iconolatry. The picture *is* the person. We never hear of a Catholic having a vision of a woman but failing to identify the woman seen: on the contrary, the Catholic at once perceives Mary – that is, perceives the picture that can only be Mary. There is no room for doubt about the matter, and it would make no sense to say to the visionary, 'Perhaps you saw some other woman who just happened to be dressed like Mary, standing in Mary's typical posture, and bathed in light.' The visionary can no more doubt that this is Mary than a child in a department store at Christmas-time can doubt that this is Santa Claus. The distinctive iconography of white beard, fur-trimmed red suit and boots leaves no *space* for doubt.

The fact that the object of faith is at this stage more of a picture than an individual person makes prayer more rather than less easy. Prayer as expressive soliloquy evoked by and addressed to a holy picture flows utterly spontaneously. The best analogy I can find is the way in which many of us who are rather reserved in our relations with our fellow-adults may nevertheless find ourselves joyfully babbling sweet nothings to a beloved animal or a baby. They do not really understand, and can be relied upon never to think that we are making fools of ourselves. They have no secret thoughts about us: they just love to be loved, love to draw out our self-expression. In some societies people go to graves to speak to their dead in in a somewhat similar way. The dead make good listeners.

Because the sacred beings are not as yet very clearly individuated, but rather function as guiding pictures that attract and channel our life-expression, the human self is not yet very clearly individuated either. Hence the phrase 'narcissistic fantasy' that I used earlier is anachronistic. It invokes contrasts, between fantasy and reality and between a self-centred and a disinterested view of things, which have not yet been drawn. To a considerable extent, the self and the world still mutually interpenetrate each other, so that at the mythical stage there is a plurality of often conflicting forces within the self and likewise a plurality of conflicting forces within the world; and elements pass back and forth across the frontier. Indeed, for paleolithic man there was no very clear frontier between the self and the world at all. He could assume without question the propriety of interpreting events in terms of his own feelings and needs. Of course the sacred world is close around me, and its denizens move freely in and out of my soul: how else could it be? The phrase 'narcissistic fantasy' is used from the standpoint of a later way of thinking which has drawn a sharp line between the inner and outer worlds and has declared that to see how things really are in the outer world we must make ourselves into dispassionate ideal observers, dissociated from our own wishes and desires. But all this was to come very much later: for the archaic way of thinking 'all things were full of gods', and there was a plurality of souls within the self. The self was like a football scrum and the world was like a football scrum: and the two scrums readily became confused so that players slipped from the one to the other.

We can begin here to glimpse the answer to a question that is rather more difficult than it looks: why did people ever come to believe in invisible spirit-beings within and around them at all?

The belief is now not so easy to recover by introspection. I recall being afraid of the dark, but even then I think I already suspected that the object of my fear was not a spirit but merely my own self-feeding fear itself. When I was a theological realist my realistic conviction was largely philosophical: in religious experience – vivid though it was and sometimes still is – I discerned nothing more distinct than a sense of massive and abiding warmth, a feeling of umbilical connection with the divine. I have perhaps come closest to guessing what it was to believe in spirits when alone in a remote place in the Arctic; but even this experience was very faint, and most of the face of the Earth is now so extensively humanized that the spirits have been driven out forever.

If this testimony is at all typical, we would seem to have become almost wholly cut off from the past. Why *did* people believe in spirits?

The received answer is a form of projection theory. The most potent explanatory concepts available in early times were personal and social. When people explained events in the surrounding world in terms of the activity of spirits they were attempting, as it were, to connect nature with society, and by personifying nature to familiarize it. This not only helped to make the mysterious ways of Providence humanly intelligible, but also opened up the possibility of negotiating with it. The impulse to project a human face on nature is very strong. Babies are so effectively pre-programmed to pick out the pattern of a face that it is not at all surprising that adults should still see a man in the Moon. We look for the personal, and we find it.

A sign of the old mentality is the way some African peoples speak of 'God' where we would use a more neutral expression like 'things' or 'it', as when the African says 'God is hot today', where we would say 'It is hot today'. But as the external world is depersonalized, 'God' as a name for all that we are up against gives place to Destiny, Fate or Chance, which in turn become Things or It.

However, projection theories are open to the criticism that we made of the phrase 'narcissistic fantasy': they are anachronistic. Judging an archaic form of thought by alien and later standards they tend to misrepresent it and summarily to dispose of it, leaving it more alien than ever. We have quite failed to understand it in the deeper sense of having been led for a moment to share it.

How are we to gain this deeper understanding, when the very idea that there are invisible spirit-beings around now seems so counter-intuitive and indeed incoherent? I suggest that we recall how thoroughly we adults continually interpret our experience by reference to an implicit world-hypothesis which we use to fill in the gaps in the continuity of things. The youngest infant does not yet have this world-hypothesis. To him the mother is *herself* an invisible person who periodically manifests herself at his cot-side. She has for him the status that will later be ascribed to spirits, because he has not yet developed the conviction that when absent from him she nevertheless persists in being as a physical object moving along a continuous track in space and time. As he sees it, when she is invisible to him she is invisible, full-stop. Perhaps he contrasts her now intermittent self-manifestations with an earlier and longed-for time when he was permanently united with her.

Infantile thought and experience may therefore have helped in the past to make belief in spirits seem intelligible and credible, and may explain two common beliefs, the belief that in a past Golden Time the gods dwelt continuously on earth among us in bodily form, and the belief that even now after they have with-drawn from our sight they may still manifest themselves to our senses, especially in time of need. Images and feelings from infancy do seem to play a large part in the longing for union with God, as in my own experience mentioned earlier.

We should also remember that there was a time when not only our world-hypothesis but also our self-hypothesis was relatively undeveloped. At that time I must have regarded compulsive feelings and moods not under my control as evidence of the activity of other personal centres within my psychic field. Here surely lies the source of ideas of possession by spirits.

Freud considered that their obviously infantile character was a reason for disparaging these ancient forms of religious experience. I do not agree. For one thing, he himself acknowledged that the feelings and thought-creations of infancy are the most powerful that we ever generate, and for another, most people's thinking remains mythical throughout life and they probably do a great deal better than us who have for good or ill become demythologized.

However, demythologized we are; and we must move on.

3

DOCTRINAL REALISM

Mythical realism is pictorial and unsystematic. By later standards, it is a disorderly collection of shared symbols, narratives and practices which are invoked as required to facilitate the expressive flow of life. Concern for the systematic organization of the self, of society, of the world, of life and time, and of the religious realm itself is by no means absent. But it is still relatively weak, because the need for it has not yet been deeply felt.

Doctrinal realism, by contrast, is religion as credal belief, the kind of religious faith to which people in Christian cultures may be dramatically converted because they find it meets profound and urgent cognitive, practical and emotional needs. It lays great emphasis on a set of distinctive doctrinal beliefs, and on membership of an organized religious society which sees itself as distinct from the surrounding civil society in which it is embedded. These credal beliefs have a number of important characteristics: they are regarded as revealed by God through the church and the Bible, they are immutable saving truths, they should have over-riding authority in your life and must never be betrayed, you must assent to the whole set of them *ex animo*, you must hold *only* these beliefs and not contaminate them by importing any other religious beliefs and allegiances, and you must put them consist-ently into practice as the law of your life in a thoroughgoing way. In addition, there is a general recognition that the authorities in the community have special custodial authority in relation to the system of beliefs, for it is their right and duty to safeguard, interpret, define and enforce it. Evidently such a conception of religious belief reflects a very strongly felt need for order, discipline and security.

Credal faith, Catholic or Protestant, is in Christian cultures both regarded as the norm and a topic of sharp controversy. The majority, who are nowadays outsiders, accept the hostile verdict on it of the Enlightenment and the great nineteenth-century dissuaders. Nothing, it seems, can again induce them to take its intellectual claims seriously, for it has been finally exposed as a system of domination to which some people are unfortunately drawn for psychological reasons. The minority of insiders take an entirely opposite view, for through the gift of supernatural faith they have found spiritual liberation, eternal truth, joy and consolation. The contrasting accounts of the nature of faith given by such figures as Marx, Nietzsche and Freud on the one hand and by orthodox theologians on the other show how great the polarization has become. Yet it also leads to a certain measure of agreement. At least it is agreed that there is indeed a chasm, that it shows that faith cannot be rationally vindicated, and that this kind of religion is true religion, the genuine article. True religion is a structure of authoritative supernatural beliefs which must remain intact. It is like a great tower of cans in a supermarket: take one away, and the whole thing crashes. On that point at least, Nietzsche agreed with the Pope.

The tendency to see religion as being *essentially* highly credal in this way has been so strong that people in Christian cultures have during the past two centuries felt it right to pay other faiths the compliment of describing them also as 'creeds'. In fact, however, no other faith is credal in quite the way Christianity is, and Christianity itself became credal between the second and fifth centuries through a very special concatenation of historical factors. Before the New Testament writings were collected, canonized and widely distributed as a readily accessible norm of faith, there was a desire to preserve the apostolic tradition uncorrupted in a very pluralistic culture. The bishops, who claimed to be the legitimate successors of the apostles, successfully seized full control of the church and the sole right to define doctrine. The Roman passion for law and organization, the Greek belief that right practice would follow right theory, and the need to fix an agreed ideological basis for the Christian Empire all played a part. Other major religions have also produced short mnemonic formulae that summarize their own particular ways: the Shema, the Five Pillars of Islam, the Eightfold Path. But these formulae prescribed mainly allegiances, observances and practices, whereas Christianity became uniquely credal.

However, patristic Christianity and the intellectual tradition that has flowed from it in the Latin and Greek churches was also interwoven with elements of classical philosophy. Metaphysically-grounded religion is to be considered later: at present we are concerned rather with a simpler type of doctrinal belief, found in popular Catholicism and Protestantism and seen perhaps at its purest in certain Reformation confessions of faith. We have here a form of religious consciousness which remains very powerful today, but which is deeply puzzling and difficult to describe and explain. The ugly modern polarization of opinions about it to which we have referred only makes it the more difficult to see the issues clearly and frame the right questions. The outsiders are too polemically hostile, and the insiders (being pre-critical) lack self-understanding and are unable to explain to us what they are up to in terms that are intelligible to us. We have to ask why the religious consciousness should take this particular form. What *is* a doctrinal belief, and what is it to come to hold one and to live by it? And how did the need for it arise?

Although doctrinal belief is, as we have said, commonly regarded as non-rational, it does in fact have its own kind of rationality. It claims, at least, to be rationally derivable from the primary sources of revelation, to be systematic and coherent (that is, free from internal contradictions) and to be applicable in an orderly way to all the circumstances of life. Furthermore, the believer obviously holds that his or her beliefs are in some strong and simple sense *true*. However, the kind of rationality that is involved in doctrinal belief is undoubtedly different from our modern critical rationality. It is closer to legal rationality, reminding us that the earliest attempts to systematize religion took the form of law-codes which collected and organized the rules governing ritual observances, the securing of institutional continuity, matters of conduct and the resolution of disputes. The passion for order which motivated such attempts was social, and not merely speculative.

In Nietzschean terms, when tribes confederated to form the first nations, the most vigorous and dominant individuals were confronted by new and difficult problems of social control. The means of control was law. Particular human behaviours had to be recognized as falling under general concepts, and trial procedures had to be devised so that in disputed cases it could be determined in a precise and consistent way whether a particular behaviour was to be classified as an instance of murder or theft or whatever. There had to be public proclamation of rules enjoining and prohibiting particular classes of behaviours; and to maximize the ruler's power and control over the whole life of his subjects it was necessary that the whole body of his edicts be closely defined, systematically coherent, understood by all, publicly recorded, and efficiently enforced with a graduated scale of penalties. This scale has itself great educative value, for it shows that the ruler does not wish to exercise all his power against every offender, but proportions the penalties according to his perception of the gravity of the offence against himself. The scale of penalties shows how the ruler sees himself: the study of his law is an education in glory. And where the ruler is a god, study of his revealed will is a training in theology.

Power thus creates its own form of rationality as a tool for securing its own fullest self-expression as social control, and the plenitude of power must *ex hypothesi* be the perfection of rationality. Even today in our kind of society we still notice the connection between power and rationality in the way that the utterances of the party in government tend to sound more rational than those of the party in opposition. Power teaches rationality. Conversely, those who studied, interpreted and administered the law, who demonstrated its systematic comprehensiveness and interconnectedness, who showed its perfection, were glorifying the power of the king or the god whose servants they were.

We see here why in pre-philosophical thought, where legal rationality is dominant, the main interest was in proving the superior power rather than the being of your god. People wanted to overcome the threat of 'forfeiture' (Heidegger's *Verfallensein*); moral lostness, wandering, dissipation, confusion. They wanted to live a unified life, a life that followed a single straight path. The perfect law of life would be a law that had the power to integrate all the diversity of human activities. It must search the heart and conscript all human energies into an army under a single commander. Such a law, if it existed, must have emanated from

an all-powerful and all-wise lawgiver, and to follow it was to see
life as lived in his service. Legal rationality thus yields a style of
religious thought which in metaphysics would come to be called
'voluntarist'. Its main interest is in God's desire for glory, his
almighty power, his revealed will, and the realization of his
sovereignty in every aspect of human life – which is thereby itself
unified and made glorious as it manifests the divine glory. This is
certainly a form of realism, but it is not at all the same as the later
metaphysical realism.

Now the leading thinkers of the eighteenth and nineteenth
centuries, from Voltaire to Freud, reacted very sharply against
this type of religious thought, which they often associated with
the Jews. They saw it from a Greek point of view, in terms of
agency and passivity. For them, where God was most dominant
human beings were most enslaved; and the God of the Old
Testament is certainly determined to be dominant. He is thirsty
for glory. However, things are not so bad for God as they look,
for I wish to suggest that in the covenant between God and Israel
there truly was gain for both parties.

God was the pure productive life-energy itself, bursting with
will-to-glory. He was 'living', and life seeks glory as its own
maximally varied, complete and splendid self-expression. God's
power and glory were manifest in the natural order, but his
paramount desire was to see himself glorified in every aspect of
human life. So he revealed his will for mankind in the form of a
great system of sacred law, and set himself to ensure that Israel
obeyed it and so glorified his name. But Israel gained also. She
had been chosen to receive the revelation of the divine glory, and
it dwelt in her midst. The life-path that glorifies God glorifies also
those who follow it, so that not only is Israel's way of life a
glorification of God, but also God himself becomes the glory of
Israel – which means, I suggest, that the life-energy and will-to-
glory of the individual Israelite itself found its own fullest self-
expression in treading the path of righteousness. If God's boundless life-energy and will-to-power expresses itself most perfectly
in prescribing a rational and coherent life-order for mankind,
then the human life-energy and will-to-power also finds its own
highest fulfilment in that same unified life-order. God's dominance
therefore does not entail human subjection and passivity, for to
obey God's will was to participate in God's lordship, to find in the

law which was the expression of his will-to-power a framework for the optimal expression of one's own. Hence to serve him was to reign (*cui servire est regnare*), as Augustine puts it. To imagine how an almighty God who loved only glory would require you to live was to imagine indeed a glorious form of life.

We have been discussing legal rationality and the ancient type of religious thought associated with it, by way of suggesting that it contributed a great deal to the formation of doctrinal realism. The alternative theoretical type of rationality invented by the early Greek philosophers did not, I think, contribute nearly so much. The pre-Socratics were not primarily interested in social control; indeed, they were strikingly apolitical. What blocked them was a difficulty of understanding: they sought to comprehend the origin or nature, the *archē*, of things and they tried to make progress by checking out models, metaphors, ratios. Inability to understand is disagreeable because it inhibits the flow of life, but it may be relieved if we can find a way of using something we can understand as a model for the nature of the thing that we cannot understand. The consequence of this is that every theology which has been strongly influenced by Greek thought cannot help but be aware of the analogical or metaphorical character of all its language. It is inevitably troubled by doubts about the adequacy of its theoretical models. But the kind of doctrinal realism that presently concerns us is typically unconscious of the problem of analogy. For this reason the Greek-minded have always suspected it of naive anthropomorphism; but it should instead be seen as representing a different form of rationality, and one which is not concerned with the quest for understanding through analogies and theoretical models. It uses instead the vocabulary of power, law and social control, speaking of sovereignty and might, of the will, righteousness and law, of command and obedience, and sin and judgment. This language, prominent in the Old Testament, also returned in the later Mediaeval and Reformation periods. It is deeply unpopular today, but we need to understand it if we are to grasp the logic of doctrinal realism.

Undoubtedly doctrines do in many ways behave like laws. They are seen as having been authoritatively promulgated by revelation, or as having been enacted (with sanctions) by the church's ruling body. They bind all who are subject to the church's jurisdiction and none who are not so subject, so that heresy and apostasy are treated like crime and treason and arouse much more ire than simple infidelity. And by being defined they bind, in a way that makes Greek-type difficulties of understanding and questions about meaning seem to be mere mischievous quibbles.

However, the doctrine-system is not simply a code of sacred law, influential though that idea is in the background. It is also highly credal, and the believer regards it as being not merely valid but also true, in a strong sense. It brings with it a considerable body of cosmological and supernatural beliefs. How does the *realism* enter, and how are these beliefs thought of as being justified?

The first step is the same in Christianity, Judaism, Islam and many other faiths: accepting the Law, one accepts the Lawgiver. From tradition we receive a religion, in the sense of a complex body of prescriptions governing social organization, conduct, ritual observances, attitudes and styles of piety that taken as a whole generate a certain form of life. Tradition leads me to regard this whole system as having ultimate authority for me, and therefore as being a Law for my life. The unity and perfection of the Law shows me the nature of the Lawgiver, and I ascribe to him its authority, wisdom, power and goodness. God is not so much a Being as a Lord, an embodiment of the principle of sacred authority.

So far we have a form of obedientiary realism, of a type to which we will return later: but, especially in the case of credal Christianity, much more is added. For revelation communicates to the Christian not only the religion, the perfect Law of life, but also outlines of cosmology and the history of salvation, and a good deal of other supernatural doctrine as well. This additional material is included in the package, and so is accepted as revealed truth. One might explain this juxtaposition of cosmological doctrines with ethical directives by saying that creation, miracles and the like were originally seen as manifestations of divine power, and not as anything like scientific theories. The revelation of God's power and glory in the Law by which you lived was clothed or surrounded by a wider cosmic revelation of the same thing.

However, at this point the problem of the stack of cans in the supermarket arises. By invoking the notion of legal rationality we have indicated that there is indeed a *prima facie* case for obedientiary realism. God is seen as the 'principle' (let us for the present be no more explicit than that) of the sacred authority of a certain form of life. So we speak of that form of life as having been revealed by God, and of God as the Lord of all life. But when a large body of supplementary cosmological and supernatural beliefs are incorporated into the package, sacred authority is also made the arbiter of many questions which may in time become open to scientific and historical investigation. Belief in (for example) the virginal conception of Jesus in the womb of Mary is made as much a matter of sacred obedience, and is given the same sort of authority, as the practice of agapeistic love. This is decidedly incongruous; but it can be contained, so long as within the culture the best available secular knowledge does not seriously challenge the cosmological and other supernatural beliefs. However, when such a challenge does come along and proves irresistible, then the falsification of just one ancillary belief that has been made to rest on the authority of revelation threatens revelation itself, and therefore the entire religious system.

Luther is a good test case. Much of his language when he is at his most brilliant is a highly rhetorical expression of obedientiary realism. But sometimes, as when he pours scorn upon the theories of Copernicus, he unmistakeably moves to doctrinal realism – and in so doing shows its dangers.

After these lengthy preliminaries we now briefly consider doctrinal realism as a phase in the development of the religious consciousness. In rapidly changing and pluralistic societies it is the kind of religion to which people are converted, and the peak age for such conversion is adolescence. We emerge from the mythic world of childhood with its non-corrosive time, and become aware of sex, death and the responsibilities of adulthood. From the age of sixteen, wounds begin to take longer to heal. We realize that we have before us – a life, and our society does not give us anything to live by. All it offers is the round of alarm-clock, breakfast, journey to work, work, journey home, supper, entertainment and bed, for forty or fifty years – and the prospect of raising the next generation for the same empty routine. A tiny minority will do rather better, but a much larger group do not have even this much to look forward to. When we realize that we have before us just – a 'career', we recoil from this appalling prospect and search for something better. That which can satisfy us will inevitably retain a good deal of the imagery of the beloved childhood world, but in a more systematic and internalized form. The heavenly father will replace the earthly, and the church will replace the mother. Between them they must supply an authoritative and coherent world-view and programme for life which has the power both to explain and to inspire. All this, doctrinal realism claims to do. Its ways of thinking retain many features of mythical realism in enhanced form. All complex totalities, including the self, the cosmos, society and the moral realm, are unified by being hierarchized, and explanation is therefore typically foundationalist. The order of the psychological, physical, social and moral worlds is thus explained and validated by being traced back to their common foundation in the creative and legislative will of God.

These ideas should not be seen as being crudely authoritarian and alienating, or even as 'oedipalizing'. On the contrary, to be the recipient of revelation, to be one of those chosen from a godless world to know the truth and to be an instrument of the fulfilment of God's purposes, is highly energizing. One is swept forward like a surf-boarder on the mighty tide of the divine will, and has, as a result, an intensely enhanced sense of life. The religious experiences of doctrinal realism are in some respects the most vivid of all, and the most personal in character.

However, for moderns it has been falsified by advances in knowledge on a great many fronts and in ways which do not here need to be recapitulated. Even in ancient times those influenced by Greek culture found it hard to understand, and sought to make it intelligible and to give it better intellectual foundations with the help of philosophy.

4

METAPHYSICAL REALISM: THE LADDER

For doctrinal realism God's nature is will, and his will is fully revealed: *ergo*, God is fully revealed. God is not mysterious, for he is known by studying and doing his revealed will. There is no difficulty of understanding, because it is only those who are losing their power over us whom we find it difficult to understand. Hence the expression, 'There's none so deaf as those that will not hear.' Conversely, a wholehearted will to obey creates perfect comprehension. God is real, because the world is seen as a power-hierarchy and he is the supreme Power, the front of the power-structure of the religious society and of the authoritative law of faith and conduct by which it lives. To cleave loyally to this society and to accept all its norms is to cleave to God. Nor can this type of religion justly be called slavish, for what can be more invigorating than to have irresistible divine power and authority running in one's veins?

This whole system is so tightly-knit, efficient and enthralling that it is hard at first to see what mere philosophy could hope to add to it. Its adherents already have a superb assurance that they are pleasing to God and are the agents through whom he is fulfilling his purposes. In the way it subordinates truth and goodness to social authority and the social order it is not only traditional, but also after its fashion ultra-modern. Hence its capacity to inspire that fundamentalist revolt against secular liberal values which so baffles and dismays its contemporary critics. It needs no other reply to these critics than simple aggressive militancy, because it maintains that naturally he who has most power is best placed to determine reality: is not that what is meant by the standard monotheistic doctrine that God being almighty creates all facts by the *fiat* of his will?

John Calvin is often said to have been deeply influenced by humanism, and the claim is not so paradoxical as it sounds. To see why, imagine that the world is like a performance of one of Shakespeare's history plays. We do not go to the theatre to spend our time in gazing at the stage-setting. We go to see a drama of *human* power-relations, for that is what, in every sense of the word, most deeply interests us. All that is required of the stage-set is that it should function as a frame to contain the human drama and should have such few features as may from time to time be required to make the action intelligible; and if the entire performance is under the control of a fully competent author-director who knows just what he wants, then the players will do well to follow his instructions implicitly in the sure knowledge that he will have seen to it that those circumstantial conditions are indeed met.

This analogy reveals the connections between some otherwise-puzzling characteristics of authoritarian organized religion. In one sense it is unworldly, in that it is not conspiciously interested in the study for its own sake of the profane natural world. Its world is the human world; and in that second sense of 'world' it is very worldly indeed, being utterly absorbed in questions of authority, power and control, to the extent that it openly locates the divine in a particular mode of power-relations among human beings. Hence, Calvin's 'humanism'. Godliness is strong personal and ecclesiastical discipline, both intellectual and moral. Thirdly, we see why it is absolutist. Mere finite power is secular, but absolute power is a most spiritual thing. Power gets to be religious precisely by being absolutized, which is why those who wish to submit unconditionally to an infallible authority are regarded by the public as being the most serious about their religion.

Why turn from all this to philosophy? New converts are in too exalted a frame of mind to be very clear-headed, but there are three points at which philosophy may enter: the system of authoritarian religion needs an internal check, it needs some internal clarification, and it needs criteria that its own logic cannot supply for conducting its external relations.

It needs an internal check, because without some moderating and corrective principle it has nothing to prevent it from over-reaching itself and toppling into megalomania. The conviction that I am a sword in God's hand has often been used to justify an insane and murderous fanaticism.

It needs some internal clarification, because pure objective theological voluntarism (as I wish to call it, to distinguish it from the existentialist type of subjective voluntarism of the individual will) is not without its own intellectual difficulties. That which, being the fount of law, is above the law cannot be described as law-abiding. So if almighty divine power has posited all the norms of truth and goodness, no standpoint is left from which it can itself be judged true or good. We are left worshipping only absolute power for power's sake – and now we wonder whether or not the God of the system is anything more than a mere personification of the system's own spiritual power and its absolute claims on its own behalf. The system itself cannot decide the issue internally, and is obliged to call in the help of philosophy to clear the matter up.

Thirdly, it needs criteria for conducting its external relations with other truth-claimants. Some of these will be other systems like itself, others will be institutions that operate by very different criteria while also claiming to produce knowledge, and there is also philosophy. The system's internal criteria work very well with its own members who acknowledge its jurisdiction, but it cannot employ them in its external relations without at once becoming involved in a bruising power-struggle. To take a simple example, the Vatican cannot usefully invoke the infallibility of the church in its diplomatic activities; but the same considerations apply quite generally, to every believer's daily relations with the surrounding culture.

The faithful believe that there is a world without these small flaws, in which the system is whole, unrivalled and self-sufficient. But we do not yet live in it, for it is Heaven. Here below there has to be compromise: some acknowledgment of alien intellectual norms cannot be avoided. The system's standard device for limiting the damage this may do is to wrap it about with irony. Good-humouredly we admit that in a fallen world we must for the moment deal with the world on the world's terms – but that is all. We do not allow it to corrupt our souls.

Church leaders who must move rapidly back and forth between conducting such external negotiations and reverting to the exercise of their internal role within the hierarchy cannot avoid irony, in the sense of being aware of shuttling between widely different intellectual standards. Hence the well-known mediaeval debate about whether an Archdeacon can be saved. But the ordinary believer is more fortunate: she or he need not be disabled by compulsory ironization, and may continue the quest for spiritual integrity by turning to philosophy. Philosophy can help her to situate faith in the world, and to connect it satisfactorily with its environment. Faith seeks understanding, and understanding seeks faith. Faith's rather sketchy supernatural cosmology and vision of history, its sense of God, his will, his revelation and the divine order for human life, and its Christ-centred doctrine of sin and redemption, all need to be situated within a larger and more general cosmological vision, a natural theology. Hence the shift from will to reason, and from an ideology of power and control to a metaphysics of being.

Strangely though, the classical tradition of theistic metaphysics was never able to deliver a sense of the reality of an objective metaphysical God which was at all comparable with that gained by the older realism of power and the will. The reason for this lies in the special character of mainstream Greek philosophy.

Metaphysical realism is not primarily a doctrine about God, but a doctrine about the natural world. The Greeks framed the concept of nature as Cosmos, a stable, ordered and relatively-autonomous physical world, which was both independent of the human mind and at the same time thoroughly intelligible to it. Where we distinguish between the finite and the infinite (and readily associate infinity with God), they typically distinguished between the Formed and the Formless; and the Formless was evil, a limitless morass of repellent goo, chaos, and unthinkable because shapeless. As they saw it, intelligibility was shapeliness and was beauty: and the physical world was formed and shapely everywhere, to such an extent that the Greeks found it very difficult to recognize the elements of randomness and mere luck in life. Being everywhere formed and intelligible, the world could be seen (especially in the popular cosmic religion and in Stoicism) as being itself divine, at least in its upper heavenly regions, or as being permeated by a directing divine intelligence. This cosmic principle, the Logos, could readily be linked with late Jewish ideas about the divine Wisdom manifested in the created order. Even in the first century, St Paul saw Christ as the Wisdom of God and St John saw him as the Logos. So it came about that the first great gift of Greek philosophy to Christianity was not a metaphysical doctrine of God, but a high doctrine of creation and of Christ as the cosmic Logos.[1]

From what, though, did the Logos proceed? Greek philosophy took very much longer to arrive at a doctrine of God that even approximated to what Christianity required, because the Greeks had to regard their gods as being Formed and shapely, and therefore as finite and part of the cosmos rather than as transcending it. Plato's Form of the Good was indeed transcendent and beyond the cosmos – but it was therefore 'beyond being'. A thing could ordinarily only be, and be good, and be an object of knowledge, insofar as it was a Form or something Formed. As for the infinite and unbounded, it was Formless, unintelligible and evil, so that, odd though it may seem to us, there was for them a kind of incoherence in the very notion of an actual and all-good Being who was infinite. It was not until Plotinus, in the third century AD, that pagan Greek philosophy finally reached something like full-blown monotheism. The eternal One or Good in Plotinus is the ultimate reality, infinite, transcendent, simple and self-sufficient, and the source of all things. But although Plotinus did find a way to affirm the reality of One who is both good and real and also infinite, the ancient conviction that the infinite or unbounded must be incomprehensible remained, and became fixed in Christian thought in the form of the Negative Theology. Our thought can never comprehend God and our language can never describe him: the most they can do is orient themselves or point towards him without ever fully attaining him. An endless vista opens. When we look down a straight railway track the lines at first appear to the unaided eye to meet in the distance. But if we set off down the track we find that we cannot reach the meeting-point, for parallel lines meet only at infinity. Plotinus' idea of God similarly suggests that the soul seeking God embarks on a very long journey, and perhaps an infinitely long journey such as a finite being can never complete.

The development towards this doctrine of God and this image of the soul's path to God had begun with Plato. For Plato the Forms being timeless, perfect and intelligible had to be separated from the world of sense which was none of these things, and

located in a higher intelligible world. He thus began to develop the
idea of an ontological ladder, a scale of being, and a corresponding
epistemological ladder to be climbed by the soul as it rises towards
the highest object of knowledge, the Form of the Good. In his
Timaeus Plato also put forward, quite independently, the idea of
a divine craftsman who shapes the world and orders everything
for the best. He thus introduced the important idea of a benevolent
Providential government of the world which, as he believed,
philosophy could trace and defend against its critics.

There were various ways of systematizing Plato's ideas in
order to adapt them to the needs of the emergent philosophical
monotheism. The Forms had to be included within the divine
mind: that much was clear. There was also need for a distinction
between the ultimate and incomprehensible One, and a second
lower-level divine being who had emanated from him and who
Formed and guided the world. This provided the required philosophical basis for the distinction in theology between the Father
and the Son. It is best preserved in the art of the Eastern Orthodox
churches, where the Father as the ultimate and unknowable fount
of deity is not usually represented at all, and it is the Son who is
portrayed in human form as a grave cosmic superperson; the
point being that 'the old man in the sky' is in the East the Son,
and not the Father as is more commonly the case in the West. It
was permissible to picture the Logos in human form because he
himself had chosen to take it.

The thought-world of middle and later Platonism is of course
very remote from ours, but it is worth saying again what has been
said so often but is rarely fully grasped: Greek Christianity's
account of God truly was very agnostic. Ladder-metaphysics and
ladder-spirituality pointed towards that which was beyond being
and thought. Plotinus himself declared that the One 'does not
exist'. One might perhaps say that the word 'God' had the same
logical status as 'my aim' or 'my ambition', in that it functioned
as the unspecifiable object of a certain intentional orientation of
the soul, that which is indicated by right worship.

From this account it is clear that the God of Plato-based theism
and ladder-mysticism, like the God of Aristotle, was somewhat
inert. He functioned as an ultimate object of aspiration that lured
the soul towards itself; and Plato was quite explicit that the soul's
purification and its progressive ascent are brought about by

refining and spiritualizing the erotic impulse. Religion just *is* sublimated and purified eroticism. Celibates, who tend to see eros as a snake in the self and the root of our egoism, think that this makes sense; but the married know that it is wrong. Eros itself educates in altruism, for lovers soon find out that the other's pleasure is more erotic than one's own, and that if one is unduly self-concerned one cannot function at all erotically. Celibates frequently equate eroticism with egoism because all they know is erotic fantasy, which is indeed highly egoistic; but erotic reality is different. It is a wholesome moral education, good and plain as fresh bread. We doubtless need to be cured of egoism, but repressing eros is no way to set about it. Far better to learn through intercourse with them to respect the manifold ways in which life expresses itself in others than ourselves.

Kierkegaard saw in Platonic mysticism a forerunner of Romanticism. Both were driven by thwarted eroticism, and in both the soul was filled with a sense of exile, of transience, and insatiable yearning after an unattainable Object. This psychology has produced great art and mystical writing, but Kierkegaard came to regard it as pagan rather than Christian.[3] Certainly its impotence and quietism are in marked contrast with the vigorous, worldly and power-relishing spirit that we diagnosed in doctrinal realism, to say nothing of the active, outgoing temper of Christian *agapē*.

We have been stressing how thin and unsatisfactory was the outcome of the classical quest for philosophical knowledge of an objective metaphysical God. All it came up with was the incomprehensible One of the Negative Theology and the sublimated eroticism of the ladder-mystics, which seems very feeble compared with the vigour and worldliness of the religion that is based on power and the will.

Yet the church was not displeased by this result. The Negative Theology had usefully shown how impossible it was for mere human reason to gain an adequate knowledge of God, and how difficult it was for the solitary mystic to attain a union with God more perfect and satisfying than that offered by the ecclesiastical system. The obvious moral was that only a tiny sheltered minority (at most) would ever find religious satisfaction through philosophy and mysticism. For the rest of us the lesson is that we must be content with the limits of the human condition. We should renounce unrealistic aspirations and follow the safe way to salvation by submission to church authority. Ingeniously, the fact that the Negative Theology had not done very much to answer the questions posed by the old religion of power and authority was itself turned to good account by being made to justify a reversion to it.

This is confirmed by the ironical fact that if a philosopher claimed to have *succeeded* in the quest for philosophical know-ledge of an objective metaphysical God, and boldly defended the thesis that we can attain to an immediate rational intuition of the divine Being, then far from being thanked by the church he was on the contrary promptly suspected of heresy, because a satisfactory philosophy of God was highly undesirable. It would make the church redundant. Among those who have made claims of this kind, Bruno and Spinoza may no doubt be judged heretical on other grounds also; but Descartes and Malebranche although most careful never to impugn Catholic doctrine both fell under some suspicion, and in the nineteenth century 'the Errors of the Ontologists', Gioberti and Rosmini, were condemned by the Inquisition. The position is that the church requires of philosophy that it prove (*a*) that God exists, and (*b*) that he cannot be known by mere reason. Even if its religious temper was in many ways very unchristian, the Platonic tradition at least had the vital merit of meeting this *dual* requirement.

Platonism had a further attraction in ancient times: it inculcated foundationalist ways of thinking which have proved extremely durable. Even today they are widely regarded as essential to religious thought. In every field the doctrine was much the same: the mind could never be fully satisfied until it came to rest in the intuition of pure rational necessity. The local, the particular, the chance, the contingent had to be eliminated. Nothing had been fully explained until everything had been explained by reference to the ultimate self-explaining Explanation or Ground of all things. The changing could be conceived only against the back-ground of some eternal and unchanging basis of change. The conditioned must ultimately be traced back to some Uncon-ditioned condition of all conditions. The contingent must be grounded in the necessary, the finite in the Infinite.

The argument could take a great variety of forms. It might be a regress along a chain of causes in search of the Uncaused First Cause on which the entire series depends. It might claim that the changing, the limited and the conditioned are only conceivable as such against the background of at least an obscure, negative or indirect awareness of Something not so limited, as when Descartes argues that my awareness of my own imperfection shows that I have an idea of Perfection. It might take the form of an asymptotic approach towards the ideal limit of a series: we arrange things we know on a scale of degrees of durability or perfection, and the scale itself prompts an intuition of Eternal Perfection as the standard that makes any act of scaling things possible. Or it might be presented as an *a priori* requirement of reason, that its questioning cannot cease until it comes to a First Principle of all things that is single, eternal, self-sufficient and luminously self-explanatory.

These foundationalist styles of argument show the continuing influence of the principle of hierarchical order. They are the intellectual equivalent of the ecclesiastical demand for an ultimate authority, and of the mystical quest for the vision of God. Yet there is something odd here. Why was philosophy in the odd position of continually awakening a hunger for the Absolute, while simultaneously insisting that the One, or God, is incomprehensible? Something had surely gone wrong at a very early stage, and we need to understand what it was.

We have seen that Platonic ladder-metaphysics encouraged religious thought to turn in an other-worldly and ascetical direction – and the result was a languishing denial of life. This is puzzling, and an account is needed of how such a thing could ever have occurred in the first place. How could the productive life-energy whose expressions we are turn in the direction of pessimism, fall in love with death, and become a ghost of itself?

We saw that the life-energy, seeking richer and more diversified self-expression, generates symbols that facilitate its own self-affirmation. Of these symbols the most primal and potent are those which represent the synthesizing of diverse constituents into an organic unity by hierarchizing them under some sovereign principle. Thus the life-energy manifested itself as our various organs, physiological states and emotions, and then synthesized them through the primal narrative of the emergence of the I. I am thus enabled to see myself as a hierarchized organic unity, and an agent.

Along similar lines, narratives of unification into a hierarchized order under a sovereign principle make possible the emergence of ever greater organic totalities, from the primal family to the descent-group, the tribe, the State, and even the Cosmos itself. Myths relate and enact the organization of the primal family by our first parents, of the tribe by the tribal ancestor, of the state by the first king, and of the cosmos by God. Religion is the total stock of potent symbolic narratives and practices by which experience is organized into meaningful hierarchized organic unities. Often they are like a series of concentric spheres, each hierarchy being taken up into the one next larger than itself.

In the largest-scale polities, cosmologies and theologies the triumph of life becomes more magnificent and the hierarchies ever grander. Jewish monotheism in particular represents a culminating affirmation of divine dominance and creative, organizing power. Provided that the ordinary individual's life-aim and ethical activity could successfully be incorporated within, and seen as being of a piece with God's self-affirmation, then the flow of life was not blocked but enhanced as God glorified his people.

However, religious alienation could occur if the imagery of dominance became objectified, if lower-level hierarchies were not successfully subsumed within higher levels of organization, and if there was some loss of confidence in the very principle of organization itself. All these things have been known to happen. The gods could be objectified to the point of transcending life altogether so that they came to inhibit life, as if the symbol no longer facilitated but now blocked the thing symbolized. In a case where the political system no longer successfully incorporates the life-aims of the citizens, the I could feel a contradiction between its internal sovereignty within the sphere of the self and its lowly status as a mere cell within the larger body politic. And thirdly, the pessimism about the phenomenal world that led Plato to separate the world of Forms from it betokened a loss of confidence in the power of our symbols to organize experience. No longer actively at work organizing experience, the Forms are reified, and become objects of aesthetic contemplation in their own right.

Religion as life's symbolic self-expression needs not merely to generate the various hierarchies but also to affirm the unity of the whole hierarchy of hierarchies. At a simple level, it needs to provide images and practices through which I can identify my own life-aim with that of my god-king. Insofar as they are functioning successfully my aim is taken up into his and his is fulfilled in me, and there is no contradiction. But if the linking imagery and practices fail, he begins to look objectified to me and I begin to experience him as alien. To overcome the alienation, I must attempt to achieve union with him so as to restore the unity of his life-aim with mine. Mysticism is therefore an attempt to restore the unity of life by 'climbing the ladder', determinedly pushing my way up through the bureaucracy of levels of organization that I perceive as separating God from me. As I ascend, I get to be more like him and more able to make a direct and personal approach to him.

There is an element of muted social protest in mysticism. It is because the hierarchies have failed that the I seeks directly to realize its own union with the First Principle of all things. Psychologically, this grandiose ambition is no doubt historically continuous with the original desire for unity with the mother, but it is now immensely magnified.

How is the programme to be carried out? Inevitably, by setting up yet another hierarchy, the ladder of levels of the spiritual life, the stages of the soul's purification. By ascending the ladder we are to attain union with the One, the Good, the First Principle of all things. Yet there is something deeply ironical in this, because Plato's ladder actually incorporates, in his separation of the intelligible world from the world of sense-experience and biological life, the very self-doubt and alienation that it purports to overcome. The Forms themselves are no longer active, but mere objects of contemplation, and the mystical goal is not one of life-affirming activity but of quasi-aesthetic and passive contemplation. It is as if life, disgusted at itself by its own failure satisfactorily to organize the world of experience, attempts a final victory by going beyond itself on a path of self-conquest and self-transcendence. It is a superb ambition, but necessarily self-defeating. This ultimate One, this final unification, is incomprehensible and unattainable. Life's attempt through asceticism to conquer itself produces not superabundance but exhaustion. Insofar as it does indeed conquer itself, it merely reduces itself to an enfeebled ghost of itself.

5

DESIGNER REALISM

We have still not yet quite touched the nerve of popular realistic belief in God. We found *mythical realism* to be a matter of vivid symbolic pictures and stories which organize and give meaning to experience. It is realistic only in a qualified sense, realistic by default as one might say, in that it simply accepts these pictures and stories, knowing nothing else; making fully confident use of them, certainly, but without any sense of needing a theory of their status. This is a pre-theoretical and unconscious realism: to become fully explicit in the modern style it would have to be made more factually assertive by being interwoven with and infused by the spirit of a secular theory of nature. Only when that development has taken place do we have thoroughgoing theological realism, design-argument realism of the type presently to be discussed.

As for the classical Platonic type of *metaphysical realism*, we have seen that it fell far short of what popular faith demands. A neat illustration of this is given by Iris Murdoch, in a 1969 essay 'On "God" and "Good" ', where she has this to say:

> I shall suggest that God was (or is) *a single perfect transcendent non-representable and necessarily real object of attention;* and I shall go on to suggest that moral philosophy should attempt to retain a central concept which has all these characteristics.[1]

The formula italicized is in the Platonic style, and epitomizes the view of God put forward by the Negative Theology. Iris Murdoch accepts it and seeks to vindicate it. She would like to see moral philosophy rebuilt around such a vision of the Good. Surely then she is a straightforward Christian theist of the older type? Yet she says she is not, and she goes on:

> The religious believer, especially if his God is conceived as a person, is in the fortunate position of being able to focus his thought on something which is a source of energy.[2]

In short, although Iris Murdoch's view of God, or the Good, is that of the Platonic philosophical theology, she thinks that it is insufficient to count as a religious belief in God because it sees God only as an inactive *telos* of aspiration, or Ideal of supreme value. Such a God may be seen as a 'final cause', to which we are drawn as iron filings are drawn to a motionless magnet, but he or rather it is not the God of religion. Religion requires that he have also the attributes of power ascribed to him by *doctrinal realism*, and be experienced as creator, judge and saviour. He needs to be, if not exactly a person, at least an agent.

Iris Murdoch's case indicates therefore that Platonic theism never in fact delivered – and, given its basic assumptions, never had a hope of delivering – anything like the view of God as an active and at least quasi-personal being that is held by the ordinary believer. So far as the mainstream theism of the pre-modern period was realistic at all, it was so only through a highly incongruous combination of the Platonic Supreme Value with the power-God and the authoritative practical and doctrinal religion of revelation and the church.

One response to this is to suggest that modern anthropomorphic theism, with its demand for a *felt* personal relation to a personal God, has become a different religion from the more austere faith of the ancient and mediaeval periods. This is a plausible thesis. Since 1800 or so, it has been very common for religious writers to attribute an anthropomorphic belief in God to Jesus. They wish to see him as a man of prayer, whose prayer was an intimate person-to-person communion with the heavenly Father whom he addressed as *Abba*. Now, whether the texts really justify this view of Jesus is an unanswerable question, for it rests on pre-critical ideas about text and its interpretation. But it is very interesting that so many people desire to see Jesus in this way, because in speaking thus about him they reveal their own feelings about what prayer ought to be like, what religion ought to be like, and how we ought ideally to be able to experience God. The best, they feel, would be an intimate one-to-one *rapport* with a vividly experienced guiding and loving fatherly presence. This they therefore attribute to Jesus; but the point to be noticed is that the need to see Jesus in this way is modern. It is very uncommon before 1800, and perhaps unknown before the Reformation. As the service-books show, ancient and mediaeval prayer was relatively formal, distant and highly ritualized.

However, the mere observation that a certain style of piety and set of beliefs about God and religion are modern and historically heterodox does nothing to prove them wrong; and this particular form of religious consciousness deserves investigation in its own right and without prejudice, for it may well be regarded as a crowning religious and intellectual achievement. Religions and world views can be classified in terms of their visions of what in the end it is that we human beings are up against and must come to terms with. It might be a disorderly plurality of spirit powers, an orderly hierarchy of spirit beings, Destiny or Fate or Necessity, one impersonal material principle, an irreducible plurality of impersonal entities or laws, Chance or pure Chaos, a more-or-less benign principle of Progress or Providence, or a fully personal God. All these varied views have been held, and others too; and it is certainly arguable that to be able to represent that with which we must deal as a benign personal God, and to maintain this faith in one's life-practice, represents a triumphant affirmation of moral, of personal and of religious values. The history of religions and of philosophy shows that there is not and cannot be any objective old-style metaphysical Truth in these matters. That notion of truth is mythical. Moral and religious truth depends only on what, within the range of possibilities presented to us by our culture, we have the courage, optimism and strength to affirm and put successfully into practice in our lives. That being so, then there must be a case for saying that the greatest triumph of faith possible is that which brings all life under the control of a single vision of an all-good, all-wise, all-powerful anthropomorphic God who maintains the cosmic order and the moral order, and who communes intimately with each individual in prayer. Disparaging talk about anthropomorphism may be dismissed as expressing the *ressentiment* of the disillusioned and embittered. Of course it is anthropomorphic: to be so is precisely its greatness.

Although popular anthropomorphic theism, the layman's

natural religion, begins to take its modern form in the seventeenth century with the rise of natural science, it has ancient roots. We have mentioned Plato's teaching in the *Timaeus* about a great Craftsman or *Demiourgos* who has framed the physical world. Whether Plato himself intended what he says to be read as metaphysics or as myth (is there a difference?), it certainly resembles the design-argument theism of later times. The *Demiourgos* is a 'soul', at least a quasi-personal being, and perfectly good. He makes the world and time together, and the world is a process of becoming, not a haphazardly lurching flux but a unidirectional temporal *course* of things, so that the physical world manifests its maker's wisdom and goodness not only in its constitution but also in its course. For Plato, the philosopher could descry not only design but also providence. And although the world, being temporal and made of corruptible material, cannot be a perfect copy of the eternal world of the Forms, it is nevertheless as good a likeness as it can be.

The *Timaeus* is a book about cosmology and not piety, and Plato says nothing about whether we can know the *Demiourgos* or commune inwardly with him. In fact, philosophers have never found it easy to explain what direct person-to-person communion between a believer and a god could be, or how I can distinguish between an imagined unseen person beside me and a real one. When I talk about my sense of the presence of an invisible spirit, or of my belief that some thoughts that have just come into my head are words spoken to me by a spirit, effective criteria for distinguishing between the veridical and the illusory are not easy to find. However, although Plato is prudently silent on such points, this type of designer theism has remained ever since as one strand in religious belief. It could not easily become a dominant theme, because it is a layman's religion. It threatens to develop into a sufficient working natural religion that is logically independent of revelation and the power and authority of the church and until the power of the church had weakened somewhat it could not safely emerge.

However, it has emerged. It says that to believe in God is to hold that there exists a being who is (I quote a modern definition): 'a person without a body (i.e. a spirit) who is eternal, free, able to do anything, knows everything, is perfectly good, is the proper object of human worship and obedience, the creator and sustainer of the universe.'[3]

This doctrine does not exist alone. It carries with it a complete popular metaphysics, a whole array of other beliefs that it presupposes and entails. It is something of a shock to discover just how extensive this additional baggage turns out to be.

There is, first, a doctrine about the world, metaphysical realism. It is assumed that there is a cosmos out there, independent of our minds and yet intelligible to us. This cosmos is ordered, its orderliness is objective and inbuilt, and the basic principles of its design are sufficiently accurately known to us to be reliable premises for an argument from the design to its designer. We must consider ourselves already to possess objective and absolute knowledge of the ultimate principles of the world's constitution. Our present fundamental physical theory must be final, and not in danger of being undercut by any future refinements or theoretical revolutions. Otherwise, there may happen to us what happened to the Newtonian theologians: Alexander Pope wrote 'Nature and nature's laws lay hid in night; / God said, "Let Newton be!", and all was light'; but a disrespectful later commentator has added, 'It did not last; the Devil howling, "Ho! / Let Einstein be!", restored the status quo.'

Secondly, within this great objective cosmos whose fundamental structure is known to us, a special standing must be assigned to human beings and their valuations. The world order must be a moral order, having moral principles and properties such as we recognize and acknowledge built into its constitution and guiding its course, so that the Universe is analogous to the State. The presumption is that if, by observing how a people live, one can infer that their conduct is guided by morally-good laws that must have been prescribed to them by a king, then one might make a similar inference from the way the constituent parts of the universe behave.

Thirdly, the idea of a spirit as a person without a body must be intelligible. To make it so, we must suppose that we ourselves are dual, composite beings, embodied minds; that we are our minds; that we could subsist as complete persons without our bodies; and that there could be such a bodiless person, much greater than ourselves, who knows all things, has great power to act in the physical world, and so forth. The only analogy available to make this latter idea intelligible is our own power to move our bodies, so that we must suppose that God is able to move every part of the world in the same sort of way as we can move some parts of our bodies.

We owe the spelling-out of these – and other – corollaries of design-argument realistic theism to R. G. Swinburne, whose books *The Coherence of Theism* and *The Existence of God* (Oxford 1977 and 1979) are admirably explicit: if you wish to be a thoroughgoing theological realist, then this is what it requires. If he were an animist, Swinburne might have been able to give meaning to the claim that there is an almightly bodiless person behind the scenes by setting him at the summit of a hierarchy of lesser, finite spirits – angels, demons and the like – whose existence and activity are already generally recognized. That is how ancient thought first made the move to monotheism: God was a judge among gods, the top god. However, modern designer-theism is keen to show that it is not animistic but scientific, and its premisses must therefore be drawn from contemporary metaphysics and natural science and from a theory of human nature. In terms of the modern world-view the human mind is the only available analogy for God, so that Swinburne must see the human mind as a distinct and complete spiritual substance, if it is to do the job of helping to make God thinkable. This makes God very anthropomorphic, but it has the advantageous corollary of making the possibility of our communion with him a little more intelligible.

In addition to this, for Swinburne there has to be an objective and intelligible cosmos out there whose fundamental structure is known to us, so that the actual existence of a rational designer-god may be inferred from *its* existence. In this kind of theological realism God borrows his reality from the world's, in the 'order of knowing' at least. Hence my comment, at the beginning of this chapter, that traditional mythical religious thought is made realistic in the thoroughgoing modern sense only by being interwoven with and infused by the spirit of a secular theory of nature. The real world is held to be something more than the sum of all our experiences of it, and as the real world transcends experience, so God transcends the real world: therein consists his reality. And he transcends it as we transcend our bodies: therein consists his personality.

The point of view we are discussing, then, is both highly

anthropomorphic, and dependent on a strongly realistic view of the existence of the cosmos and of the objectivity and finality of our scientific theory. This can lead to problems. We have mentioned the case of Newtonian physics: another is that of biology, for during the eighteenth century it was widely thought that scientific theory ruled out any natural explanation of the origin of species. The various biological species were not eternal, could not have arisen by spontaneous generation, could not have arisen by the transmutation of other earlier species, and could not with any calculable probability have risen by a chance collocation of atoms. Therefore only a supernatural explanation of the origin of species remained – and therefore also, this type of designer-theism suffered a nasty blow when biological theory changed. Clearly designer theism will seem most persuasive in a period when scientific theory is stable and is believed to be final.

The mind-body dualism so essential to give designer theism intelligibility involves a strange dualism of the worlds of thought and being. Knowledge must be seen as a replication within the mental world of the structure of the physical. Thus, I have before me at this moment a pair of scissors. Mind-body dualism commits me to saying that I have before me two objects. There is an object out there, and a picture of it in here – a picture that, within the mental world, I bring under the concept 'pair of scissors'. Provided, then, that the mental picture is an accurate copy of the object, I can justly maintain that the object out there is one of the natural kind, pairs of scissors, just as the picture in here falls under the corresponding concept, 'pair of scissors'; and the better informed I get to be, the more detailed becomes the structural match between the mental world in here and the material world out there. In God's mental world the divine ideas are the archetypes of natural kinds, and in our mental world our concepts of things are copies of natural kinds.

But this is bizarre. I am not looking at two things, but just one, the scissors. A philosopher colleague just came in, and I checked with him. He agreed, 'Yes, that's a pair of scissors'. About something else we disagreed, but not about this; and the only distinction needed to account for this gratifying unanimity is the distinction between experience and language, the social and rule-governed activity through which, among other things, we formulate a common construction of the world of experience. In terms of a distinction we made earlier, language brings us forward from the subjective pole to the objective, from the formless and private to public order and meaning. The distinction between experience and language corresponds to the deep old mythical distinction between chaos and cosmos, the world as a structureless flux of proto-experience and the world ordered and made intelligible by language. There is no way we could ever detect the establishment of a 'real' intelligible world order out there independent of us, because we can none of us know anything prior to or apart from our own initiation into the linguistic, world-ordering human community. As for the supposed two parallel worlds of material bodies and of minds, they are mythical. To explain the way things are, no more is needed than language and experience. To see this, compare two possible worlds: in World One all experience is just as it is now, whereas in World Two all experience is just as it is now but in addition there is a real world of material bodies, natural kinds and the like. Where's the difference? Since in World One natural science would be just the same as it is now, there seems to be no gain in postulating an additional world beyond the world of experience.

To make realism intelligible and give it content and plausibility, various arguments in support of it are brought forward. It is argued that a real material world transcending our experience is needed to be the cause of our experience; but a uniquely odd causal relation is involved here, for how can we check the relation of all experience to something unexperiencable that is supposed to stand on the farther side of it? It is argued that the real world must be postulated to account for the fact that our experience is sufficiently stable, coherent and shared to give us a common public world; but it is precisely the function of language to order experience in this way. It is argued by Sartre that consciousness is essentially transitive, in that it is always consciousness-of; but this is only to say that experience is indeed . . . experience. It is argued by Kant that objectivity is presupposed by the very possibility of our being able to have experience and a point of view, but this need mean no more than that, once they are distinguished, the objective and subjective poles within our experience are seen each to imply the other. It is held, in different ways by Hume and by the later Wittgenstein, that objectivity is a natural belief built into all our thinking and language, which cannot meaningfully be denied; but this means only that our linguistically-constructed common world in which we find ourselves is indeed indispensable to our sense of ourselves. That is a fact, but it is only a fact.

There seems to be no argument for realism which singles it out and gives it distinct intelligibility and plausibility as a doctrine. The arguments that are advanced can readily be met, in one way by George Berkeley from his point of view, and in another way by a modern constructivist.

Furthermore, experience itself is always culturally moulded or, in the jargon, 'theory-laden'. There is no way of detecting structure in it prior to our act of putting a construction upon it. There is, for example, no way of testing whether our way of apprehending space and time and colour, and in general of classifying things, is 'correct' as compared with the way these things are done in some other culture. That we feel we must operate in the way we do shows neither that our way is objectively founded nor that it is uniquely privileged. There are, it would seem, an indefinitely large number of possible ways of world-making.

There is no wholly pre-conceptual or uninterpreted experience, for prior to all interpretation nothing is present but a mere physiological state. So the formula is that our physiological states, plus the culturally-supplied symbols and concepts that transform them into expressive and intelligible representations, become our experience; and because experience is from the first evoked and shaped by a common culture, experience is from the first capable of being organized into a common social world through language. The only – but powerful – constraint upon the whole process is that we must make a world in which we can function, a world in which we can live, find our way around and interact with each other. The productive life-energy that expresses itself successively in our emergent physiological states, our experience, our social life and our common world, since it seeks maximally varied and vigorous expression, must seek coherent expression. It must seek a language, a total stock of social practices and symbolic forms, that hangs together and generates a sufficiently coherent social order and world order. As society becomes more large-scale, the quest for vigorous and coherent systematic expression requires us to develop philosophy, natural science and the like, all of which work out the implications of, and try to resolve the problems left by, the way the basic stories, symbols, concepts and so forth were set up from the first. Eventually the knowledge-systems we generate get to be so complicated that we reify them, attribute to them an objectivity independent of ourselves, and talk as if we think that our present physics, for example, copies the order of a *physis* (an order of nature) that was objectively established long ago before there were any human beings at all. The impulse to objectify in this way is understandable, because our present physics represents the stage we have reached in trying to systematize awkwardnesses that were already implicit long ago in the ways our basic concepts of space, time, thinghood, activity and so on were first set up, and which subsequently became built into the syntax we have inherited. Hence the appearance of objectivity. But in another sense the objectivity is clearly mythical. Instead of thinking of the designer God as fixing just one great pattern of cosmic order long ago and then inserting us into it, it would be better to identify God with the productive life-energy within us which is continually generating our evolving patterns of social life and our constructions of the world order. Physics does not copy an antecedently existing cosmic order. Rather, our physics, with all the technologies and practices based on it, *constitutes* the presently-known cosmic order.[4]

If in this way we move to an expressivist viewpoint we can, surprisingly, return to scientific realism and see it in a more sympathetic light. For the cosmic order can now be identified with the present state of development of our physical theory and technical practice (including here the theory of the world that is embedded in our everyday language and working practice, as well as the highly elaborated and refined supplement to it that we call physics). And scientists are right, we are suggesting, always to talk as if they think the world is just what current theory says it is, because our present construction of reality does indeed constitute all there can be for us to say just now about how things are.

We may also look more sympathetically at the rise of the anthropomorphic designer God since the seventeenth century, and the turn of religious thought since then in a more humanist direction. A revolution had occurred, and a new truth-power was established. Less than a century earlier, Christian art had still portrayed God the Father in the likeness of the Pope, but now

Galileo had introduced the habit of speaking of him as a mathematician and engineer. The God of the new mathematical-mechanical cosmology expressed a growing confidence in new ways of ordering the world. He was a kind of personification of the spirit of scientific optimism. He inhabited, understood, unified and controlled the cosmos as easily as we do our own bodies: 'All are but parts of the stupendous whole / Whose body Nature is, and God the soul.' In him one saw the objective, archetypal and final triumph of the productive life-energy within us, so that there was naturally an analogy between the macrocosm and the microcosm.

We see now why it is that designer theism is highly realistic while at the same time being easily transformed into expressivism. A ghost of the older ways of thinking, a thin veil of myth, was retained to prevent it from becoming fully aware of itself, so that it could continue to regard itself as discovering rather than inventing, and as copying a pre-established cosmic order rather than constituting a new one. That thin veil of myth made it possible to argue from the striking analogy between A and B to a metaphysical conclusion, instead of recognizing the identity of A and B. Thus design arguments were able to find metaphysical significance in the analogy between contrivance, order and beauty in nature and the same things in works of human art, because they did not acknowledge that the vision of nature as beautifully ordered and contrived was itself another work of human art. When they found that in physical theory, other things being equal, the more elegant and economical theory is to be preferred, they thought that they must be thinking God's thoughts after him, and forgot that they were building a cosmology and that to make it powerful their building activity *must* be guided by these criteria. They marvelled that when they contemplated Nature they saw something not hostile and chaotic but framed, beautiful and intelligible: but they did not realize that it was they themselves whose achievement it had been to make it so. All along, they saw themselves as copyists and not creators, so that for them there were always two things, the pre-existent cosmic order and the copy of it in Newton's system, whereas for us with our hindsight there is only one.

They saw God anthropomorphically, as a cosmic mathematician and engineer. Did this not suggest to them that he was a kind of personification of the spirit of science itself? No, because the veil of myth that still hung before their eyes maintained the distinction between the cosmic order out there and the scientists' representation of it, between design in Nature and the design of our theories, and so long as the distinction held God could be understood in a way that was both highly realistic and highly anthropomorphic. The texts written at the height of the cult of Newton may at first seem to a modern reader to bring Newton and God very close together. The poet James Thomson, in a commemorative ode written after Newton's death, invokes him in the language of prayer: 'look with pity down / On humankind, a frail erroneous race!'[5] D'Alembert, in the introduction to his *Elements of Philosophy*, declares that 'the true system of the world has been recognised, developed and perfected',[6] and Laplace in passing remarks that 'Newton established the principle of universal gravitation';[7] the sort of comments that seem quite unexceptionable until a later philosophical shift makes us suddenly aware of an ambiguity in them. At the time, however, the ambiguity was not and could not be apparent. Metaphysical realism about the objective cosmic order, and scientific realism about Newton's system as an accurate but secondary and distinct representation of that order, both held firm. God was the great Architect, and Newton was but the student of his works. We may have been demythologized by hindsight, by knowledge of the history of science, and by the legacy of German idealist philosophy and the social sciences; but they were not. They had established designer-theism as a layman's natural religion, logically independent of the doctrinal realism of the church – deism, it was called by its orthodox critics – and for the present they were well content with that.

Yet when all this has been said, designer-realism continues to exercise an immensely powerful hold over us. As both Hume and Kant acknowledged, it has a kind of primacy and inevitability which still in our own day enable it to survive, even in the face of the problem of suffering, rapid change in scientific theory and devastating philosophical criticism. It is sustained, no doubt, by an archaic need to feel that we are not alone, and by the conviction that human consciousness cannot be self-originating but can only arise as a response to Another. Both these hunches might be explained in terms of our early psychic life, but they are greatly reinforced by the old mythic impulse that leads us to think that beyond our own construction of the world there has to be a Real state of things that duplicates, supports, explains, justifies and may also correct it.

Cicero remarks that man is the being who must create for himself a 'second Nature'. Unable to live directly in the wild, he uses natural materials to build an artificial environment for himself. It has various layers: clothing, houses, farmlands surrounding them. Today we have reached the point where we have to reverse Cicero: man is the being who is not content with the house of meaning, the world to live in that he has built around himself, but must in addition surround it with a Second House to protect it.

Because the need for the Second House is so strong, designer realism is undoubtedly a potent form of religious consciousness, especially among people who are confident in the strength and stability of their world view. Of all forms of religious belief it is much the most vulnerable to the problem of evil: indeed, it is decisively refuted by it. Yet the very fact that people today feel so strongly the weight of the challenge to belief in God that the world's suffering presents is indirect testimony to the continuing influence of designer realism, just because other kinds of belief in God do not feel the challenge so acutely.

The great attraction of designer realism to most people, apart from its engaging anthropomorphism, has been the fact that it is relatively non-political. Most other forms of religion in the Western tradition, from the oldest orthodoxies to the newest sects, regard submission to an all-too-human power structure as being of the essence of faith. Christ's teaching that you must lose your life in order to save it has been understood by us in such a way as to legitimate our impulse to surrender our intellectual and moral freedom to some authority in return for its consoling guarantees of forgiveness and salvation. It is no accident that the first modern designer realists were lay writers of the late seventeenth century who styled themselves 'free-thinkers'. They were seeking to describe a religion free from tyranny because it was based on nature and not on society, and designer realism has therefore attracted liberals ever since.

What has finally undone it in recent times has been the strange way in which the first house has overwhelmed the Second House since the rise of technological civilization. Technological society sets out to remake everything. It acknowledges no fixed order of things whatever. Nature is merely a source of raw materials for it. Human nature and society are clumsy unplanned artefacts of past history, and therefore are just as much up for reshaping as everything else. All life becomes dominated by questions of technical expertise, efficient management and restructuring. In earlier world views the ideas of being, order and truth functioned as reminders of a permanent framework within which human life is lived. But all conceptions of such a framework have themselves been demythologized by being shown to be cultural products: they were the ideological fictions by means of which social cohesion and control were maintained in the past. Now, they also are up for reshaping.[8]

In technological society attempts by religion to recall people to older conceptions of a fixed and unalterable order of things are futile. Reactionary religion of that type will find itself being viewed merely as a technical problem. It will be understood, tolerated, and managed into ineffectuality. It will be tolerated, because it will be seen as part of what is nowadays called our culture or our traditional way of life, and as such it is of some value as a tourist attraction; but that will be the limit of its influence on public life. Some philosophers, such as Heidegger in his *What is Metaphysics?* (a lecture of 1935, published in expanded form as a book in 1953), have attempted to diagnose what has gone wrong with technological civilization and to reinstate the older concern with Being, but we all know that such efforts will have no influence whatever on the way things go in the world.

The only publicly-effective form that religious and ethical activity can take in technological society is commitment to the struggle to influence the process of social change. In the most developed countries this struggle can no longer take a revolutionary form, because the means of social control are now far too powerful. Revolution cannot occur, because the State can so easily monitor the first emergence of revolutionary groups and manage them out of existence. But party politics and pressure-group politics remain: one can at least attempt to influence the direction of public policy. Indeed, the struggle to do so is now the chief ethical imperative. There may, then, be a place for a form of religious belief, free from metaphysical nostalgia, which begins from the idea of lived obedience to the commands of God and which seeks to bring the world under the rule of God. To this we now turn.

6

OBEDIENTIARY REALISM

Designer realism, being the simplest and most popular form of realistic theism, has been much discussed, and its difficulties are well known. They include the logical problems of the design argument itself, the facts of evil in the world, its naively mythical anthropomorphism, and the puzzle about what the kind of disembodied person it envisages could possibly be. Most disabling of all is its curiously weightless quality; it often seems to differ little in practice from a mere expression of innocent cosmic optimism.

Obedientiary realism, in spite of the rather dreary name I have invented for it, is a much more serious matter. It is less all-things-bright-and-beautiful and more adult; a protestant, moralized and internalized version of doctrinal realism. Like designer realism but more vehemently, it rejects the external control of reason and conscience by any human power structure, including that of the church; indeed, especially that of the church. Unlike designer realism, though, its logic is biblical and practical rather than inductive and theoretical. Pessimistic about nature and sceptical about the power of natural human reason, it denies that philosophy can grasp what God's reality is for us. Instead it holds that the objective reality of God is made known to us only by the way we need him, the way we believe in him and above all by the way he is to be obeyed. The reality of God cannot be fixed by us theoretically, but shows itself in our reception of it and in our practice. Obedientiary realism detests idolatry and repudiates every sort of worldly objectification of religion, seeing life as a pilgrimage through a dark world in which the man of faith puts his trust in nothing whatever except the guiding will of God as it is revealed to him. The classic exemplar of this type of faith is Abraham.

Obedientiary realism is a kind of religion to which we now find it particularly hard to do justice. The reason for this is historical: we cannot help recalling how completely, between Kant and Sartre, the Protestant hero of faith became secularized into the existentialist hero. Like his predecessor, the existentialist was also a solitary pilgrim, a lover of freedom who refused to bow the knee and looked only to his own inner resources to guide him through life. But the existentialist hero, as seen for example in the novels of Albert Camus, was an atheist; and in any case with the decline of individualism he seems now to be passing into history along with his Protestant forerunner. All this may well lead us to suspect that old-style heroic Protestant individualism was never a very stable and distinct form of religious consciousness, but was merely a transitional phenomenon bridging the gap between medieval and modern forms of selfhood. Maybe, and maybe not: at any rate I hope to show that in its day and on its own terms it made sense, that it had its own grandeur, and that it is still a stage that many of us must pass through. And it was a genuine form of theological realism.

Nevertheless it must be acknowledged that many of its basic assumptions are now strange to us, and we shall have to make a detour in the attempt to understand it. Obedientiary realism was intensely dualistic and even paradoxical in the way it suspended the spirit between sharply conflicting attitudes that were held simultaneously. Thus it was world-affirming in that it emancipated the monk and the nun from the cloister, told them to marry, and insisted that they could and must live together a holy life, pleasing to God, as they pursued their secular callings. But at the same time it also took a very pessimistic view of sexuality, of human nature in general, of the prospects for a full Christianization of society, and of the physical world. The darkness of life persisted even while faith was from moment to moment overcoming it. By rejecting the old traditions of natural theology and Aristotelian philosophy the Reformers had lost much of the ancient confidence about the physical world, without yet gaining the renewal of optimism that was to come with the first great successes of natural science. As a result they lived in an interim time when thoughts of sin, corruption, death and judgment were close, and signs of (mostly hostile) supernatural intervention abounded. The sixteenth century was in many respects a sombre age. Augustine's long shadow still hung over it, and many late-mediaeval attitudes persisted. Even while they were considerably modifying its import, the Reformers used the language of heteronomy in a most extreme form. Man was a dumb beast, unable of himself either to know or to do right, and incapable of finding his own way. He had to be ridden, and if he was not ridden by God then he would be ridden by Satan. One or the other of them must be his master, and there was no third possibility. Finally, the new technology of printing could put thousands of identical copies of a text into the hands of individuals, and so made the Bible available as the needed guide to life. It was a portable oracle, the medium through which God's will was made known to each individual, a compendium of all the knowledge most necessary to us, the world in a text, the epitome of everything from A to Z, a complete, perfect and infallible tutor.

How is the rise of this type of religion to be explained? Psycho-historical explanations easily become fanciful, but it is worth remembering that Protestantism began among people for whom the relation of time to salvation had become a matter of urgent concern. Many of them were German and Swiss townspeople, merchants and small craftsmen, clockmakers and printers. These people knew all about calculation, precision and the payment of bills on time. They were devout, and were imbued with Latin Christianity's odd combination of searching moralism with legalism, its highly juridical conceptions of sin as a crime against God's majesty and of the penalties that must be paid for it. It is not exactly easy for us now to imagine a period when one saw people in the evening of their lives as being just about to commence serving sentences of several hundred thousand years of extremely unpleasant punishment, but Jacques Le Goff has recently explored the intellectual and social significance of the concept of Purgatory.[1] In addition, these folk were beginning to feel the impact of the individualism and humanism of the Italian Renaissance. Put these various factors together – irreversible and uniform linear clock-time, the quantified legal theology of sin and punishment, and individualism – and it is not difficult to imagine the extremes of religious anxiety and dread that were possible, and which the

church did not fail to exploit. It was inevitable that people should
seek urgently for some way of deliverance from the monstrous
burden and the threatened penalties of past sin. The quest for
salvation took the form of a struggle to wake out of religious
nightmares and to find a way of life based on a solid present
assurance of God's forgiveness and one's immediate relation to
him.

Again, all these ideas may seem remote, and to make them
intelligible we need to use some later material. We begin therefore
with the primacy of the ethical, and with Kierkegaard's well-
known remark that life can be understood only backwards,
whereas we have to live it forwards. That is, all theoretical
knowledge and understanding are inescapably retrospective,
being based on things that have already happened and so have
become fixed. As such, theoretical knowledge can certainly show
us the burden and the legacy of the past, but it cannot tell us
anything about the way to freedom. The possibility that my life
may *change* cannot become visible on the basis of my study of my
own past, which reveals me to myself only as one bound by the
law of cause and effect. However, I am not merely an observer of
my own past, crying over spilt milk; I am an agent in the present
moment. For me as agent now, the centre of the universe, the
point at which everything decisive is happening, is this present
moment of action. In this present moment and here alone my
eternal destiny is being decided; what I am to be and will hereafter
always be is becoming crystallized through my action. God and
Satan, Heaven and Hell, loom about me right now. And I cannot
be delivered from my past by theoretical knowledge, which is
merely knowledge of the past, and tells me nothing about how I
am now to act. My eternal destiny depends only on the set of
practical principles that at present govern my action – and this is
what is meant by the primacy of the practical. Government makes
reality. What I am is in this present moment being actualized by
him whom I obey, who rules my action. If the law that rules my
life-action is the will of God, then God is making me his and I am
God's eternally.

Thus at the leading edge of reality, in this present moment of
decision, everything depends on that which rules my action and
so creates me. But I cannot be delivered from the burden of my
past by a law that is itself merely natural, theoretical and of the

past. I must repudiate everything that is merely of the past, merely natural, merely theoretical, merely based on what has been. To be delivered from the past I must be converted. I must change my life and come under the rule of a new law of life that is supernatural, the law of Christ. This new law of life shows its own supernatural and transcendent character precisely in its power to deliver me from my past and set my feet on a new path. Thus conversion and obedience can reveal objective transcendence. In my new life not some but all of my good works are done by divine and supernatural grace, for nature and the past can know nothing of moral goodness. No good works can be done except by grace. Past-grounded and merely natural knowledge can show me only my past wrongdoing, and from its point of view there is no reason to expect anything but the continuance of my well-established evil habits. Since it can know nothing of freedom, my past traps me in nature and can show me only an inevitable downward slide. I can make the move from the sphere of nature to that of freedom only by coming under the rule of a set of authoritative transcendent principles of action, a supernatural law of life that I can in faith appropriate and live by from moment to moment. If I do this, then I have eternal life while still living in time, and am assured of salvation. Thus what I need is God's forgiveness, grace and rule in my life. And by God I just mean that transcendent and creative moral Power which I find delivers me from my past and sets my feet upon the path of freedom. This Power alone enables me to do good works and to face the future with hope. It is through the Bible and the word of preaching that I hear of such a God and find his will for my life made known to me.

Like the neo-orthodox Protestant theologians, I have had to borrow from the later language of existentialism in order to make classical Protestantism intelligible. This is not accidental, because Kant and many of the pioneers of existentialism were themselves Protestants by birth and were entirely conscious of continuing certain Protestant themes, as is particularly obvious in the way they contrasted the worlds of nature and of freedom, in their stress on the primacy of the practical, and in their doctrine that by moral action we can escape from bondage to time. But although existentialism thus resembled Protestantism in its stress on the individual's action in the present moment, it never took so realistic a view of God. For existentialism, we could make the conception of ourselves as rational agents intelligible to ourselves only if we assume that we have an *autonomous* capacity to step out of the sphere of nature and into the sphere of moral freedom; whereas for classical Protestantism we had no such autonomous capacity. According to Protestantism, by nature we are bound. We may indeed at first have been created free, but that freedom had been lost. It was the divine will and the divine grace alone which could release us from bondage to Nature, and thereafter maintain our freedom by governing our lives. For existentialism freedom creates reality, whereas for Protestantism God alone creates reality. Good works, freedom, and reality-production are all seen as past-transcending creative expressions of the divine will active within us. Classical Protestantism was thus firmly theocentric and, in its own way, heteronomous, whereas existentialism steadily developed into an atheistic doctrine of autonomous human freedom.

The Kantian contrast between nature and freedom is a philosopher's moderated version of what was originally a much more extreme contrast; for the classical Protestant contrasted natural determinism and theological determinism. Sin is a life ruled by the past, by nature, by Satan: faith is the freedom of a life that is wholly ruled by God. If I make the mistake of putting theoretical knowledge first in my scheme of things, I allow the present to be naturally determined by the past. But the past is sin, and the chains of habit. If I look at myself only in the light of my past I can see myself only as Satan's. My will is bound; I may perhaps feel remorse, but I do not have the freedom to change or escape. I am in bondage to the world, stuck in the mass of perdition. For Protestantism, the moral condition of natural man in the world is just like that of a motorist caught in a traffic jam. I cannot turn, I cannot change, I cannot do any good works. I may fume impotently, but I cannot achieve the world-transcendence or world-mastery of which I (very obscurely) remember I am capable. But if I put the ethical and the present moment first in my scheme of things, if I repent and break the entail of the past and by faith accept the saving will of God as the new law of my life, then all things are made new. The new world that I now see coming into being through my action is God's world, being created by him as I do his will.

We have been using as a general principle of interpretation the

rule that the productive life-energy in us seeks maximally vigorous
and varied expression. However, at certain periods the prevailing
historical and cultural conditions are experienced as blocking its
flow. These blocks to life's expressive and ethical flow, these
barriers to our ethical life-affirmation, are then experienced and
described as evils, metaphysical, natural and moral. They include
finitude, death, suffering, craving, and moral ignorance, impotence and sinfulness. They are always characterized in universal
terms as if they were conditions of bondage to which all human
beings everywhere have always been subject, but in retrospect it
is clear that this is not exactly the case. The details of the various
particular analyses of human bondage that are given are always
culturally determined. But however they are described,
salvationist religion is always an attempt to escape from the
conditions that are currently experienced as binding us, and
the imagery of salvation is much the same everywhere: it is
emancipation, deliverance, release, victory, illumination, healing,
fulfilment and the like, the common theme being that a way has
been found to overcome the barriers to life's flow. Following
Freud's account of the formation and function of our dreams, we
might say that the productive life-energy, unable to find direct
expression, generates a religious ideology and set of practices
through which it can find a way round the obstacles in its path.

At the time of the Reformation the obstacles seemed wholly
insurmountable. A highly heteronomous politics of absolute
sovereignty, time-dread, world-pessimism, and a sense of intellectual and moral impotence threatened life with utter stultification.
But if the life-impulse was stopped completely, how could it renew
itself? Only by so-to-say alienating itself from itself, and resuming
its activity on the far side of the barrier. It dies and is reborn: it
dematerializes itself on this side of the barrier, and regenerates
itself on the far side. Death, sin and the Devil between them have
brought my old natural life-expression to a halt and I am dead;
but on the far side of that total loss of life I experience a
supernatural renewal of life. This self-renewal of life I experience
as my own regeneration by the grace and forgiveness of the living
God. However, the old stultified natural order remains. Society,
my own nature and the environing conditions are still what they
were. So I can live, act and pursue my new supernatural life only
on the basis of continually accepting the nullification of my old

natural life-impulse and continually accepting my new supernatural life-power as if from above. My evil impulses and deeds continue and are products of my old selfhood, but through faith I continually repudiate them and allow the new life-impulse to affirm itself in me. I am 'at once righteous and a sinner', my evil impulses being all mine and my good works being all God's.

Protestant doctrine is then an extraordinary *tour de force* of the life-impulse, achieved under particularly trying historical conditions. Instead of lapsing into quietism or fleeing from the world – the typical solutions of earlier periods – it found a way of returning to and acting in the very same world that it nevertheless knew to be still under the dominion of sin, death and the Devil. At the time of its origin its highly heteronomous and paradoxical language represented the only solution to the religious problems it confronted. But by the end of the seventeenth century conditions had already changed so much that the language of classical Protestantism, which had once been so liberating, was itself in its turn also beginning to sound artificial, alienating and oppressive. Since that time the liberating power of the language of full-blooded Protestantism has worked effectively only in certain restricted contexts. The chief examples are when individuals find themselves blocked by the psychological conflicts of adolescence, when social groups find themselves politically and economically so tightly inhibited that they cannot act effectively in the wider society, and when people have lived through such violent and rapid social change that their past, through which they would normally identify themselves, has become dead to them. I have seen theologies of the Reformation kind visibly working in all these contexts; but they are restricted, and if one strives to hold on to an orthodox Protestant faith in life-conditions to which it is no longer appropriate the results are disastrous. A sign of this is that curious and rather depressing situation which is so familiar in certain churches: it is only those who are very liberal or ironical in their faith who approximate to being tolerable human beings.

There are indeed certain moments of severe conflict and frustration in our lives for which the classical Protestant form of religious consciousness represents, if not the only, then surely the most powerful solution. St Paul has described them in the first half of the *Epistle to the Romans*. But inevitably the solution reflected, and so preserved, the initial contradiction. The believer (let us try the effect of the feminine pronoun) cannot experience her new life as being truly her own: her righteousness is merely imputed. Her initial natural condition of total depravity and life-frustration had been so severe that salvation could only be believed in if it was pictured in the language of unconditional election and prevenient, irresistible grace. This extravagantly heteronomous imagery had to be used, to safeguard the purely given and supernatural character of the new life and to preclude even the least hint of synergism; but the consequence was that the believer remained fixed in a schizoid mentality. To maintain the triumph of faith in herself she must continually disparage nature, reason and everything merely human, and give all the glory to God in a sustained act of ecstatic self-transcendence. Magnificent; but *corruptio optimi pessima*. Once the first supernatural joy of the conversion experience had faded, the believer maintained her faith and bore witness to God's free grace precisely by the unremitting vehemence of her self-disparagement and self-mistrust – that is, by an intropunitive and ascetical psychology. Her experience of grace no longer came to her spontaneously as life's own solution to a life-problem, so she began to force it psychologically. The old self in her though dead would not lie down, and must constantly be mortified. Her prayer had to take the form of the self-abasement of a sinful human being before a holy God, and she was using it not to heal but to maintain and even to exacerbate the split within herself. The forcibly self-divided psychology was a necessary condition for her experience of God's saving grace, for only insofar as she detested herself and utterly despaired of herself could she receive grace. By a tragic paradox, she bore witness to the reality of an absolute liberation by being uncompromisingly repressive.

The contrast at this point with designer realism is most instructive, and shows clearly why the two forms of religion are so sharply opposed to each other. For designer realism, as we saw, God borrows his reality and his goodness and wisdom from the reality of and the goodness and wisdom displayed in the cosmic order, whereas for thoroughgoing Protestantism nature has to be equated with Satan and Satan's dominion, and the reality of God appears only when everything merely natural has been renounced and put to death. God must first kill before he makes alive.

The full-blown Protestant conversion experience, arrived at in a moment of the direst extremity, undoubtedly represents one of the supreme moments in the spiritual life. Those who have never passed through it (or at least, something like it) are unfortunate; but those who have failed to move on from it are more unfortunate still. For what happens if we hold on to the view of things that we took in the moment of conversion, and make it the basis of our theology and our life-practice? Inevitably, in our attitude to life and our moral relations we will feel called upon to bear witness to God's sovereign grace by condemning the merely human in others as we have learnt to condemn it in ourselves. (And I invite the reader to consider: was the feminine pronoun *odd*? Do we ordinarily see the psychology of classical Protestantism in very masculine terms?)

It is customary in attempts to explain the decline of high Protestantism to point to philosophical and biblical criticism as having steadily eroded the belief that there can be an absolute, revealed and complete moral code to live by and that in the Bible we have been given it. That story can indeed be told, but it is insufficient as an explanation. At a deeper level, the cultural and religious conditions of the early Reformation period demanded and created the ideology of the Bible as a complete revelation of God's saving will for human life. Given those conditions, it was a necessity of life that the Bible should be everything the Reformers said it was, and should continue to be so for as long as those conditions held. Reason is the servant of the life-impulse, and as long as the life-impulse required people to find in the Bible a coherent and sufficient rule of faith and guide to life, then they found it. But when the ambient conditions changed and the life-impulse became able to express itself in other ways, then the maxim *sola scriptura* was no longer the life-imperative that it had been. On the contrary, it had now itself become a new form of bondage from which people needed to free themselves. Criticism thus did not create, but rather followed, a deeper shift.

Why should this deeper shift have occurred if – as I fully acknowledge – the thoroughgoing Reformation theology represented as profound a diagnosis of the limits of the human condition and as great a victory over them as there has ever been? It must be because the Protestant way to salvation left the self still intolerably divided. To overcome the barrier of sin, death and impotence that blocked its path, the life-impulse died and was reborn. It renounced itself on the near side of the barrier, and renewed itself on the far side. To make this extraordinary event intelligible, the renewed life had to be represented as being wholly supernatural and extrinsically bestowed, having nothing in common with the old natural life that it was superseding. 'I live, yet not I': the old natural self and the new regenerate Christ-self still for the present co-existed. The believer inhabited two opposed worlds simultaneously – and the heteronomous and dualistic theology forbade him or her to unify them, for if that were done the cutting edge of the gospel would be blunted.

In the Protestant gospel we see both the highest achievement of thoroughgoing theological realism, and its inevitably transitional character. The antithesis between God as an absolutely sovereign, holy and gracious Lord and man as his weak and sinful creature makes possible a marvellous way of deliverance from bondage, but also makes impossible the subsequent full integration of the believer's life and personality. In him life is still at odds with itself because the old dualism between nature and spirit, God and man has not been overcome – and it shows.

We have worked our way through the five main forms of theological realism and have seen how remarkably diverse they are. The *mythical realism* of a traditional society that lives within its stories, and accepts them implicitly because it has no other forms of religious understanding with which to contrast them, is perhaps the most beautiful and the one for which we feel the greatest nostalgia; but we lost it irretrievably long ago. The others remain live options, after their fashion. The attractiveness of *doctrinal realism*, in which truth is created by power, is for many people, unfortunately, enhanced rather than diminished by the fact that it demands submission to authority and a sectarian view of the world. In the main Catholic and Orthodox traditions of Christianity doctrinal realism is interestingly blended with and mitigated by mystical Platonic *ladder realism*, which relativizes it and thereby creates more spiritual space for the soul to move in. But at its heart ladder realism is so negative as scarcely to be realism at all. *Designer realism* is the popular anthropomorphic natural religion of a scientific age, liberal but somewhat weight-less. *Obedientiary realism*, in which God's reality is positively contra-natural and is shown in his Lordship over the regenerate believer's life, is grand and religiously extremely weighty. At one time I felt its full force; but its psychology soon becomes unendurable, and the view of the Bible that it requires has therefore become incredible.

We turn next to two forms of semi-realism.

7

PROTESTANT ETHICAL IDEALISM

For several decades now, we have had an uncomfortable suspicion that large areas of our traditional moral vocabulary are becoming redundant and slipping out of use. Words like conscience, duty, obligation, moral law, sin, guilt, commandment and repentance may still be heard in specialized and conservative arenas like the lawcourt and the church, but are vanishing from everyday speech. Morality, it seems, is suffering attrition, being secularized and therefore demythologized, and undergoing displacement or change in the same sort of way as religion. For this reason the form of religious consciousness I am now describing as 'Protestant ethical idealism' is less common than it was. Nevertheless, it is certainly historically important, and is by no means extinct. In many large charitable and international organizations, for example, there are still to be found numbers of people whose effective religion is universal idealistic humanitarianism, a partly-demythologized ethical Christianity of a kind that Harnack, Tolstoy and Schweitzer would have recognized; and very admirable people they are.

This form of religion traces its pedigree to the ethical teaching of Jesus and the Israelite prophets, and also to Plato. For in addition to his contributions to the Western tradition that we have already mentioned, Plato bequeathed something even more important, a whole series of connected theses about morality and its religious significance. The ones that really count are very simple and general, and until quite recently their truth seemed obvious to almost everyone. They include the beliefs that the question of morality – what is the good life, and how are we to live it? – is more important to us than any other; that philosophy can answer this question; that virtue is a unity and is rational, in that the virtuous man has a unified, harmonious and healthy or properly-ordered soul and his life is in harmony with and is properly proportioned to the real nature of things; that our value-terms and other moral words stand for objectively-existing constituents of reality; that by living the good life we fulfil the whole or at any rate the greater part of our religious duty; and that the good life is the only sort of life that we can in the end judge to be fully satisfying to us.

In effect Plato, at least in his early and middle periods, saw true religion and morality as being more-or-less coextensive. Furthermore, because the general concepts we employ in moral and religious thought stand for objectively-existing Forms and the Forms are timeless, true religion and morality were for Plato timeless and unchanging. And when during the development of the Platonic tradition the Forms, ranged under the Form of the Good, were all incorporated into the divine Mind and became the divine Ideas, then it became all the more natural to speak of the good life as an imitation of God and as the rational way of responding to God – as Plato himself had indeed already done. God was objective absolute Goodness, incorporating and unifying all values within himself, and a human being whose soul was truly pure, virtuous and harmonious was a small-scale image of God. True religion was moral attunement between the soul and God.

Notice that this kind of religious thought is not dependent on the notion that we should aim at one-to-one intimate personal fellowship or intercourse between ourselves and God. That notion does require a realistic and anthropomorphic theology but, as we remarked earlier, it is relatively modern. For Plato, what matters most is moral attunement between the virtuous soul and ultimate reality. This attunement is not really a datum of experience; rather, it is established by philosophy. It certainly does require the objectivity of values and the transcendent unity of all value, and the Good sufficiently represents to us that unity of value. But it is not necessary to go on to postulate any vividly personal or interventionist kind of realistic theism. Hence my use of the term semi-realism in this connection: God was the Good, the goal of the moral life and the unity of all value, rather than a distinct personal being over against us.

To see how all this may work out in a modern context we may consider the case of Tolstoy who, though of course not strictly a Protestant, was very much a follower of Kant and a typical exponent of Protestant ethical idealism. Like many of the liberal Protestants of his time, Tolstoy came to believe that the essence of Christianity was ethical, and detested the doctrinal realism that had dominated the Latin and Greek churches since the time of Constantine. Dogmatic theology was a tool of oppression, irrational, authoritarian and allied with worldly power. His study of the Gospels during the years 1877–1885 led Tolstoy to find the essence of Christianity in five great commandments issued by Jesus. They forbade anger, lust, retaliatory violence and swearing, and enjoined universal love, starting with the love of our enemies:

> The fulfilment of Christ's teaching, expressed in the five commandments, would establish the Kingdom of God. The Kingdom of God on earth is the peace of all men one with another. Peace among men is the highest blessing attainable by man on earth.[1]

That is from chapter VI of *What I Believe* (1884): in chapter VII of the same work Tolstoy makes clear that he regards the belief in personal survival of death as an egoistic or 'Epicurean' idea. By exploiting it, the church has committed great evils.[2]

It might be objected that Tolstoy's interpretation of Christ's teaching is itself authoritarian and legalistic. But in a late letter where he discusses the 'Christ-myth' theory then being put forward by a few radical Gospel critics, he writes:

> They are attacking the last of the outworks, and if they carry it and demonstrate that Christ never was born, it will be all the more evident that the fortress of religion is impregnable. Take away the Church, the traditions, the Bible, and even Christ himself – the ultimate fact of man's knowledge of goodness, which is from God directly through reason and conscience, will be as clear and as certain as ever; and it will be seen that we are dealing with truths that can never perish . . . [3]

Thus for Tolstoy, at the end of his life at least, Christ's teachings are intrinsically authoritative. Once we have understood them and have grasped that their truth is unconditional, they become independent of the original teacher, and Tolstoy's religion is therefore as timeless as Plato's. In a paper on 'Religion and Morality' (1893), he ends with the definitions:

> Religion is a certain relation established by man between his separate personality and the infinite universe, or its Source. And morality is the ever-present guide to life which results from that relation.[4]

Tolstoy did not altogether approve of Plato, but we have here his version of the old idea of attunement. We also have a rather vague notion of God. What precisely did Tolstoy mean by God, and how far was he a theological realist?

By God, it seems, Tolstoy meant 'that which makes it possible for us to say Yes to life, that which enables us to find meaning or value in life'. It was not enough that God should be merely an idea, or a willed fiction, for 'I seek that without which there can be no life'.[5] The clearest statement is to be found in *A Confession* (1882), XII, where Tolstoy describes his own oscillations between faith and despair. Repeatedly he found that when he lost belief in God he fell into despair as the life-impulse in himself failed, but when he was able to believe, life returned:

> What is this animation and dying? I do not live when I lose belief in the existence of God. I should long ago have killed myself had I not had a dim hope of finding him. I live, really live, only when I feel him and seek him. 'What more do you seek?' exclaimed a voice within me. 'This is he. He is that without which one cannot live. To know God and to live is one and the same thing. God is life . . . Live seeking God, and then you will not live without God.'[6]

A little later, Tolstoy spells out the nature of his return to faith in terms that are interestingly different from the dualism of the Reformation theology we discussed earlier:

> And I was saved from suicide. When and how this change occurred I could not say. As imperceptibly and gradually the force of life in me had been destroyed and I had reached the impossibility of living, a cessation of life and the necessity of suicide, so imperceptibly and gradually did that force of life return to me. And strange to say the strength of life which

returned to me was not new but quite old – the same that had borne me along in my earliest days.[7]

God, it seems, is the ground of the possibility of our primal ethical life-affirmation; something known instinctively and unconsciously by children and peasants, the archaic wisdom of humanity. We think we begin to understand what Tolstoy is after: God is the basis of life and goodness. But in the next paragraph, as he spells this out, the fog begins to descend:

> I returned to the belief in that Will which produced me, and desires something of me. I returned to the belief that the chief and only aim of my life is to do better, i.e. to live in accord with that Will. And I returned to the belief that I can find the expression of that Will in what humanity, in the distant past hidden from me, has produced for its guidance: that is to say, I returned to a belief in God, in moral perfection, and in a tradition transmitting the meaning of life. There was only this difference, that then all this was accepted unconsciously, while now I know that without it I could not live.[8]

Tolstoy nowhere becomes more explicit than this about what he means by God, and it reminds us of Matthew Arnold's 'the Eternal not ourselves that makes for righteousness', and 'the stream of tendency by which all things seek to fulfil the law of their being'. In effect, belief in God amounts to the same thing as belief in the objectivity of ethics. For we cannot joyfully commit ourselves to the task of becoming virtuous if goodness and life are hopelessly at variance with each other: to live, we must believe in a deeply-hidden Ground of the unity of nature and morality. Otherwise, Tolstoy fears, the very phrase 'the good life' might be found to express a contradiction. So, like Hans Küng's 'fundamental trust', belief in God expresses a primitive wordless conviction that the good life is a coherent possibility and that in living it we are attuned to the ultimate reality of things. God is known only as the ground of the possibility of life – that is, a good and meaningful life such as one can will to live and view with satisfaction – and this knowledge of God is therefore purely ethical. Nevertheless, *via* the ethical, and only by that route, it makes a veiled and implicit ontological claim. The only evidence we can produce for the truth of the claim is what Matthew Arnold describes as 'the experimental sense of *life*, of being truly *alive*, which accompanies righteousness';[9] and it is because this cannot be further elaborated that we describe this form of Protestant ethical idealism as being semi-realist.

However, the trouble with Tolstoy's position and the reason for its vagueness is that he does not have and cannot have Plato's confidence that goodness and being are convertible, the most good being necessarily the most real and *vice versa*. The objectivity of ethics cannot mean to Tolstoy quite what it had meant to Plato, for, as a student of Kant and Schopenhauer and as one living after Darwin, Tolstoy knows perfectly well that the world of fact, the world as represented by natural science, is non-moral. It is a struggle of conflicting wills-to-power, and it knows nothing of the evangelical morality. Tolstoy himself recognizes the split between the world of fact and the world of absolute values by finding the principles of true morality in Jesus' unconditional prohibitions of violence and lust and his command to love our enemies, by describing Jesus' ethic as a set of timeless truths evident *a priori* to reason and conscience, and by then contrasting them with the way things actually go in the natural and social worlds. We all know, and Tolstoy knew, that sex and violence are the very stuff of our biological life. To establish his own puritan ethic based on Jesus' teaching, he had to join Kant and Schopenhauer in opposing true morality to nature. True morality became a matter of rational allegiance to pure ideals, exalted above the violence of nature. Yet on the other side of this thought Tolstoy wants to differ from Schopenhauer, and to claim that the Will that has produced us is ethical, that God is life, and that we should see life in terms of doing his will; and of course he extols the ancient unconscious wisdom of the peasants. He wants God to be not only a pure ideal set up in contrast to nature, but also the ground of actual life as we know it.

God is life, says Tolstoy, and when I believe in God I can live. But what is *life*? Not mere biological life, for that is a competitive and violent struggle, a war of all against all; and not just the course of human social life as we know it, because that is no better. Indeed, it is worse. Furthermore, Tolstoy himself was dualistic, for as is well known his puritan moralism contradicted his own nature, which was domineering, quarrelsome and highly-sexed. Within his own make-up life was divided against itself, for 'life' as he uses the word in *A Confession*, the text from which I have quoted, is evidently not at all the same thing as the driving creative libidinal energy of the man Leo Tolstoy. The best he can do is to return to his formula, 'I live, really live, only when I feel God and seek him. Live seeking God, and then you will not live without God.' That is, for us humans the will to live and mere natural libido are not enough; we only truly feel ourselves to be alive when we seek to transcend mere biological life and to moralize it. To believe in God is to believe that this is possible; that libido can be moralized and so life can become good. But in that case the idea of God is eschatological rather than cosmological, and the good life is more of a future hope than an initial datum – which is not easy to reconcile with extolling peasant virtue. For on this account God, the moralization of life, is an ideal waiting to be actualized rather than something given in a deep unconscious way from the very beginning.

Tolstoy, then, has a difficulty of which Plato could have known nothing, for it has become hard for us to conjoin the ideas of good and life *at all*. Nietzsche saw the problem and proposed to solve it by revaluing all our values, revolutionizing our idea of goodness so as to bring it into line with life. He went all-out for a life-affirming biological naturalism which rejects as futile the old habit of contrasting the way things are with the way they ought to be, and which also rejects the device of trying to view one's own life impartially and from the standpoint of eternity. Nietzsche rejects idealism of every kind and urges us to be frankly egoistic, because when it is a matter of our moral assessment of our own lives, no other standpoint than our own is morally relevant to us. And in spite of what people mistakenly think about Nietzsche, egoism thus understood as a moral necessity is quite compatible with love, friendship, kindness and self-discipline. Tolstoy hates all this, but he has difficulty in producing a sensible reply to it, for Nietzsche can always ask him, 'Look at yourself. What can be the point of a morality that is anti-life? Why this vain pretence that things can and should be other than they are? And how can you Protestant ethical idealists hope to give your moral ideals ontological grounding in God or whatever? – For why should God create Nature and then promptly discover that the world he really wishes to see is after all one quite different from that which he has just made? Alternatively, if you describe your moral ideals as timeless intelligible essences exalted above the flux of becoming, then they had better stay immobilized in their world-above and keep quiet, because they can have no healthy influence on the way we shape our actual lives here below.' Nietzsche holds that idealism poisons life by making us discontented with it.

Tolstoy then runs into trouble in appealing to 'life' in the way he does – what *does* the word mean? – and he runs into even more trouble by being very critical of life (i.e. the world in general, and human nature in particular) as it is, by invoking absolute moral principles exalted above the flux of life, and by then seeking from them some ethical-ontological foundation for our life. It is impossible to do all these things at once; and that is the trouble with Protestant ethical idealism.

However, in the paper on 'Religion and Morality' (1893) Tolstoy makes yet one more effort to clarify his position.[10] He is discussing, or rather savaging, the English writer T.H. Huxley. He agrees with Huxley that we cannot base morality on 'the law of evolution', because when we regard man from a biological point of view then it is true that 'the struggle for existence and the survival of the fittest is the eternal law of all life'. He also agrees with Huxley that true morality must be seen as a protest against the law of evolution. Does this then mean, asks Huxley, that to achieve goodness we must extirpate the life-impulse altogether like the ascetics of old? No: for Huxley believes that morality can be given a naturalistic foundation in our social needs. We are both rational, and intensely social, animals. To flourish we must curb our aggressive and antisocial impulses and learn fellow-feeling and compassion, for the sake of the group we belong to; and to learn to do this, says Huxley, is advantageous for all of us.

Tolstoy protests violently, because this line of argument merely lifts morality from individual egoism to collective egoism, and because he regards all existing societies as morally evil. Take for example 'English society, as it exists today – with its Irish problem, the poverty of its lowest classes, the insensate luxury of the rich, its trade in opium and spirits, its executions, its slaughter or extermination of tribes for the sake of trade and politics, its secret vice and hypocrisy'[11] – is that moral? Since this catalogue of woes scarcely needs to be modified a century later, we must concede that Tolstoy has a point. But if the principles of true morality cannot be derived either from the way the natural world works or from the way the social world works, and if they are severely corrupted and submerged in the existing religions, then after so comprehensive an indictment where are we to get them from? Tolstoy answers, from religion; and religion is a way of relating oneself to the universe as a whole, or its Source.

In an essay called 'What is Religion' (1902) Tolstoy is a little more specific. Reason irresistibly prompts us to consider ourselves not only as belonging to nature and to society but as 'part of the whole infinite universe existing eternally'; and when we establish our relation to 'the whole immense Infinite in time and space' and draw guidance for our action from this relation, then that is religion; 'and as all men stand in one and the same relation to the universe, it follows that religion – which is the elucidation of that relation – unites men' (II, IX).[12] Like the deists of old, Tolstoy maintains that beneath their superficial diversity and corruption all the world's major faiths bear witness to a small set of basic rational and universal principles:

> These principles are: that there is a God, the origin of all things; that in man dwells a spark from that Divine Origin, which man, by his way of living, can increase or decrease in himself; that to increase this divine spark man must suppress his passions and increase love in himself; and that the practical means to attain this result is that you should do to others as you would they should do to you.(XIV)[13]

Tolstoy has recoiled from the wickedness of Nature and society, but he is not content to regard his principles of morality as being valid autonomously and *a priori*, in the manner of Kant. He still wishes to find some cosmic backing for them: and the result is feeble. He knows that he cannot derive his morality from such knowledge of the universe and our place in it as is given to us by our natural sciences, but what other knowledge do we have that is strong enough to outweigh the bad news they give us? Tolstoy sometimes talks as if from the mere fact that the universe is very big and we are all very small it follows that we should all adopt an egalitarian ethic of love. But this is no more logical than it would be to argue that, since we are all so insignificant, we may as well kill each other. And if Tolstoy is any kind of realistic theist, he cannot avoid the difficulty that the Origin of all things, if it has ordained the ethic of love, has also previously ordained what

Tolstoy himself describes as 'the eternal law' of the struggle for existence and the survival of the fittest.

Protestant ethical idealism therefore fails twice over. It fails, first, by too sharply separating morality from nature, which divides the self and uselessly locates our values in a timeless realm separated from the imperfections and the flux of nature and history; and then it fails again by nevertheless attempting to ground moral values in the One who is also the maker of nature and history.

Can it be made more consistent? There are hints, at least, in Albert Schweitzer.[14] He gives up a metaphysical God and the doctrine of Creation, insisting that the world of nature is indeed as amoral as Schopenhauer and Darwin have said it is. But we are rational and moral beings, and we must seek to moralize nature. The way to do this is not by Tolstoy's method of opposing Christian love to the sex-drive, but from within, by gradually transforming the life-and-sex drive into agapeistic love. The linking idea is environmental agapism: to learn to love and respect the drive to life in yourself and in all other living things. The good life is precisely an attempt to make *life* . . . good, to moralize the world of biological fact. We will not ever wholly succeed in making the world of nature into the kingdom of God, but we should attempt it. God, being perfect goodness fully actualized, is not anything that yet exists, and perhaps he is not anything that ever can exist. But he is a very potent eschatological symbol, standing for what we should seek to achieve. We pray to him in order to bring him into being and to make him good, and we pray by loving: 'He prayeth best who loveth best / All things both great and small.'

Such a consistently earthly ethic of love represents a genuine Christian alternative to Nietzsche. A Buddhist story tells of a monk who offered himself as food to a starving tigress. It may seem fanciful; but in 1985 a zoologist in Africa though armed with a rifle allowed himself to be charged down by a white rhinoceros rather than shoot a member of an endangered species. He survived.

Schweitzer, then, accepted the old liberal Protestant programme of working towards the realization of the kingdom of God on earth. But he knew his Schopenhauer and recognized the difficulty – perhaps even impossibility – of the project, and he avoided projecting his ideals into the sky. Instead we should stick close to the earth and seek the moralization of nature from within, immanently. The divided self is to be avoided; nature and the passions are not to be suppressed but affirmed, in oneself and all others. We moralize them by the way we affirm them, and not by the way we repress them.

At this point Nietzsche's instinct was sound, as everybody nowadays recognizes. Schopenhauer was a *bon viveur* who thought that we ought to adopt the view of life and the morality of an Indian ascetic, and Tolstoy adopted an interpretation of Christian ethics that directly contradicted his own life-impulse. Both became outrageously difficult old codgers, because the attempt to impose upon the self a religion and a morality that does violence to it invariably produces a last state that is worse than the first. Self-discontent leads to world-discontent and, as Nietzsche would ask, What can be the point of a lofty morality that makes you into a thoroughly ill-tempered and disagreeable character?

By contrast, suppose we solve the problem of moral evil by adopting the maxim, Never *complain* about evil. Suffer it if you must, work peaceably to overcome it, or indeed combat it vigorously; but never complain, because complaint is always a symptom of that poisonous idealism and self-dissatisfaction which cannot bring itself simply to accept that things are what they are.

Thus Protestant ethical idealism can be made self-consistent, but only at the price of giving up its idealist component. It need not seek old-style cosmological grounds. Tolstoy need not have said to himself, how can I go beyond nature and society and relate myself to the universe as a whole? He need only have said to himself, Being what I am, and placed as I am, how shall I live and what stance in life shall I adopt? The cosmic reference adds nothing: it merely encourages the old temptation to reify our values and represent them as subsistent eternal verities that function as a standing reproach to life.

Liberal Protestantism was curiously addicted to the belief in eternal truths, in things that remain always the same. That belief, and the implications of questioning it, now need to be studied in a different context.

8

OBJECTIVE SYMBOLISM

This book is interactive. It does not claim that everybody's life-journey moves and must move along just one line. Its wiring is parallel rather than serial, and it cannot realistically aim to do more than list and describe a number of the principal junctions in the hope that you will recognize some of them, and perhaps wish to work out the track through them that you personally seem to be taking.

Such individual tracks may be very erratic. After beginning (as I suppose) with *Genesis* (1) and *Mythical Realism* (2), which I have here imaginatively reconstructed, I was taught *Designer Realism* (5) at the age of fourteen. I assimilated it, but then it faded and lost its hold on me, and I had to be rather abruptly converted back to religion four years later. What I returned to was I think *Doctrinal Realism* (3), but this soon proved to be too extrinsic. It made truth too much a matter of external institutional power and authority, and I turned to the more autonomous and Protestant position of *Obedientiary Realism* (6). However, the influence of science and empiricism made me uneasy with such a dualistic and intellectually-estranged outlook (I was at the time still studying biology). I flirted for a while with *Protestant Ethical Idealism* (7), especially the very moderate Platonic version of it taught by W. R. Inge. Through him I was led to read the Western mystics, and so to settle on *Ladder Realism* (4). It was orthodox, Catholic and religiously-rich, while yet allowing some spiritual and intellectual room for movement. Throughout my twenties it suited me very well, and if it was out of touch with the facts of modern life that was rather a recommendation than otherwise. I felt I belonged to a great and ancient tradition, and a deviant or even reactionary stance may – as numerous writers have shown – give the believer an alternative perspective on the world which makes many things stand out all the more clearly. However, the relentless pressure of all the new ways of thinking that arrived after Kant, and especially the influence of Kierkegaard, gradually forced a series of further shifts of perspective that I have documented elsewhere.

I happen to have been a member of a church with lively Protestant, Catholic and liberal traditions and a strong sense of history. That has made it easier to explore the main stations in all three traditions and set them out in their approximate historical and logical relations – and therefore in parallel rather than in series, as the diagram after the contents page indicates. Real life is however less tidy, and individual journeys through the principal stations may be made by very irregular routes.

With *Objective Symbolism* we now switch back to a more typically Catholic path, because it is the natural successor to ladder realism in a historically-minded age. It is a position common among liberal historical theologians, and I was somewhat involved with it in my thirties.

I use the word 'symbolism' in the technical sense of the doctrine that all dogmatic statements are symbolic, the adjective 'objective' adding the rider that though inadequate, changing and drawn from human experience the symbols are nevertheless believed to be symbols *of* something. They are not merely expressions of human subjectivity, but have objective and transcendent reference. If I pray before an icon or read the Bible, at one level I am perfectly well aware that the thing I am using to assist my devotions is a fully human historical product. I know that historians can explain, often in minute detail, the historical conditions under which this object took shape and which led to its having the form it has. Every word and image in the Creed is human and has a human history; every doctrinal assertion made in the Creed is a human product with its date, to the trained eye, written all over its face. Whatever materials we use in religion – texts, customs, images, music, institutions, values – they all are human with a history that is in principle traceable and explicable. At one level it is aesthetically pleasurable to bathe the imagination in so much history. But at the same time there is no difficulty in also using this material in a much more serious way, as one's window upon eternity. To the believer, this set of symbols is a uniquely effective and authoritative way of portraying, and even learning to do business with, the conditions that ultimately determine our existence. Through all *this*, the eternal God is known. And if through the pace of historical change it is borne in upon us that certain ancient symbolic structures are becoming alien to us and no longer usable, then we need not be discouraged. Historical change is bound to demand a continual effort of reinterpretation and reformulation.

So far, so good. Controversy begins when it is recognized that this effort of reformulation may require us to develop and justify new ways of reading and expounding the text of the New Testament. During the past two centuries it has become a commonplace that the people who wrote the New Testament had a world-view and ways of thinking very different from our own. What is to be done about this? The task of reinterpretation can be seen in a whole spectrum of different ways. Karl Barth, emphasizing revelation and seeing the biblical message as being simply God-given, aims to expound revelation so fully in a sustained dialogue with modern thought that we will modify our present ways of thinking and bring them into conformity with the New Testament's. We will then presumably be able to lift our noses out of the book and return to the present-day world as fully Christianized and effective individuals. Rudolf Bultmann believes that there is a permanent and fundamental structure of the human spirit as such, to which the gospel message is addressed. If we remove the merely contingent mythological dress in which first-century thought unavoidably clothed the gospel message, something perfectly intelligible and adequate to the needs of modern people will appear. Leonard Hodgson, whose words are often quoted by Dennis Nineham, instructs us to ask ourselves, 'What must the truth be, and have been, if it appeared like that to men who thought and wrote as they did?'[1] This also seems to presume that there is something called 'the truth' which is a constant, and which we can distinguish from the various symbols and thought-forms in which different ages (including, of course, our own) happen to have dressed it up. The metaphor here of a body which is seen in a succession of different suits of clothing (New Testament, Patristic, Mediaeval, Reformation, etc.) invites the retort that someone who has always seen bodies clothed and has never seen one naked has no basis for making any distinction between the body and its clothing. To vary the metaphor, you can distinguish between the kernel and the husk only after you have successfully broken open a few husks and have found that there are indeed distinct, indubitable kernels within them. In the case of the New Testament, however, many people feel strongly that the book is all kernel and strongly object to the suggestion that any of it is husk that can be distinguished, and ought to be separated off and discarded. Even among those who accept the kernel-husk distinction, there is no general agreement as to which elements constitute the permanent core of truth, and which belong to the disposable husk of outmoded beliefs. It is because he is highly aware of all this that Nineham's own words are notably more cautious than Hodgson's. He remarks, for example, that where people today 'seem to need help above all is at the level of the imagination: they need some way of envisaging realities such as God, creation and providence imaginatively in a way which does no violence to the rest of what they know to be true. They need to be able to mesh in their religious symbols with the rest of their sensibility in the sort of way supra-naturalist and messianic imagery meshed in with the sensibility of first-century people.'[2] Nineham here sounds like a thoroughgoing symbolist who seeks to describe the situation in a way that does not invoke the idea that we are able to pick out any core of unchanging truth. A critic would say that Nineham is post-liberal and such a strong historical relativist that for him the New Testament is in effect all husk and no kernel. Husks are all we can have. Reality is thoroughly historical, with the result that we see only the series of historically-conditioned symbolic constructions and never the eternal reality or unchanging truth to which the symbols are believed to refer. The theologian's task is indeed to create a new symbolization of Christian truth for our time; but, for Nineham, he cannot do this by so-to-say teasing out the elements of eternal truth from previous symbolizations and then reclothing them in imaginatively effective modern dress. What then is he to do? He uses his imagination to enter the faith-world of the past era – the New Testament, for example – and seeks to grasp the religious and moral *force* of that faith-system for those people in that historical context. Then he returns to the present day and waits to see if the after-echo in his imagination of what he has learnt can germinate and give rise to something that has analogous religious and moral force in our own context. Since there are no constants which can simply be transferred from then to now, the entire content of faith must be completely re-imagined.[3]

Nineham's method assumes that by the exercise of the historical imagination we can enter into the mind of a past age and feel the way their religious beliefs worked for them. It also assumes that there could be something for us in our age that does for us essentially the same job that their religion did for them. Nineham recognizes that both these assumptions are highly contentious. Many people think the world has changed so much that we can no longer clearly understand an alien fully-religious world view, because we no longer have the concepts that would make such understanding possible; and by the same token there cannot be in our pluralistic, man-centred and secularized culture anything that has just the force for us that their Christian faith had for the New Testament writers. If these doubts are well founded then Christianity cannot now be reinvented even by Nineham's method. The German philosopher H.-G. Gadamer says that we cannot 'reproduce the original production': we cannot fix something that we have a right to call the 'original' meaning of the text, and therefore our reinvention must be freer even than Nineham envisages.[4]

Subject to this *caveat*, however, Nineham's position represents the least mystifying and most truthful version of objective symbolism available, because it accepts without reserve the historical character of modern reality. We can never directly compare the symbols with the thing symbolized because we can never jump out of our own historicality and achieve a direct and history-transcending intuition of timeless truth. We are stuck within our own human and history-produced symbolizations. They are all we can have. Thus Nineham is a consistent symbolist; but he is I think still an *objective* symbolist, in that he believes that in every historical epoch there will be some particular system of symbols and rituals which can efficaciously point the soul towards the Eternal, and even be the vehicle through which we experience the Eternal's gracious activity towards us. Only, we are stuck on the near side of our symbols: we cannot get to the far side to see how they work. There is a transcendental signified, as the French call it; but it is not directly accessible to us. Does this imply that Nineham is a fideist, one who commits himself by a pure act of the will to a set of dogmatic representations, without any way of telling whether they manage to describe anything or not, but merely in the hope that they point to something? Not quite; and 'fideism' is an unfortunate term, for Nineham's view is after all only a modern historically-minded version of the teaching of Aquinas, and nobody would call Aquinas a fideist. For Aquinas, we use theological language in the faith that it manages to say something about God who is the source of all being and meaning, but there is no way that we can lay our language about God out alongside God and demonstrate how it manages to say something about him. We know nothing of God except that our language about him is inadequate. Thus for Aquinas we believe that our language about God has objective reference, but we cannot explain how it manages to have objective reference.[5] Our use of it is genuinely 'intentional', or objectively orientated and grounded, but we cannot spell out just how it manages to latch on to its object. Nineham need only add to this our modern recognition that all our language is socially generated, and that the usage of all words is in continual slow historical change. We will therefore have to choose different words if we are to produce in the twentieth century an utterance that has the same sort of religious force for us that an utterance of St Paul had in the first century.

However, this promptly brings us back to the *caveat* that we entered earlier, because the modern recognition of how deep historical change goes does after all make a big difference. A historical theologian like Nineham, if he is to secure the identity of the Christian tradition, needs to hold that a modern student can get into the mind of a New Testament writer to feel imaginatively what his faith was like for him, and then return to the present world and imaginatively generate something that will have analogous force for us. But this presumption of a possible analogy sounds too much like a new version of the old appeal to constants. It assumes that we are still enough like them for it to be possible for us to have a faith that is for us like what their faith was for them; and if we are being consistently historical we cannot make that assumption.

The problem is that the human condition is not something

given, prior to history, but is itself internal to history and so subject to change. We have to recognize that philosophy, cosmology, ethics and the rest really are included within history. We do not start with philosophy of nature, theory of knowledge and so forth, and then insert history into a pre-existent framework: no, history really does come first and all frameworks, world-views, sciences, moralities and the like are internal to it. There is no transcending our historicality. And given that in their cosmology, their conceptions of knowledge and of morality and so on the New Testament writers really were quite different from us, then we cannot assume that there must be something waiting to be for us what their religious faith was for them. Indeed, it is a commonplace among historians that the devices by which a society seeks to represent to itself its continuity with its own past are always ideological fictions. They are inspired not by considerations of historical accuracy, but by a present-day need for legitimation. Undoubtedly, religious communities need to feel that they have kept the faith, and that in spite of historical change they still believe much the same things in much the same way as their ancestors. But that need is merely a piece of social psychology, and all the stories about the tradition of apostolic faith, dogmatic immutability, and so forth that are produced to meet it are mythical. History shows us that different cultural totalities really are different from each other; so much so that we never actually know the past just as it was, but can only attempt to imagine it from the perspective of our present concerns.

The modern objective symbolist who has digested all this must find it hard to avoid being very much more pluralistic than Aquinas, as pluralistic as a Hindu, and in a way that spins the objectivity as fine as gossamer. For it has to be allowed that, scattered across time and space in different cultural totalities, religious symbolic structures may be of many different kinds and work in many different ways. We cannot lay down *a priori* any limits to the possible number of symbolic forms under which people may have dealings with the Eternal. Nothing can be said of the Eternal that is not couched in the vocabulary of one or other of these forms – except that none of them is adequate. And now there is no longer anything we can get hold of that will clearly differentiate objective symbolism from the subjective symbolism or expressivism which sees every particular religion as a work of folk art, and all of them as being equally true as expressions of the human spirit. All that remains of objectivity is the will-to-realism, a conviction that there is 'something there' which cannot be any further elaborated or justified.

Here one enters into the peculiar agony of the modern educated believer. She goes to church and joins in worship because *all this* gives her a soul-nourishing sense of eternity. She knows enough of the facts of historical change and the nature of symbols to be aware that *all this* is at one level simply expressive symbolism, an historically evolved product of folk art; and she loves it as such, because it connects her with the past and the faith of her ancestors. At the same time, the influence of theological realism leads her to feel that she cannot in good conscience worship purely at the level of expressive symbolism. The love of beauty, of the past and of the dead is not by itself religion at all. Faith, she thinks, has to be objectivist or it is no more than a beautiful dream. But she cannot find any very clear rational grounds for deciding between objective symbolism and expressivism, so that she hovers in perpetual uncertainty between the two. When she was younger, objectivism seemed to come more easily to her; but the pitiless years are demythologizing her and faith seems to be slipping away just when she most needs it. Some other people seem able to find a kind of psychological lock by which they can hold on to their faith. She is too self-aware to be able to do that, but the way her problem has developed historically seems to preclude her from finding the rational basis for objectivist faith that alone would set her heart at rest.

When discussing ladder realism and the Negative Theology we noted that it was already so agnostic as barely to merit the description 'realistic', and in fact in antiquity Platonism itself had a way of slipping into scepticism. Modern objective symbolism faces a similar predicament. It is repelled by the austerities of the Negative Theology, and instead casts about for some device that will enable it to cling to a realism that is in danger of becoming attenuated to vanishing-point. How can this be done? Karl Barth attempted to stop the rot by declaring that the constellation of religious ideas to be found in the New Testament has been revealed by God and is uniquely authoritative, immutable and intelligible to every generation. Rudolf Bultmann's dyke is a philosophical anthropology, adapted from the early Heidegger, that assures him that at a deep level the human condition and the (demythologized) gospel as the remedy for it are alike unchanging. Leonard Hodgson follows an old English tradition in believing that we can distinguish between the truth itself and its changing vestments. Dennis Nineham's semi-realism seeks to combine a full acknowledgment of the historicality of human life with the hope that we may be able to work out something that is for us at least analogous to what the faith of earlier ages was for them, a set of representations through which we in our generation may be able to have dealings with a gracious Eternal One.

These four positions are only samples from a much wider range that could easily be quoted, and they illustrate the interesting modern development by which theology is now turning into philosophy of religion. In the past things were rather different, for theology was a curious blend of law and philosophy. On the legal side it asked what opinions were licit, and was preoccupied with questions of authority and tradition, precedent and case-law, orthodoxy and heresy. Official doctrinal statements resembled laws, and theology developed somewhat as a legal system developed. On the philosophical side, however, religious beliefs were treated as if they were assertions in dogmatic meta-physics that needed to be explained, placed, justified and tied into a general world-view. On the legal side of theology problems of meaning scarcely arise, but on the philosophical side they predominate. Now since the Enlightenment theology has been studied principally in the universities. It has become less comba-tively denominational, less interested in defending orthodoxies and more concerned with its place on the map of culture as a whole; that is, with its relation to critical history, philosophy and the natural and social sciences. All this has meant that the philosophical side of theology, already prominent in some medi-aeval universities, has more than ever come to the fore, and the legal side is fading away. This background helps to explain our current absorption in problems of whose very existence the old canon-lawyer's type of theology was almost unaware. We are asking, what sort of thing *is* a religious belief? What is the status of religious theories? Just what kind of existence, being or reality should be attributed to religious objects and powers such as God?

Perhaps on the analogy of a person's being alive or dead, either present with us or absent from us, we tend to operate with a very simple binary model: existence is a univocal term, and things either exist or do not exist. There is a great domain within which our concepts are or are not exemplifed, and we call it reality. The objective symbolist feels the need somehow to locate God within this domain. However, sustained attention to the diversities of religious language and the movement of the religious life is dissolving away that over-simple picture, just as it is doing so in philosophy as a whole. Although in deference to long-established ways of thinking – the term 'realism', as it is currently used, goes back at least to Kant – we have classified the major positions in religious thought so far considered under the general heading of realism, it has become clear that for each of them reality is something different. They each construct reality in different ways, and still further diversity is found internally within each of them. It begins to look as if we shall soon need to abandon the concept of realism, because it depends upon and presupposes the existence of a single mind-independent field of reality out there against which our various constructions are to be checked. But we are not in possession of an agreed definition of any such thing. It would be better to say that our ordinary notion of reality is a myth, one of those big slovenly protean and clinging ideas that we have inherited, and which confuses more than it clarifies. There are in fact many 'realities' – and *we* made them all.

The persistence of the myth of 'Reality' may be due to our tendency to suppose that because physics has a universe, philosophy has one. We are so impressed by the vast yet finite and beautiful universe of modern physics that we take it to be *the* Universe, in the philosophers' sense of the Absolute, all there is. This is not so, for the universe of physics belongs only to physics and is a highly specialised theoretical construction. It is not at all the same kind of thing as the Cosmos of prescientific thought, for it is only one world of many. The various other worlds that we also construct and project out – the worlds of sense experience, logic, morality, art and religion – are incommensurable with the universe of physics and will not fit into it. There are many worlds, and there is as yet no replacement for the old philosophers' Universe, in the sense of a single generally-recognized unified orderly total objective scheme of things in which each of these diverse worlds finds its place. The nearest we can come to such a total vision is to start from the idea that all the various worlds of logic, nature, art, society and religion are in various ways thrown out by us. ('Objective' means 'thrown out'.) They are the different modes of symbolic expression through which we encircle ourselves with our houses of meaning. Unfortunately, though, we do not yet have a fully comprehensive science of man the maker of meanings which will provide a co-ordinated account of all our diverse meaning-making activities.

When the universe of physics is taken to be 'reality' and understood as if it were an object like the Cosmos of old, gauche attempts are made to fit our other concerns into it, as when people imagine God causing the Big Bang to occur. But from the philosophical point of view the order of things, so far as we can represent it at all, is as we have been describing it here: the productive life-energy that shapes us and powers our mysterious symbolizing and world-making capacities comes first, and it passes through a succession of stages of representation. I have described them in terms of the development of the spiritual life because our religious representations are the most potent and wide-ranging expressions we produce, and I have drawn upon the vocabulary and the historical development of the Western and Christian tradition because that is, for me and for most of us, the school through whose various grades we have been passing. And from the account given so far it is plain that the end of theological realism is a major event. Life at last fully returns to itself and becomes conscious of itself: we begin to grasp what is our true situation, one of extraordinary freedom.

The reason for the fierce last-ditch resistance is that people mistakenly perceive what is happening as the death of God. Realism, that clinging slovenly myth, generates a hazy notion of God as a superperson out there, existing as a constituent of reality independent of us. But when we focus on that myth, clarify its various component strands and make all the thoughts it involves more definite – then it is dispelled. So people think: 'This is the end of reality, the end of the Cosmos, the death of God!' This response, however, is over-excited. Philosophy neither brings things into existence nor annihilates them but merely changes the angle of vision. Everything that was there is still there, but seen more clearly from a new vantage-point. The various worlds of sense-experience, natural science, morality and social relations, of art and of religion, are all still in place, just as they were. God continues, because what people say of God and the part he plays in shaping their lives remains exactly what it was. The chief difference is that we now remind ourselves of the shift in our angle of vision that has taken place by learning to talk always about meaning and about the functions and the explanatory powers of theories, instead of about existence and old-style truth. So, in the case of natural science, we do not suppose that our theories are replicas of objectively-existing cosmic structures, but instead think of them as tools that we use in that special way of organizing the world of experience which is natural science. As tools they are, we may claim, the best currently available, the most powerful, the most prolific in generating explanations and in opening up new possibilities, but tools wear out, and it is reasonable to expect that in time they will all need to be modified or replaced. Similarly in religion we shift linguistic emphasis from the existence of God to the power of God, and make two very obvious points: first, that God is the power of God because God is the role God plays in developing our self-understanding, focussing our aspirations, and shaping the course of our lives; and secondly, that the right God for us at any one time is the God that is most religiously powerful for us at that time. Progress and development in the spiritual life is brought about by changing one's idea of God. That is why every stage in the spiritual life is a distinct position in the philosophy of religion. You have to be prepared to move fast, from God to God. You need the God that is right for you just now, and still more do you need the God that will be right for you next. Ideas of God need to develop to prevent dogmatic ossification, just as scientific theories need to develop to prevent dogmatic ossification. In the old days when people were dominated by realistic myths they always had to put up a rather comical pretence that their current scientific theories were either already constitutively true or (more often) were just on the point of becoming so. This promise that a fully adequate fundamental science of nature is only just around the corner has been made so often that it has discredited itself, and realism with it. Now we say only that we stick to our current theories because they are the ones that work best at present, but when the time comes we will unhesitatingly trade them in for new ones. That is beautiful, because it has grasped that absolute knowledge is a debilitating mirage; forget it, turn away from it, and suddenly you feel much stronger and better.

Similarly in religion, the reason why objective symbolism produced and still produces such chronic faith-sickness is that it remains captivated by the mirage of absolute knowledge, the dream of a final and necessary truth of things in which alone the spirit can come to rest. That dream must be shattered if we are to be cured. The spirit lives and is strong only so long as it is on the move.

9

THE CRISIS

It is possible to avoid passing through a crisis of faith, for there are several routes by which people can and do move smoothly and painlessly from belief in a personal and interventionist God to the various forms of non-realism.

Some of these routes appear to lead towards the secularization of religion. For example, in public discourse during the eighteenth and nineteenth centuries there was a steady drift from God to Providence, and then on to a wide range of idioms in which people spoke in a quasi-religious way about progress, the spirit of improvement, development, history, destiny and the life-force. The legacy of this drift is still with us, for social psychologists report that the population of the United Kingdom is about equally divided among people who believe in a personal God, people who do not believe in God at all, and people who hold the intermediate position of believing in some kind of 'Power' or 'Life Force'. This intermediate position might be described as a form of semi-realism. It seeks to avoid the small-town optimism of those who think God will make sure that nothing very unpleasant will ever happen to good people, while yet retaining a vague and more generalized hope that those who are trying to make the world a better place will eventually prove to have been on the winning side. Some power beyond ourselves is active in the world process to bring it about that the right will prevail.

This is a philosophically puzzling kind of religious belief. How does it manage to be so sustaining, when it is so fuzzy? It is incorrigibly unspecific and unfalsifiable. It seems impossible to distinguish it from a mere hopeful attitude or a spirit of secular

optimism. Yet people are quite genuinely sustained by it, feel it
has content, and certainly show the difference it made when
events have caused them to lose it. We may judge it to be
transitional and half-secularized, like Tom Paine's theism but
further along the line: but we should also note that these vague
transitional forms of belief can be very important to people.

Other routes to non-realist faith have rather more religious
weight. A Protestant Ethical Idealist in any case always did put
morality first in his or her understanding of religion. From the
outset, he tended to see God as a cluster of values or as representing
the ideal unity and perfection of Christian values. He may
therefore quite easily pass to a form of religious humanism in
which God is either a mere metaphor or unmentioned, without
ever having to suffer any major hiatus in what he always regarded
as being the principal business of religion, namely the practical
living of the Christian life. Nowadays we hear people of this sort
speaking about 'the human spirit', 'the spiritual dimension of life',
or 'religious awareness' – and we realize that these expressions
have unobtrusively replaced older idioms about a personal God.

There are also cases where an Objective Symbolist moves over
to a tacit form of Subjective Symbolism or Expressivism without
much trauma. Many people of a Catholic turn of mind, and many
historians, see God chiefly as a bond of community and as a
symbol of the continuity of tradition. Such a person may come to
speak less and less about God, and more and more about the
church, its life, and the unbroken tradition of faith down the
centuries – and nobody turns a hair. The change has taken place
unnoticed.

Most weighty of all, in the Platonic mystical tradition there has
been since early times the recognition that as we progress in the
religious life symbols and images must fall away and we move
into ever-deeper darkness and unknowing. For the orthodox
ladder-mysticism it is a normal and expected part of the religious
life that it will eventually require us to give up belief in a personal
God. The loss remains painful, but the discomfort is reduced by
the fact that we received advance warning that it would have to
come.

In all these four main areas of religious thought – cosmic,
ethical, institutional and mystical – the transition to non-realism
often takes place gradually and inconspicuously. Perhaps that is

the way to be preferred. But there are also people who suffer an acute crisis of personal faith. For them it is an overwhelmingly important event which may lead to the total loss of religion, or may become the starting-point for rapid subsequent religious growth.

The central theme of the crisis of faith I have in mind is the sudden loss of belief in an objective and personal God. It is often thought that this event is a peculiarly Christian phenomenon, made possible as a result of what had happened to religion in the West since the seventeenth century. According to this analysis, the secularization of the physical universe and of society forced religious belief to become privatized and psychologized. Faith in God increasingly became a special kind of inner emotional 'lock' within the self – and therefore something that might be abruptly gained or lost as a result of a personal psychological upheaval. But in non-bourgeois and non-Western cultures, where religious belief had not become so psychologised or so anthropomorphic, we should not expect to find people either gaining faith or losing it in the way that is so familiar in Christianity.

There is much truth in this account, as we shall see. After all, it scarcely needs pointing out that there is no Buddhist Billy Graham. But the crisis of faith in an objective God is not an exclusively Christian problem. Among the Jews, the eminent conservative rabbi and academic R. Rubinstein, in his book *After Auschwitz*, openly rejected the traditional Jewish idea of God; while from Islam the most-discussed of all modern Arabic novels, Naguib Mahfouz' *Children of Gebelawi*, is about the death of God. The two writers differ significantly. Rubinstein rejects the traditional rabbinic eschatology, and thinks that Auschwitz has decisively refuted the belief in a God who acts in history and preserves and protects the Jewish people. With no belief in an objective God or life after death, Rubinstein thinks that Jewish thought must become more naturalistic. It must forget dreams of salvation and confine itself to loving life, accepting death, and believing in the renewal of life. Thus Auschwitz is followed by a rebirth of the Jewish people in the state of Israel. As for God, he is simply the final Nothing from which we came and to which man and the world will at last return.[1] Mahfouz, for his part, also stresses the problem of evil and the felt absence of God, but his emphasis is on the cruelty and intolerance of the God of popular religion. Men made a despotic God and then made themselves in the image of their God. However, Mahfouz is not quite an atheist: he calls himself a 'Sufi socialist' and a critic of 'an idea of God that men have made'. Like many of us in the West he wants to go behind the personal God to something different, something that for a long while yet people are going to find it hard to understand.[2]

These two notable writers both indicate that the modern crisis of faith in a personal God is a major event, one not confined to Christianity; and it is a major *religious* event, pregnant with new possibilities. That said, however, there remains something distinctive about the specifically Christian experience which deserves more detailed analysis. It is that, for Christians in particular, the end of faith in a personal God is psychologically the end of a love-relationship.

Suppose we ask ourselves, How do people ever come to acquire faith in a personal God in the first place; and having acquired it, how can they ever come to lose it? Christians in the modern West differ somewhat from their Muslim and Jewish neighbours in the more strongly emotional and anthropomorphic character of their religious imagery, and in the prominence among them during the past two or three centuries of the complex of ideas usually classed under the heading of bourgeois individualism. For example, traditional Christian graves were unmarked: only kings and other major figures had permanent monuments with their names on them over their tombs. But from the seventeenth century tombstones became progressively democratized, and by the late nineteenth century every Tom, Dick and Harriet was being given almost the sort of monument that once only kings had had. Funerary rites, which until quite recent times were usually austerely brief, theocentric, impersonal and penitential, now increasingly take the form of a tribute to the dead person who — especially in America — receives a eulogy. The first English Memorial Service was, I think, that for Queen Victoria. Now more and more of us seem to get one. That's democracy for you. Judgment and Hell have largely vanished, and God has been almost purely benevolent for over a century.

Religious changes such as these, though long prepared in the Christian tradition, have been accelerated by the spread of humanitarian sentiment and the influence of the Evangelical Revival, with its constant talk of personal religion and a personal faith. In consequence, the state of believing in a personal God has become psychologically very like the state of being in love. There is the same intense emotional attachment, and the same heightened sense of life. A glance at a thesaurus is a sufficient reminder of the very large linguistic overlap between the two states; and they both belong typically to youth, the time of life when eros is most determinedly object-seeking and our feelings are quickest to twine themselves tightly around the beloved.

From infancy human beings are among the most dependent of animals: is there any other mammal born so immobile that it is unable even to make its own way to the breast? Certainly there is none other that remains profoundly dependent for so many years. It is not surprising that we long retain the habit of forming fiercely tenacious attachments, first to the parents and then by extension to the fetish or toy, to the pet animal, the special friend, the leader, the hero, the star, the cause, the group, the lover and the god; and in all these cases we are, as they say, prone to *idolize* the object of our devotion.

Social attitudes to the lover are ambiguous. A familiar tradition, going back to the Middle Ages, uses religious imagery to describe his transports, ecstasies, raptures, infatuation, worship and enthusiasm; while at the same time he is regarded as being blind, mad, sick, enfeebled and moonstruck, and is treated with derision or at best indulgence. By an equally old tradition, the lover himself acknowledges this ambiguity, and describes it in terms of the traditional paradoxes of faith: in the eyes of the world he may seem to be enslaved, but in reality he is liberated; to be poor, but really he is rich; to have been blinded, but now he sees clearly – and so on. Thus for centuries there has been a strong tradition in the Christian West that assimilates faith in a personal God to a state of erotic fixation or enslavement. The initial stock of images, the free employment of erotic metaphors by the mystics, and then the more recent psychologizing of faith in bourgeois culture have all conspired to bring this about. There is one strong parallel, in the *bhakti* movement in mediaeval India,[3] but we find only weak parallels in early sufism[4] and in Jewish mysticism.

All this, I suggest, accounts for the special prominence and intensity of both conversion and the loss of faith in the Christianity of the past few centuries. Conversion is psychologically almost identical with falling in love, and the loss of faith in a personal

God is psychologically identical with bereavement or divorce, and the end of a love-relationship. In each case there are just the same intense feelings of grief, guilt, depression and disorientation and the same few months of mourning to be undergone.

However, the case of God is the most extreme. The peak age for conversion to personal faith in a personal God is the age when we are most heterocentric, that is, when we most need to find personal fulfilment through giving ourselves to another whom we serve. Eros seeks an adequate love-object. It is also the age when we are cognitively and morally most actively awake and in search of a view of life and a cause to live for; and it is an age when we urgently seek psychic and moral unification. What could be more overwhelmingly adequate to our needs than One who is a supremely perfect love-object, and at the same time both a cause to live for and a universal explanation? No wonder we lock on to faith so ardently.

The analogy between the love of God and other loves extends to some interesting details. For example, lovers gain a sense of immortality, and we all feel that our parents while they remain with us keep death at bay for us. They shield us: so long as they are around it will not be our own turn for a good while yet. When they leave us, we feel death closing in. But God is an immortal parent, and so has in perpetuity the power to keep our death at bay. Hence the psychological connection between belief in a personal God and freedom from the fear of death: underneath are the everlasting arms. Conversely, the loss of faith in a personal God is always experienced as like being orphaned, because it suddenly brings death very close to us personally. The famous phrase 'the death of God' may be theological nonsense, but psychologically it makes very good sense.

Belief in a personal God, understood in this way as meeting our deepest emotional needs, is very powerful. It gives us someone to love, a sense that we matter and a shield against death. It assures us that we have been singled out to be loved, protected and accompanied. How can it ever be lost? Yet it is lost, and the loss must be accepted and even willed, for precisely those reasons. It may pass itself off as a form of self-surrender, but in fact it is the opposite. It is a naked expression of blind, wilful egoistic need-love, eros throughout and not agape at all. Kierkegaard, sensitive as usual to the natural egoism of love, remarks in his *Works of Love* (II, 4) that

> if a man seeks to become the object of another person's love, he deliberately and falsely seeks his own, for the only true object of a human being's love is love, which is God, who therefore in a deeper sense is not an object at all, since he is himself love.[5]

That is, if love is to become non-egoistic, unattached and disinterested, then God must be de-centred. He must be seen, not as a person who loves me, but simply as – Love, full stop. To put it in something like Kierkegaard's own terms, God educates us in love by progressively de-centring himself, withdrawing as an individual personal object of love and leaving behind only pure love, which is his essence. We experience the difficult *command* to love precisely through the withdrawal and vanishing of the God who was a personal object for the involuntary and uncommandable erotic type of love. God's self-decentring for Love's sake is the instrument by which he brings about the believer's own de-centring. He dies to make us die too, so that love may live. This is why the death of God and the loss of faith in a personal God – which to the world seems to be the end of religion, and indeed in a certain sense *is* so – is yet also the crux of our religious education. In modern Western Christianity, we have suggested, there has been a strong tendency for historical reasons for belief in God to become an emotional fix and a self-regarding fantasy. The more this becomes the case, the more people will have to pass through the crisis of the loss of faith in such a God, and the greater the risk that they will interpret it as ending, rather than beginning, their relation to Christianity. Hence the need to proclaim the death of God, and not just of Christ, as a necessary stage in the religious life; for, in general, if you undergo the loss of faith in the personal God involuntarily you are likely to end up being quite non-religious; if you pass through it in a spirit of revolt you will probably become an atheist; if you let it happen tacitly or unconsciously you will one day wake up to find yourself an agnostic; but if you enter the crisis voluntarily, accepting it as a religious necessity, then you have the best chance of making it the stepping-stone to something new and constructive. The spirit in which you enter the crisis is likely to determine the route by which you leave it.

Interestingly, the last threads are the hardest of all to cut, and the semi-realist may prove psychologically and at heart to be still quite as much of a realist as any fundamentalist. To illustrate this, imagine a person whose marriage is breaking down and who is already living apart from the spouse. Divorce proceedings may already be in train. Then the spouse dies – and the grief, the guilt, the sense of irreparability and the sheer *loss* is just as intense as it would have been if they had remained happily married until the end. Indeed, it may be worse.

It is not, however, easy to understand why the break should be so difficult to make in the still stronger case where it is made deliberately, and in the knowledge that it is inevitable because a religious imperative that will not be gainsaid requires it. Perhaps we should say that it is hard to leave childhood behind, especially when one has some anticipatory notion of just how bleak adulthood will be in comparison. At any rate, after the initial period of mourning is over death comes close and settles permanently inside us. It will henceforth always be present, growing silently. With it comes also the vast sense of cosmic homelessness, nothingness and abandonment, in which the individual feels like a spaceman who has been cut off from the mother-ship and now falls away alone in the interminable void as he waits for his oxygen to run out. The condition has been often enough described: the great merit of Heidegger's analysis of it is that he makes clear the connections.[6] Bereaved, I am jolted out of my previous self-forgetfulness and immersion in the business of living, and am forced to conduct a solitary reappraisal of my situation. I see that my existence is essentially temporal, and that I live between a past from which I am struggling vainly to get free and a limited future for which I am alone responsible. The cosmic dread I felt was produced by the realization that my life and my world are finite. They will come to an end. My being is being-towards-death, and since death is nothingness it closes or seals up my life and gives it to me as mine, my span and my task. I am thus forced to assume the full responsibility for what I make of myself in the time I have left to me.

The unawakened self may be in a state of 'forfeiture', absorbed in and scattered by worldly preoccupations; it may be stupefied by myths and illusions; or it may be paralysed and made impotent by dread. That which calls me to wake up, choose myself and accept full responsibility for my life, Heidegger names conscience, and that to which it calls me he names destiny. In Bultmann's Christianized version of Heidegger's teaching, the preaching of the gospel functions as the alarm-clock that summons us to authentic existence. Either way, our immediate point is that the first sign that we are emerging from the crisis of faith is a moral stirring; and Heidegger's analysis helps to explain how it begins. More than almost any previous philosopher, he attempted to look head-on at death and nothingness, and precisely from that vision extracted a summons to new life and action. It was no doubt for this reason that Bultmann could find Heidegger congenial and see him as standing in the Protestant tradition.

Yet the question arises, How is it possible for the new life to be still a *religious* life? Certainly many people do not see how this can be the case; and since the point is so important we set out formally seven reasons why.

First, the new life has begun as the outcome of a self-reassessment that was not merely partial or relative but was religiously ultimate in character. Secondly, the crisis was experienced as a death and rebirth of the self. Thirdly, the new life is experienced as summons and gift, because we went so deeply into nihilism and dissolution that we could be revived only by a spontaneous upsurge of the life-impulse itself. Fourthly, when we emerge from the crisis we find the world swept bare and new-washed. Fifthly, we therefore find ourselves in a situation of extraordinary freedom in which our value-choices will remake us and our world afresh. Sixthly, we are of course as free to reconstitute our lives on a religious basis as on any other; but we will be the first human beings to admit our full responsibility for our own religious beliefs and practice. Our religious representations will no longer appear to us through a veil of ignorance, for we will know that they are indeed ours. Seventhly, those who raise the question of how a consciously and autonomously chosen life can be a religious life may have missed the implications of Hebraic voluntarism, for in ancient Jewish thought reality was created by acts of choice. The believer was directed simply to choose God and the life-order that the God represented. To that we say Amen: we will do just that.

Thus all the forms of religious consciousness that we shall be considering from now on are voluntaristic by comparison with what preceded them. We shall indeed distinguish between more active and more contemplative paths, but it will be under the general rubric that from now on everything is creatively chosen.

On the historical map, we are now at last approaching the twentieth century and the age of modernism and post-modernism. The period of theological crisis had occurred around 1780–1840, when first Kant overthrew the old theistic metaphysics and then the early biblical critics, culminating in D.F. Strauss, demolished the old view of the Bible. During this period between Kant and the young Hegelians (of whom Strauss was one), the old theological realism came to an end. There followed an intermediate period of what we have called semi-realism, in which ideas of progressive historical development to some extent took the place of the old belief in divine Providence. The two most famous names here are Hegel and Marx; but the optimistic historicism that they represented broke down at the end of the century. Nietzsche is the key figure, and the heyday of the modern movement from about 1890 to 1920 is marked by the sense of a radical break with the past, and a new beginning.

Of the naturalistic strain in Nietzsche's thought one might say that in him the self is dissolved down into the life-impulse of which it is the expression, and comes up again as Dionysos, united with life and saying Yes to life as never before. His teaching was in fact a naturalistic version of the Protestant gospel of salvation by faith alone. With this new beginning and new life-affirmation Modernism completed something that the Romantic Movement had begun, the full transfer of divine creativity from God to man. Art, now seen as creative self-expression rather than as copying, became the central and typical human activity: we make by making symbols. Inevitably, as Modernism developed, the very idea that language or any other form of human symbolic expression works by replicating the structure of an external and pre-established order of things came increasingly under fire. Instead, our various forms of symbolic expression (including our practices) were seen as themselves creatively establishing the various orders of things that we inhabit. The various post-crisis forms of religious consciousness that we are now to consider may be seen as responses to this new situation.

10

AESTHETIC EXPRESSIVISM

We have just been speaking as if all post-crisis forms of religious consciousness are revolutionary, involving a radical break with the past, and can have arisen only in the present century: as if the believer after the statutory period of mourning is over suddenly finds herself emerging with joy and gratitude into an entirely new world. Sometimes, that is how it is; but not always, and we must now backtrack a little. For the first major form of post-realist religious thought that we have to consider is two centuries old, its roots reaching back to the earliest stirrings of Romanticism and German Idealist philosophy. It has been around long enough to have passed through a number of distinct phases, Romantic, modernist and post-modernist; and although when it first appeared it was innovative, its temper had often been not at all revolutionary, but conservative and nostalgic.

Aesthetic expressivism is the natural successor to objective symbolism. We were discussing in chapter 8 those who find themselves gravitating very reluctantly towards it. It is a thorough-going symbolist view of religion that has renounced objectivity, and no longer tries to go beyond the symbols and relate them to something else that they stand for. We have only the symbols, and it is not possible to justify them or to ground them objectively. So we cannot spell out any way in which the symbols may correspond to, copy or represent alleged referents behind them, and this forces a shift from metaphysics to aesthetics. We now see the symbols simply as expressions and assess their play, their interplay and their counterplay – in short the ways they work – by the sort of criteria that we use in assessing art. The death of God means the end of every sort of foundationalism. Instead we just look at the surfaces, the manifest phenomena, and see how they work.

Aesthetic expressivism is thus both very old and very new. Very old, because a line of thought running back almost to the beginnings of Western philosophy has said that only God has immediate and intuitive knowledge of things just as they are in themselves, whereas our merely human understanding is always discursive and mediated. Indeed, one of the historical functions of the idea of God, still evident in Kant, was to force us to recognize the necessarily imperfect character of all human knowledge. God set us longing for an immediacy that we knew we could not have, for all that is directly given to us is never reality itself but only seemings, appearances, phenomena – or in modern terms, sense experiences, words and symbols. Some philosophies promised nevertheless to find a way of leading us from the world of appearance to the world of reality; but there was always another tradition which said, Why torment ourselves with an impossible dream? Why stigmatize the whole of human experience as being defective by contrast with some other supposed state of things which *ex hypothesi* is beyond our reach? Let us give up this futile nostalgia for an alleged homeland which we can never have inhabited and will never inhabit, and simply say yes to things as they are. We need to learn what Nietzsche has called good-will to appearance – and this is very new, for it reminds us of the Derridean maxim that 'there is nothing outside the text'. Forget the whole business of trying to relate the symbols to something beyond them and be content with their unending play, interplay and counterplay. Old-style metaphysics always saw truth as a relation of correspondence, matching or isomorphism between two entirely disparate worlds: thought and being, words and things, appearance and reality. And it was attempting the impossible because, as indeed it simultaneously admitted, we are shut up in one of the worlds and can never actually set the two worlds side by side and directly demonstrate their correspondence. So we must forget the whole picture of a more-real world-beyond and a correspondence theory of truth, and instead see the truth of any symbol-system such as a text or a religion as being like the truth of art.

This explains why aesthetic expressivism is so often conservative and traditionalist, and why it loves what is beautiful and old in religion and is therefore drawn to Catholicism and Eastern Orthodoxy. In effect, it identifies the faith with its manifest cultural expressions. Christianity is simply what it has been: it is the text of scripture, the liturgies, the institutions, the art and music, the patterns of symbolism and doctrinal themes, the lives lived. The faith is what is available to the historian, the given tradition, and is identical with its own historical-cultural expressions. You can play one bit of the tradition off against another, and you can expound and extend the tradition in an endless variety of ways. There is plenty of freedom. But it is an illusion to suppose that you have access to some supra-traditional occult essence of the faith that you can use as your standpoint for criticizing the tradition as a whole. Hence the tendency of aesthetic expressivism to become contemplative and conservative, and to be suspicious of religious activists and reformers. Unless the new material they introduce is aesthetically richer and more complex than the old material they seek to abolish, the activists will be doing more harm than good. And hence also the tendency to aesthetic expressivism on the part of all who are historically-minded.

This outlook first appeared at the end of the eighteenth century. The thinkers of the Enlightenment had inherited from Descartes a very dualistic metaphysics which sharply contrasted subject and object. The human mind, a free, rational and disembodied spirit, confronted a deterministic physical world of inert bodies, a world that could be completely described by mathematical physics and was destitute of any intrinsic religious, ethical or artistic value. It was just a machine. Enormously impressed by the magnificent achievement of Newton, the Enlightenment thinkers had the ambition of unifying the philosophical world by extending his type of science to include within it man and society. The subject of knowledge would thus himself become part of the field of determinate objects known. Fine: but if the Enlightenment thinkers were to succeed in this programme they would surely destroy human freedom, and perhaps reason too. They could scarcely desire *that*, especially as another part of their programme required them to justify morality by setting it on new systematic and rational foundations. So Enlightenment thought was caught up in a number of sharp contradictions or polarities, between freedom and necessity, subject and object, morality and nature, and so forth; and there was an urgent demand for some new initiative in philosophy that might offer a way of escape from them.

The last great thinker of the Enlightenment was Immanuel Kant, in whose first two Critiques, those of Pure Reason and Practical Reason, the contradiction between the world of natural necessity and the world of moral freedom seemed to be as stark as ever. However, Kant was an idealist who had gone further than most of his predecessors in stressing the constructive activity of the mind in building our empirical knowledge. This suggested that we are like creative artists, world-makers: it is we ourselves who turn the chaos of raw experience into the cosmos of empirical knowledge. But Kant wished to avoid being a subjective idealist, and argued that though we do indeed paint the world we paint by numbers, so that it is ordained *a priori* what kind of world we must build. He sought to prove *a priori* the validity of all the categories and principles we must use in our world-making. Just as someone who paints by numbers or makes a tapestry uses a blueprint pattern which directs her to fill in certain bounded spaces with particular colours according to rules, so Kant provided an *a priori* pattern on to which the mind must paint the colours given in experience. The result is the world of nature, the world of empirical and scientific knowledge. Kant therefore sees us as operating within predetermined limits, but nevertheless he did allow the entry of the idea that the world of fact is a man-made fiction. He had to do this in order to clear some space for morality. As he saw it, the deterministic universe of Newton's science was only an organization of phenomena according to *a priori* rules. On the one hand its structure was compulsory, but on the other it was no more than 'representation'. At a different level, there was still space for us to be free moral agents. So, at least, Kant claimed; but his first two critiques leave the reader very puzzled about just how the deterministic world of nature is related to the world of moral freedom.

However, his contemporaries were greatly struck by the way in which in his third critique, *The Critique of Judgment* (1790), Kant rather tentatively hinted that art might mediate between nature and morality. In Kant's text they read that the aesthetic realm is autonomous. It has its own very mysterious and perhaps even inexpressible logic. Artworks manifest a 'purposiveness without purpose' which gives us 'disinterested satisfaction'. Though it is a particular, the work of art hints at the universal, so that the beautiful can function as a sensuous symbol of the Good.[1]

Although these were the merest hints, they were enough: they provided the basis on which within a century Nietzsche could declare that all human activities should be viewed on the model of artistic creativity, that the world itself is a work of art, and that it is only as an aesthetic phenomenon that the world itself is eternally justified. More immediately, Kant's young Romantic readers seized on his fragmentary remarks as offering a way of escape from the legacy of the Enlightenment. The typical earlier view had been (I caricature) that the external world is barren and that value resides only in human psychological states. Moreover, these states can all be analysed as being in various degrees pleasurable or painful. It seemed that the most that could be said of a great work of art was that it caused pleasurable sensations in the spectator. And how did it do this? – because the eye was pleased by its quasi-mathematical properties of harmony, proportion, formal correctness or fidelity to nature. From this dismal doctrine Kant seemed to offer release, and such writers as Schiller and Schelling were soon making the philosophy of art central to all philosophy.[2]

Given its basic assumptions, it is not surprising that the Enlightenment should have left religious thought in very poor shape, and Kant himself had administered the death-blow to the philosophical arguments by which the old metaphysical realism and designer realism had been sustained. But the new art-centred philosophy promised to rejuvenate religious thought, if people could only be persuaded to recognise that religious meaning and truth are not metaphysical but aesthetic. For example, art has the power to evoke in us a primal feeling or 'aesthesis' for all things as comprising one infinite living organic Whole of which we ourselves are part, in a way that may give new meaning to talk of God. The power of art to lift us out of our mundane egoistic calculations into disinterested contemplation may be seen as giving meaning to talk of prayer, and its reconciling, unifying power may give meaning to talk of redemption. Furthermore, the Romantics held that all cultural life, and also the life of each individual, began from a primal unity of myth, poetry and religion.

To achieve redemption in our alienated modern society we need to move in a great circle to regain that primal unity: and this aspect of the Romantic project resembles those religious teachings that say that we must seek the Redeemer in the Creator, be reborn, and become again like children.

In this way the idealist philosophy of art might readily enter into alliance with religion as they together sought to reinstate the creative imagination, aesthetic experience and myth at the centre of the culture. A religion could be seen as a great historically evolved and accumulated work of folk art, embodying the yearnings and the unconscious wisdom of humanity. Like all artworks it is a mysterious production that springs according to its own unknown laws from the very depths of the human spirit, and is greater than its makers. And also like all works of art, it has the power to reconcile and unify things that elsewhere in our culture have become painfully sundered: the self and nature, work and play, freedom and necessity, the ideal and the actual, sensuousness and formal order.

Such ideas as these are already emerging in the first great work of aesthetic expressivism, Schleiermacher's *On Religion: Speeches to its Cultured Despisers* of 1799. In his first edition at least, Schleiermacher was a definite non-realist, though at the time his critics did not of course use that term, preferring such confusing and inadequate epithets as 'pantheist' and 'spinozist'. Schleiermacher made no attempt to rehabilitate the kind of metaphysical realism that Kant had destroyed, but instead demythologized religion into art, or (better) rehabilitated religion as art. Faith in God was understood to express a fundamentally aesthetic and reconciling response to the world as an infinite Whole of which we are part; and so bankrupt was the older type of theology that this approach did not seem reductionist to members of the *avant-garde* circles to which Schleiermacher belonged. He exercised a considerable influence upon Fichte, Schelling and others in Germany, while in France Chateaubriand, Cousin and others were soon introducing aesthetic arguments into religious thought.

In this first phase of its development, then, aesthetic expressivism was optimistic and progressive. It was confident that Christianity was true because it was aesthetically beautiful, and aesthetic beauty was going to be central to culture, for it would be publicly established as the philosophically highest and ethically most powerful kind of truth. That is to say, aesthetic expressivism could be sure that it was going to be the future of Christianity insofar as it had reason to be confident that the Romantics would succeed in their programme of rebuilding first philosophy and then the whole of culture around art. But the Romantics did not succeed. Even in their heyday, the new science-based industrial culture founded on bureaucratic, technical rationality was getting under way, and since then it has progressively elbowed religion and art aside, reducing them to the status of marginal leisure activities.

More recent forms of aesthetic expressivism have therefore become much less optimistic and confident. The Romantic critique of the spiritual alienation of men in late-Enlightenment and early industrial society has hardened into a general culture-pessimism, and the Romantic project of moving in a great circle to restore the original unity of culture in childhood, poetry and myth has often become escapism coupled with a bitter and obstinate rearguard action against modernity. The modern aesthetic expressivist often sees himself as battling to conserve a heritage of old texts, artworks and customs for which the world seems to care less and less. He lacks the interesting and optimistic rationale for what he is doing that the Romantics put forward, because no more than the rest of us can he seriously believe that the Romantic programme of overthrowing the hegemony of science and technology and reconstructing culture around art is actually going to succeed; and his soul is inevitably somewhat soured in consequence.

Perhaps the most attractive and widely influential alternative rationale available to him is that proposed by C. G. Jung. Like Heidegger in the 1930s to 1950s, Jung saw that in the objective culture of the public world the dominance of technical rationality is now so complete that people no longer even possess the means of knowing what they have lost. As Heidegger put it, 'the darkening of the world, the flight of the gods, the destruction of the earth, the transformation of men into a mass, the hatred and suspicion of everything free and creative, have assumed such proportions throughout the earth that such childish categories as optimism and pessimism have long since become absurd.'[3] Neither philosophy, psychology, art nor religion have the faintest hope of stemming such a vast and ungovernable tide, and no other option remains but an *emigration à l'interieure*. Heidegger accordingly retreated to his Black Forest hut and Jung to Bollingen, and from these fastnesses each issued his oracles to the faithful.

If the outer world was for the present lost, at least one could secure the inner. Jung located the sources and the meaning of religion and art in the inner world of the psyche. In order to secure his citadel and to avoid charges of arbitrary fantasy Jung argued that the inner life of the psyche was not subject to the constraints of the mechanistic metaphysics that had become dominant in the outer world, and also that the main capacities and typical products of the psyche were universal to all humankind. This gave them their own sort of objectivity, so that Jung could hold that the inner world was at least as real as the outer, and could maintain therefore that he was in flight not from reality, but rather *to* it. He could thus in good conscience be his own sort of religious believer in his solitary reverie, the leading themes of religious doctrine enacting themselves in his soul, while being confident that he was not alone. Everyone's psyche was a kind of Underground station buried beneath the city and linked to all the others, so that everyone if they would but pause and wait would discover the same deep realities in their own souls as Jung had found in his. The objective world was reduced to the status of mere appearance; deep down, Jung's truth was the more universal and lasting.

An old-fashioned empiricist might ask whether Jung's theory can ever be falsified. More searchingly, we might recall that Jung had begun his career studying the delusion-systems produced by the insane. Such systems defend the patient by persuading him or her that although he may appear to be in a minority of one, nevertheless there are hidden reasons why he is right and all the rest of the world are wrong. Can Jung show that his own system is not of that type?

It would be a mistake, though, to view all modern aesthetic expressivists as being mere middle-class culture-pessimists retreating into the past. Recently some people have been first converted to this form of faith. It is what they begin with, rather than something they have fallen back on, and they join in the practice of religion (whether Catholic or Eastern Orthodox Christian, or Orthodox Jewish) without being at all introverted about it. They join the church to be part of a communal project for investing human life with religious 'depth' or significance, and find that they have no difficulty in joining in worship and prayer and listening to sermons whilst interpreting all this material in a thoroughgoing symbolist sense. Furthermore, they seek to live the religious life, by bearing the Christian symbols habitually in mind and using them to guide their practice. In this way they employ Christianity as a *technē* to live by, using the term *technē* in the old Greek sense of an art or practical skill that enables one to do something well. The aesthetic beauty of prayer and worship gives them a sense of eternity that liberates them from self-concern, and does so all the more effectively because they are not realists. Realism is always associated with anxiety, scruples, intolerance, dogmatism and an impulse to control or to change things: in short, realism always has an itch of egoism about it, whereas the non-realist easily learns a Buddhist lightness and good-humour in the use of religious externals.

The reason for this is straightforward. In every philosophy there is always a close link between the ideas of God and the self. The more strongly 'centred' the idea of God, the more strongly centred the self becomes; and conversely, when God is decentred the self is decentred.

How far is this more recent type of expressivist still nostalgic? An element of nostalgia can creep in, because much in Christian symbolism invites it. When it does enter, the expressivist begins to sound like an ironized version of the traditional Romantic. To see this, interrogate her about her idea of God. She replies that God for her lies in the power of worship and prayer to free her from small-mindedness and egoism and drawn her forward out of herself and into an ecstatic sense of eternally belonging to a greater Whole. Worship has this power in a way that an orchestral concert lacks, because worship is more ethical. It comes as part of a package of practices – prayer, brotherly love, community loyalty, constant recollection of the guiding symbols – all of which help to ensure that when we are drawn out of ourselves we are drawn, not just into Dionysiac pagan ecstasy or passive reverie, but into active neighbour-love. Worship moralizes ecstasy. It requires each individual's full participation; each individual is put under the spotlight, so that whereas a pop concert turns its audience into a mass, worship turns the worshippers into an organic and ethical society.

This form of belief might be described as mythical realism

encapsulated within consciousness, and it is much more common than is generally recognized. It resembles Romanticism in regarding secularization and the loss of myth as leading to spiritual fragmentation. Only myth can unify, because myth alone unites world-view, community-structure, art and morality; and, simply as a matter of fact, if you seek spiritual integration you must turn to that social institution which is based on the primacy and the unifying power of myth, namely religion.

However, these modern expressivists are unavoidably more self-conscious than the Romantics about what they are doing. The Romantics expected art actually to accomplish the reintegration of culture at the public level, and so to bring back the Age of Gold. We moderns no longer have that expectation. It is evident that in the public domain the primal religious unity of culture, in which cosmology, art, social structure and ethics are all held together by myth, has been lost at least since the seventeenth century. Inevitably, therefore, joining the church and embracing myth is an act of dissent or defiance which cannot help but have a slightly ironical, bracketted and self-conscious air about it. Nevertheless, the expressivist can still say that she is not a cognitive deviant or reactionary. She knows what she is doing. Even in our secularized world there still is a church, the church is a society, and it happens to be the only society still founded on the essential prerequisite for a spiritually-integrated society, namely myth. A religious person is one who seeks spiritual integration, and for such a person the rational thing to do is to join the church and practise living by myth – consciously.

Now, though, if we interrogate this stance further, the element of nostalgia begins to appear. For let us ask the modern express-ivist, does she believe in God? and let us suppose that she is completely candid in her reply. She says: 'The old type of public belief in God is possible only insofar as the objective culture is able to unify all the major areas of our experience, because God simply is the supreme Subject for whom and in whom all things hold together. But the objective culture became fragmented in the seventeenth century, and this event was the so-called death of God. Obviously the modern world is godless, and equally obviously as a citizen of a modern state I am godless. Even in the church we can now believe only in a bracketted and ironical way. But at least it can be said that our type of conscious believer lives a more unified life than could otherwise be lived, and that only within the church are to be found the resources from which one day a more integrated public culture might arise. If along Schelling's lines, or Hegel's, or in some other way the objective reunification of culture were to be accomplished, then old-style belief in God would become possible again. Meanwhile, within the church we at least postulate God and choose to live by the idea of God. That much at least we can do. We can wait, and bear such witness as we can to the possibility of God-again. Traditionally such waiting-for-God has been regarded as a perfectly valid form of belief in God, because in some ages it is the best that can be done.'

With this statement an element of nostalgia and of historicist mythology has at last definitely appeared: and our expressivist has dated herself. For the speech she has just made voices the condition of religious thought in the later Modern period, especially the 1930s to 1950s. It was the period of Simone Weil's *Waiting on God* and Beckett's *Waiting for Godot*. Heidegger summarized it in his formula, 'Only a god can save us'. There is nothing to be done except to prepare oneself, by the practice of religious reflection and poetic creation, for the appearance of the god, or (as it may be) for his failure to appear 'in the time of going under'.[4] In the Modern period people were still troubled by a residual historicism which assured them that the present was peculiarly derelict and godless, and there was nothing to be done in the interim period except stay in one's fall-out shelter, practise the secret discipline, and wait, and hope.

In the post-modern period, beginning (roughly) at the end of the 1950s, we seek to escape from that nostalgia by questioning the historicism that gave rise to it. For after all, pejorism – a word we need: it means the belief that things are getting steadily worse – is just as historicist as meliorism, the belief that things are steadily improving. Neither point of view is rational, because if we are to be consistently historicist we must acknowledge that all standards of evaluation are internal to particular historical places and times. We have no history-transcending standards, no point of view outside the process from which we can issue a general pronouncement to the effect that things as a whole are getting either better or worse. Awareness of historical change and of our radical historicality had a very odd effect on the Western mind.

It gave rise at first to historicism and then to historical relativism, and it took people a surprisingly long time to grasp that in the end it delivers us from history and simply precipitates us into the here and now, where we are. The paradox that took so long to grasp is that radical historicality eats itself up: it ends the tyranny of 'History', and so brings in the postmodern age.

It was in France at the end of the 1950s that the decisive shift took place. In Hegel's *Lectures on the Philosophy of History* the end of philosophy, and therefore of history, was its reaching its goal, its completion, its termination and its arrival at its *telos*. Even Nietzsche, often thought of as the destroyer of historicism, remained partly in thrall to it, because he had a traditional type of eschatology: the death of God, the crisis, the time of affliction, the coming of the Superman and the Great Noontide. But for the postmodernists the end of history means not its *telos* but the vanishing of all remaining ideas of *telos* and directionality in history, and therefore of History itself. Meliorism and pejorism both go, along with the ideas of alienation, the dereliction of the present, the *avant-garde*, impending crisis, and a deep truth lying beneath the surface of things and waiting to be revealed. In short, the exposure and dissolution of the whole Modernist mythology is a very considerable event, and the postmodern age is more different from the Modern than is yet clearly realized.

Now the question arises, can Christian expressivism become fully postmodern by liberating itself from the attachment to tradition, the nostalgia, the negative attitude to the present, and the passive waiting for a more satisfactory future that have hitherto usually characterized it?

We need an example. The 'attitudinal Christianity' described by the philosopher R.M. Hare at the Yale Divinity School towards the end of the 1960s (and unfortunately not fully published) is perhaps the clearest, and it can be guaranteed free from the least taint of historicism.[5] Holding on orthodox empiricist grounds that supernatural beliefs do not have clear and verifiable descriptive meaning, Hare treats religion simply as piety: a temper of mind, a body of attitudes cultivated and expressed in practices such as worship. So regarded, religion does not need to be justified but only to be practised, a practice which shapes one's character and the way one lives the moral life.

Hare's purely attitudinal and non-cognitive Christianity may,

then, be taken as an example of post-modern aesthetic expressivism. Will it work? There are difficulties. It is bound to be ironical
– and to a degree, indeed, that non-intellectual persons notoriously
regard as disgraceful. It must have a starting-point, and so attaches
itself to tradition. Since post-modern theories of interpretation
are decidedly permissive, it may be claimed that the choice of a
single tradition as a point of departure does not foreclose any
options. Nevertheless, the choice of a starting-point does flavour
the whole subsequent enterprise, and the need to have one may
itself be questioned. It is very noticeable that, throughout the
present discussion, when we have spoken of the aesthetic we have
been talking of the spectator who contemplates and interprets a
work of art rather than of the creative artist who produces
it. Post-modernists, an incestuous group, sometimes seem to
envisage the coming of a world composed entirely of critics,
interpreters and literary theorists. The faith as text, the church as
a seminar, the religious believer as an imaginative literary critic,
her life as her own hermeneutical variation on the creed delivered
to her: we pause just long enough to recognize that these themes
have a certain dire plausibility – and make haste to move on.

11

PURE RELIGIOUS VOLUNTARISM

Forgive the jargon I am using: when trying to clarify new concepts one cannot avoid introducing new and often ugly terms – but the two spiritualities that I call aesthetic expressivism and pure religious voluntarism are almost perfect antitheses of each other. The one is the non-realist and modern successor of the ancient Way of Affirmation, and the other of the Way of Negation. The one values the vast unconscious solidarity of believers who live peaceably within the ancient house of meaning, whereas the other is taut, intellectually puritanical, highly-conscious, individualistic and often rebellious. The one starts from everything, and the other from nothing; and I mean, Nothing.

The contrast between them can be brought out by considering the question of consciousness. Aesthetic expressivists are people who like the received tradition and say yes to all the images. They are traditionalists, lovers of art and history who extol the beauty of holiness. They are at one end of a broad and continuous spectrum which ranges from orthodox doctrinal realists at one extreme through objective symbolists to their own position at the other, and they have no desire to make explicit exactly where on that spectrum any given individual may stand. They cordially dislike the philosophical impulse to pin things down precisely and to crystallize delicate nuances in the soul's life into sharp-edged 'positions', because such distinctions tend to become divisions that disturb the peace of the church. Least of all do they wish to become too explicit about where precisely they themselves stand. They see the Crisis as the loss of faith and do not wish to hear about it, so that although their own standpoint is in fact post-realist they may well be unaware of its being so. Many have not themselves passed through the Crisis, and even those who have done so see no need to advertise the fact. They would prefer simply to emphasize that to be a believer always was and still is to affirm the images and to live within and by them. All else is mystery, and should remain so.

By contrast, pure religious voluntarism is ultra-conscious and individualistic. It is Protestantism-squared, a religious outlook whose general contours can best be gathered from a radical and anti-realist reading of Kierkegaard. It vehemently rejects the cosy, dormant, collective and passively aesthetic faith of Christendom as being sub-Christian, and demands instead that faith must be in the highest degree conscious, autonomous and individually willed. It regards the Crisis as being not the loss of faith, but the supreme moment in the life of faith when at the time of the greatest possible challenge the true nature of faith is decisively revealed, so that the Crisis becomes the firm foundation of one's whole subsequent existence.

Pure religious voluntarism is still image-guided, but the images most potent for its interpretation of Christianity are images of the loss of all imagery, and of re-creation *ex nihilo*, out of nothing, not out of anything at all. They are the images of the end of all things, of the death of Christ and the believer's participation in Christ's death, and of Creation *ex nihilo*, rebirth and the resurrection of the dead. From these images it concludes that the only route by which anyone can enter upon a fully Christian form of existence is by passing through a state of total loss, death and nothingness. This state may be called the Nihil. In it everything is dissolved, and God, cosmology, society, values and the self all evaporate. We see ourselves as being nothing suspended in nothingness. We are as impotent as the dead.

This state would be indistinguishable from an extreme form of clinical depression, but for one thing: we entered it voluntarily or, perhaps preferably, we accepted its coming as being a religious necessity. This uncanniest of all guests was standing at the door, and we chose to admit it. For religion is about the quest for perfect goodness and holiness. It is to be filled with a kind of love which is subjectless and objectless, universal, and no longer egoistically and moralistically selective. To reach it, God and the self must both of them be de-centred: the god must die and I must die with him. We die together for love's sake. One might say that just to will the death of God is atheism and just to recognize and accept the Void is Buddhism; but to accept that for Love's sake one must die in union with the god is Christianity.

How does this work? The experience of the Nihil breaks the grip of egoism by showing us that we have no proprietary entitlement to existence. On the contrary, human existence is not securable. The self cannot save itself, for the Nihil has broken down the self's own fortifications and it is overrun. I see then that I cannot claim my life as my right, but must continually accept and receive it as a gift. I have no other option but from moment to moment to live and let live, to be and let be.

The question of just how, having once entered it, we ever get out of the Nihil is crucial, and it is important to guard against misinterpretation. For the voluntarist is readily seen as an extreme individualist and value-creationist who deifies the finite will and overcomes the Nihil by an act of Promethean self-affirmation. He is thought to be saying that when I am in the Nihil everything external to me is gone and I see that nothing can get me out of the Nihil except a pure and naked act of my own will. I must choose, posit, affirm and create my own life, my values, my world and my god to live by. When I am in the Nihil and confronted by the primal Chaos, and in default of anyone else to say it, I am forced to recognize that I and I alone have to say 'Let there be light!' This primal creative act of the will then gets me out of the Nihil and reinstates me in my world. The experience reveals to me that I myself am henceforth my only god, who must continually choose and therefore create myself, my values and my world. And then the voluntarist is understood to be saying that *this* is the real meaning of the protestant Christian doctrine of justification by faith alone: I exist authentically and my life is truly my own insofar as I recognize that at a deep level I must continually choose and affirm my own life and my values. To live on any other basis is to live in a state of forfeiture, bondage and illusion.

A number of critics have read my own accounts of the Nihil, its lessons and how we escape from it, along these lines.[1] It is not surprising that they ask: In the Nihil, who is *there* to do the willing? And they understandably suggest that the voluntarist doctrine thus read may resemble the egoism of Max Stirner or some forms of atheistic existentialism, but it can scarcely claim to be a genuine form of religious faith. If *anything* is anti-religious, this is.

I agree, and in particular I think I have always insisted that because the Nihil invades and dissolves the self itself, the atheistic existentialist's way of overcoming it will not work. Furthermore, I have also suggested that the religious person enters the Nihil voluntarily and in the full knowledge that it involves the death of the self. She does not actively seek the death of the self, but rather recognizes that a religious imperative requires it, because the self is an obstacle to holiness. The atheistic existentialist panics and pulls out too soon, seeking to extricate himself by an act of the will before the Nihil can dissolve away the self: whereas the religious person is sufficiently disciplined to be able to wait until the end.

How then does the religious person emerge? It is clear that we run up against the limits of language, because at the very bottom of the Nihil all representations are lost. The productive life-energy is annulled, and no longer expresses itself in representation at all. For a time out of time, there is total silence and darkness. We are voluntarists rather than intellectualists because in that moment when the Nihil is absolute, no reason, objective ground or explanation can be found for the life-energy's resurgence. As many of the old theologies used to insist, the act of creation or re-creation is gratuitous and inscrutable. Because it arises *ex nihilo* and no reasons can be given for it, it is more like an act of pure unconditional choice which so-to-say is its own reason for itself and cannot be further interrogated, than it is like an act or event which can be accounted for in terms of causes and reasons. A pure religious voluntarist is therefore not a person who deifies 'the will', as if *it* were an explaining cause, but rather one whose experience of the Nihil has taught her the radical gratuitousness of existence, and therefore of faith also.

The atheistic existentialist believes that he has learnt the absurdity of existence, and aims by an exertion of the will to impose value upon it. The Christian existentialist, by contrast, went more deeply and trustingly into the Nihil because she was in search of selflessness. She emerges thinking of all life as pure gift. On that basis, agapé is possible. She has passed through the dialectic, life-death-eternal life, and is an individualist because she thinks each individual must experience the Nihil in order to gain salvation. Aesthetic contemplation of the image of Christ's death on our behalf is not sufficient: one must die with Christ.

From a state in which there are no representations at all the productive life-energy spontaneously surges up, and its re-entry into representation naturally takes the form of myth. We are reborn, raised from the dead, and the world has been re-created *ex nihilo*. And since myth is here the primal language and the one that is closest to the facts, it is worth exploring this theme of the creation of the world to see if we can shed more light on the act of faith. In particular, I hope to show how a religious voluntarist understands religious beliefs, and how it is that she sees the act of faith as an act of will that creates *ex nihilo*, and so conquers the Nihil, without her being a straightforward Promethean atheist.

Doctrinal realism portrays creation as a free act performed in eternity by God, which brought the world and time into being out of nothing. There has always been a tendency to regard it as being the chronologically first event, brought about by a First Cause, that initiates cosmic history. Theologians deny this, saying that creation is an eternal act which establishes a permanent and standing metaphysical relationship between each created thing and its Maker. But the background of mythical narrative that still shapes the order of the creeds continues to encourage the old habit of representing Christian teaching as a cosmological drama in which the creation of the world opens the Old Testament story, just as the resurrection of Christ is the basis of Christian faith; and this strengthens the tendency of the imagination to view creation as the first cosmic event.

It is noticeable that on this account the world of our present experience is viewed not as chaos but as a ready-made Cosmos. Without any help from us, and indeed long before any human beings existed, God and God alone impressed upon the world a single pattern of intelligible order. The world was thus pre-established as a fit habitation for human beings, with the clear implication that there is no need for us to move the furniture around and that we have no permission to do so. There is no scope for any human action to be truly creative, for the world is fully created already. We are here in the thought-system of a traditional society which discourages innovation.

In the Christian tradition the novel, the fictional and the imaginary were long seen as satanically-prompted, but even as early as the Renaissance Tasso had suggested that the poet has in him something of the divine attribute of creativity. In the eighteenth century the large-scale transfer of the power of creation from God to man got under way. The *Oxford Dictionary* sees Sheridan, in 1775, as having been the first English writer to speak of the human imagination as being creative in the grand, almost theological, sense. By now we are entirely accustomed to the idea that there are not only creative artists and writers, but also creative thinkers, scientists and even theologians, for through the diffused influence of Romanticism and idealist philosophy the idea of creativity has spread across the entire range of human activities.

At the same time we have also become aware of the diversity and the historical change of cultures and world-views. This has led us increasingly to accept that it is we ourselves who through our language and our social practices construct our worlds around ourselves, that we are always in one way and another putting a construction upon our experience and ordering our world, and that all the ways in which we do this are not only of our own making but are also in continual historical change.

The upshot is that the old idea that there is just one pre-established and unalterable cosmic order of things has gradually disappeared. The world as such – if indeed we can speak of such a thing at all – is no more than a featureless flux of becoming, which different cultures simply order in different ways.

We therefore no longer have a fixed and divinely-made cosmos of the old type, but only a mutable and man-made one; and the creation of the world, which was once thought of as being done solely by God, is now thought of as done by the human imagination. Because the traditional understanding of creation was so objectified, setting creation in the past, regarding it as basically done already and seeing it as God's work which men were not allowed to tamper with, it has been wholly rejected, and most people cannot see any practical use for the belief in divine creation.

Yet the rejection of the old belief in a Cosmos has meant the disappearance of all fixed and enduring structures in the world and in human nature. External guidelines and reference-points have been lost, and human life seems to hang in a void. How are we to live with that thought?

In the English-speaking world the realization of the full implications of this has been delayed. For as long as we could, we clung to realism and our traditional empiricism. We held that there was a real objective order of things out there which could be copied by our theories, and that our theories could be tested against objective data that were fully independent of them. The assumption was that we could recognize and collect these independent data, without compromising their independent status. They were objective and they had a real structure of their own which the mind could grasp without in any way interpreting them or imposing a theory upon them. But gradually we found ourselves forced to admit that pure objectivity and intelligibility will not go together. To understand anything we must appropriate it, interpret it, and see it in the light of some theory or other – which means that it ceases to be purely objective and independent. We cannot have the purely objective and theory-neutral apprehension of the world that is required on the realist model if we are to check the supposed correspondence between our theories and the world. All we can ever check is, not theory against objective world, but one theory against another. With this realization we began to lose the idea of an intelligible mind-independent world described in our theories, and to realize that all we can hope for is a provisional consensus that a certain set of theories hang together well and seem to work well. We can have a world-picture, of our own making; but the world itself we have not.

We see now why those who, in the face of all this, still cling to the old doctrinal realist understanding of creation must regard the modern world as being radically atheistic. Doctrinal realism sharply polarizes God and man, and then insists on ascribing all creativity to God alone. There is only one cosmic pattern of order, and it is divinely pre-established. Doctrinal realism must regard any assertion of human creativity as an act of Promethean revolt against its basic assumptions – and so we are deadlocked. To make any progress we need to go behind dogma to myth; we need to look at what the ancient creation myths were saying before the speculative theologians got to work on them and converted them into metaphysical doctrines. For when the theologians got at the old myths, when they turned *muthos* into *logos*, they repressed many features of the old stories because they considered them embarrassing. And it is in the repressed material that we shall find the clues we need.

This, by the way, is the reason why deconstruction is a valuable technique in religious thought today. The developed dogmatic theology is up a blind alley and immobilized. We must retrace our steps, resolving *logos* back into *muthos* and looking out for the repressed elements, in order to make any advance.

What do we find? The oldest surviving creation-myths were recited or enacted ritually at key moments or crisis-points in human experience, when the cosmic order was annually renewed, when a king was enthroned, at the dedication or the commemoration of the dedication of a temple, to cure barrenness and to revivify people who were despairing or downcast. The myth functioned as an inspiring model of renewal.[2]

The myths picture the Creator as being himself in a state of darkness or sleep, confronted by a formless void within himself as well as around him, and struggling to become conscious of himself. Chaos presents itself to him as a primeval Deep into which he must sink in order to bring up some earth from the very bottom, or as a threatening monster with which he must do battle. Creation stories are, in short, exemplary myths of the mind's struggle to free itself from the monster-ridden darkness and helplessness of unconsciousness and impose light and order without and within. So it is out of mud drawn from the depths of the primeval ocean that the Creator makes the world, and it is out of the divided carcass of the very monster itself that he frames the sunlit paradisal Cosmos. He divides the Cosmic Egg. He sunders light from darkness, heaven from earth, land from sea, human from animal, male from female. In all this his victory is also a becoming conscious of himself, for there is no doubt about the affinity between creation myths and myths of the emergence of consciousness and an organized selfhood. That is one of the crucial repressed features which I mentioned.

This work of creation was then not accomplished in a metaphysical realm quite outside human life, but was regularly enacted within human life. In the Hebrew Psalms God's victory over the monster, and his temporary descent to the bottom of the primal Deep, are repeated in the believer's soul. They function as myths of death and resurrection by which the believer's affirmation of the world and life are renewed. The psalmist finds himself overwhelmed by hostile powers and sinks beneath the waters of chaos. He feels himself dissolving and disintegrating. But in the darkness the power of re-creation awakens in him and enables him to struggle free, overcome his enemies and regain firm ground.

Now when speculative theology expurgated these old myths, objectified the creation and made of it a suprahistorical event which was all over before any human beings appeared, the effect was to deprive us of any real participation in it. Creation was made into a non-religious First Event brought about by the First Cause. But the original myths were wiser: they were about the Nihil, what is it like to be in it and how one emerges from it. They see the god as the archetype of that mysterious creative energy by which as we confront nihilism we are enabled to conquer it, to impose distinction, order, value and symbolism, and generally to constrain the world to become a friendly and habitable cosmos for ourselves.

Creation understood in the usual objectified way has been refuted by modern developments, but Creation understood as a primal sacred myth modelling for us the way we ourselves are to struggle out of the Nihil and transform chaos into cosmos (within ourselves as well as around us) makes sense. By the same token, however, it is clear that if indeed we are along these lines to recover the meaning of myth and bring ancient religious ways of thinking back into use again, we shall be obliged to break down a number of entrenched theological distinctions – above all, that between God and the self.

It has become a commonplace in recent years that Western reason, the *Logos* of theoretical man, first came into being by differentiating itself out of its background in myth, and then repressing and denying not merely any resemblance between itself and its parent but even the very memory of its parentage. *Logos* then pictured itself as standing alone, a nonpareil, the only way to truth, a uniquely privileged, precise, unmetaphorical and luminously clear mode of understanding. Once these claims were established *Logos* became very difficult to dislodge, for by invoking reasons against Reason you merely confirm its authority, and in Descartes and Hegel the absolute sovereignty of Reason remained as secure as ever. More recently, though, as reason's expression has become more narrowly scientific and then bureau-cratic-technical, its hegemony has been increasingly oppressive and people have looked for ways of recovering other modes of expression such as poetry and myth. The new styles of interpretation introduced by Marx, Freud and others suggested that it might be possible to develop undermining techniques that would successfully unmask Reason's pretensions. The idea that the next task of Western thought is to renew itself by demythologizing Reason itself may seem paradoxical: but as we saw earlier, the Romantics in their day had also hoped to unite philosophy with poetry and to recover myth. The more recent programme aims to deconstruct Reason by resolving *Logos* back into *muthos*. One favourite move, made by Nietzsche, Heidegger, Foucault, Rorty and Derrida, is to point out the extraordinary extent to which Reason's authority depends on the persuasiveness of a small set of beguiling and persistent optical metaphors that were first introduced by Plato.[3]

All this is highly relevant to our present travails in religious thought, because doctrine differentiated itself out of myth in the same way as Reason did, and the need to repudiate the parent was even greater. Myth is fluid, unsystematic and multivalent, and freely confuses God and man; but doctrine is about power, and if you wish to maximize your power your edicts must be unambiguous. They must be lucid, unconditional and systematic, and they must themselves incorporate, and inculcate, a clear-cut representation of the source from which they emanate. The King's Law must show what the King is, and God became the embodiment of the unconditional sovereignty of doctrine itself. Doctrine's primary expressions were a series of very sharp disjunctions between God and man, spirit and flesh, heaven and earth, nature and grace, and between divine and human agency, authority and power, these disjunctions being the analogues in the religious realm of the similar series of disjunctions that Plato impressed on Western philosophy.

Pursuing the analogy, the old absolute sovereignty of doctrine and doctrine of absolute sovereignty remained vigorous until Calvin, and even for long after him: but it is now hopelessly unworkable and oppressive. To make any progress, we must deconstruct it and go back to *muthos*. That means we must reject doctrine's disciplinarian dualism.

Now we return to the pure religious voluntarist. She is a Christian existentialist who has been schooled by Kierkegaard. The Nihil, and faith's victory over it, is the basis not only of her religious thought but of her very existence. She is a voluntarist in the sense that an existential philosophy must begin from *Dasein*, human-existence, which in turn is continually maintained by a primal act of acceptance and affirmation that creates it *ex nihilo*. As I have described it – but these are only words – her coming-to-be out of the Nihil starts with a spontaneous resurgence of the life-energy, which promptly expresses itself in the language of religious myth, whose function in turn is to inspire our own choice and affirmation of life and value. And the voluntarist will say, you do not truly have *faith* unless you spontaneously and auto-nomously accept, affirm and will the life-impulse's self-expression in you that is you; and this affirmation must be gratuitous. It must arise from nothing.

Doctrinal realism objects, and tries to force a dilemma. If existence rests on something like a choice, then just who makes the choice, God or us? Either we accept our own existence as being entirely the gift of an objective metaphysical God, or we are atheists who think that by willing our own existence we create ourselves. But we reject the implicit dualism of this. Did not the old theology itself say that God is known only through his effects; that is, God is the work 'God' does in framing and facilitating the act of faith? Religious language is mythical, that is, its meanings are given by the manifold ways it shapes the religious life-story; and the pure religious voluntarist is not an atheist because she cannot describe the basis of her own existence except in religious language. Choosing to live, she chooses God; choosing God, she chooses to live – and she resists attempts to divide the unity in that primal choice of life, God and self.

I have spilt much ink elsewhere in describing various forms and nuances of religious voluntarism, and will not add more for the present beyond two brief comments.

The first is that although we began by describing aesthetic expressivism and voluntarism as antitheses, they do have some points in common. Both are post-realist, and both use religious language and symbolism regulatively to guide practice. Witt-genstein, indeed, combined elements of both outlooks: though he was somewhat uncomfortable in doing so, a discomfort which leads me to my second point. For aesthetic expressivism tends, we have suggested, to be nostalgic and quietistic. It loves tradition and the peace of the church, and finds within the faith delivered to us symbolic resources quite sufficient to meet all our spiritual needs.

Religious voluntarism is different. Having passed through the Crisis it has traversed the philosophical universe from pole to pole, from absolute nihilism to pure unconditional affirmation. It has a special love for Kierkegaard and Nietzsche, because they were twice-born characters who were impelled to seek out the extremes of what the human spirit can experience. Moreover it does not regard the two poles as places to be visited just once in a lifetime. Rather, faith's conquest of nihilism is the continuing ground of the believer's existence from moment to moment. Every day she dances in the void: she looks death in the face and sings, gratuitously affirming the gratuitousness of life. With such an outlook she must be provoked by the shadowy half-life, the armoured triviality, in which most human beings seem content to live. How can she get through to them? How can she wake them up? They are very well defended. She must be cunning. Her ethic will have to be one of subversion.

MILITANT RELIGIOUS HUMANISM

A militant religious humanist is a person whose religious expression is very markedly combative, this-worldly, extraverted and ethical. He is militant because he cannot be content to see the moral task as consisting merely in the pursuit of personal goodness and holiness, within the framework of a given social reality. Such a view is for him too narrow and individualistic, and exhibits too much concern with personal decontamination. Instead, the moral task is to strive on behalf of others to change present social reality. As he sees it, the command to love God and one's neighbour is not two commands that can be conceived of as directing attention towards two distinct objects of concern in two different realms, but just one command that precipitates him into the fight to change the world. God is not the God of the present order of things, but of the future: that is, God-language should be invoked, not to validate the present social order, but rather to inspire a struggle to push the present order speedily into the past.

Morality and religion are for the militant not separate domains, because God is in Christ and Christ is in the neighbour, and my neighbour's plight demands a practical response from me. In philosophical language this means that the function of religious language and imagery is to guide the moral struggle. Religion clothes morality in symbols that dramatize its claims and enhance the objects of its concern. To love God in the neighbour is to see morality *as* religion, to see my neighbour's need as directly imposing a sacred obligation on me that requires me to commit my whole life-activity on his behalf. Hence religious humanism: the sacred is thoroughly humanized and moralized, and we are likely to find such people devoting their lives to pressure-group politics, to trades-unionism, to Christian socialism or the co-operative movement, to philanthropic activities, to the struggle for human rights and to revolutionary struggle for people's liberation from poverty, injustice and oppression. To be preoccupied with personal belief and conduct is bourgeois individualism rather than Christianity: the real test of orthodoxy is the form of your social practice, and in particular whether or not you are on the side of the dispossessed.

This religious-ethical struggle is also a struggle for value because, like the Romantics to whom we have already referred so often, the militant religious humanist is liable to regard the present time as being peculiarly bereft of value.

If he does think that the modern world is particularly deficient in value, he will need to produce some historical analysis of how and why things have gone wrong. In doing so, he may represent capitalist economics as being the chief villain, saying that it has progressively stripped the world and impoverished our culture by reducing all the rich diversity of human values to the single abstract, quantified power-value of money. Alternatively, he may press the analysis further and see behind money the mechanistic philosophy of nature, the Cartesian conceptions of matter and motion, and the ever-expanding hegemony of the bureaucratic-technological form of rationality which has grown out of them. Which comes first – technical rationality, the physical force, or the social force of capitalist economics – may be disputed, but at any rate these things are likely to be regarded as the great destroyers of value.

However, nothing obliges him to construct any story of a lost paradise. He may dismiss nostalgia and say simply that the human condition is perhaps more-or-less constant. Faith is always future-orientated, and always a struggle for change. In an uncertain, but certainly-afflicted, world at least we know that large classes of people at present live in chronic poverty, sickness and hopelessness. If we wish to live well, there is no need for us to spend too much time in rationalizing the situation or in philosophical contortions. Too much of our 'thought' is merely the devising of excuses for inactivity. What we should do is as plain as a pikestaff: we should take the side of those people. Few are prepared to do this, but to do it is religion.

Very well: but we must point out a crux here, to which we will return. It matters a great deal whether or not the militant religious humanist has the support of a story that backs his efforts by telling him how things came to be this bad, and by promising him that his labour is not in vain because things are going to get better. In the past a variety of such legitimating and encouraging narratives sustained Christians, men of the Enlightenment, socialists, liberal humanitarians and many others. Nowadays we are all of us having to learn to do without them, because in the post-modern period they have all broken down. This makes a very big difference, for the militant Christian humanist may well find he has to adopt the standpoint of Michel Foucault: every present reality must be combatted, in perpetuity. We cannot specify what a better world would be like, we can have no grounds for expecting it ever actually to arrive, and whatever does come will itself then immediately have to be contested just because it is now present. The goal has been lost, and morality has become a ceaseless struggle to sabotage the present, a struggle we engage in as *infinite protest*.

Demythologizing religion into commitment to political and moral struggle in the way he does, our militant Christian is clearly a non-realist about God. He may or may not have passed through the Crisis and become conscious of the situation, but either way he is a modern for whom what now matters most about God is not what the word stands for but the way it is used. And the right way to use it is as a symbol of protest, a metaphor of the moral claim the poor make upon us, and a call to fight for them. However, the militant Christian can scarcely avoid being a definite realist about the objective social world, for he takes it as the whole field of his religious activity, he sets himself to struggle within it on its own terms by mastering the forces presently operative within it, and he therefore very properly insists on an objective analysis of what it is and how it works. All this implies that he is a strong realist, in both the popular and the philosophical senses. But the more 'real' you take the given and present natural and social world to be, the more you will move in the direction of naturalism, materialism and probably determinism. In this way, your acceptance of present reality as the one and only field of your religious expression will come into conflict with your ethical repudiation and down-grading of that same present reality. The realist (in the popular sense) is the sort of person who says that you can't change human nature, and must accept things as they are; whereas the moral activist is surely bound to be like an early Christian who asserts that this world is passing away. He must disparage present reality and assert the superior reality of his inner vision, dream or ideal of the way things ought to be. Our militant Christian humanist therefore seems to be both a realist and an anti-realist at once: a realist about the objective social world that he chooses as the field of his action, and an anti-realist in the way he chooses to fight against it.

The philosopher F. H. Bradley considered that at this point there was a contradiction in the very nature of morality itself. It could not take a fully consistent view both of what is and of what ought to be. Morality is 'a demand for what can not be'. It must somehow suppose that the ideal it envisages is 'more real' than present reality, and is realizable. But how is this claim to be justified? It cannot be, for the fact is that 'reality is not wholly good. Neither in me, nor in the world, is what ought to be what is, and what is what ought to be; and the claim remains in the end a mere claim.'[1]

Bradley is saying that morality starts from, presupposes and is motivated by a perceived sharp disjunction between the ideal and the actual. Without that disjunction, morality does not even arise: but given the disjunction, how can moral action succeed? Unless the moral ideal has some reality in it already, how can it get any effective leverage for changing present reality? To be justified, moral activity must be capable of succeeding by bringing about the coincidence of what is with what ought to be. But if that were ever to happen, morality would be at an end; and in any case, what is the basis for supposing that what is and what ought to be ever *can* coincide? So morality is internally at odds with itself, because it finds itself both presupposing and denying the conflict between what is and what ought to be.

Bradley could not bear the thought that the moral struggle might be an infinite incoherent cry of protest, so he went on to conclude that morality must pass over into religion. God is the 'real ideal',[2] both actual and perfect. He is everything he should be and that we should be, and just by being himself he therefore solves the paradox of morality. Unfortunately the same conflict then recurs, for religion also is a striving, practical activity. It finds itself simultaneously affirming the present absolute reality and perfection of its object, while at the same time it has to be for ever struggling to attain him. As the real ideal self, God is at once real and still to be realized.[3]

The paradox of morality is like that of the greyhounds at the dog track: to keep them running at full stretch they have got to be made to believe that they are just on the point of catching that rabbit, and, *also* to keep them running at full stretch, that belief has got to be perpetually false. The paradox of religion is slightly different: to be God, God has to be quite perfect just as he is; but to be the object of religious striving God has to need a little help from me so that his full self-realization in one bit of the universe, namely me, can be improved. The oddity is that in religion I have to feel a bit dissatisfied about my relation to an object that I have posited as being infinitely satisfactory.

Bradley cannot stand for this. He retains moral and religious striving as the highest practical expressions of the human spirit, but to solve the theoretical puzzle passes beyond the God of religion to the all-inclusive Absolute in which (one wonders how) all things are reconciled.[4] Like so many other thinkers of his own time and earlier Bradley feared fragmentation and spiritual dissolution. Science was alienating man from himself, thought from being, and nature from spirit; by its huge success it was discrediting and banishing other and more unifying forms of response to the world, aesthetic and religious. Again in the style of the Romantics, the fall into multiplicity must be followed by a counter-movement back towards unity. Fragmentation must be countered by totalization. So Bradley was one of the last to feel the need to posit a final monistic vision in which all things come together again.

In this Bradley is still in the grip of the ancient myth of the One that goes out to become the Many and then returns to itself, a myth that has taken so many forms in philosophy, religion and politics, and is perhaps the ultimate archetype of all legitimating narratives. Even today it remains attractive to those who are nostalgic about the past and pessimistic about the present, and therefore accept some form of fragmentation-thesis.

However, it is hard to see how the fragmentation-thesis could ever really be justified. Historical periods are different from each other, and values change. Some old values become lost, and new values appear; and as has been said before we have no God's-eye view of the different values of different periods. We can look down different perspectives, but we have no perspectiveless evaluative standpoint, for values are historical, and all acts of evaluation are made from particular viewpoints within history. The Middle Ages look different to Catholic and to Marxist historians, and they look different to typical historians of the eighteenth, the nineteenth and the twentieth centuries. In the light of all this, how can the fragmentation-thesis be regarded as anything but an ideological weapon and a presently-useful myth? Although his own books on the history of ideas and social practices are conspicuously disenchanted, Foucault found himself obliged in all consistency to insist that they too were only fictions that he had devised for the purpose of combatting present-day reality.

Accordingly the militant religious humanist will be wary of Bradley's totalizing Absolute Idealism, wary of utopianism, and wary also of the fragmentation-thesis and the nostalgia for a past Golden Age that it implies. At least, if he retains them it will be in the full awareness that they can be no more than useful fictions. He will not seek a mythological solution to Bradley's antinomy, but rather will simply accept it as another aspect of the tragic absurdity of the human condition.

Something of all this emerges at the very end of the Modern period in Albert Camus' *The Plague* (*La Peste*, 1947). The book is of course about moral action and the problem of evil, and operates with a realist notion of God; but there are signs that Camus is aware of the possibility of an alternative to realism. Rieux, the doctor, says that 'if he believed in an all-powerful [and, in effect, realist] God he would cease curing the sick and leave that to him. But no one in the world believed in a God of that sort: no, not even Paneloux [the priest], who believed that he believed in such a God. And this was proved by the fact that no one ever threw himself on Providence completely. Anyhow, in this respect Rieux believed himself to be on the right road – in fighting against creation as he found it' (Part 1, 7).[5]

This suggests the possibility that the church should not understand its own faith in a realistic way. To do so is hard to reconcile with protest against natural evil, with the performance of works of mercy, and with prudent provision for the future. There is also a hint as to what was meant by the eccentric old man who declared that obviously 'God did not exist, since otherwise there would be no need for priests' (Part 1, 6). The old man was correct, in the sense that from a history-of-religions point of view the whole vast machinery of organized religion is based on the absence of the gods. When they withdrew they left behind them the apparatus of scriptures, priests, rituals and so forth to remind us of them and to sustain us in their absence. So is not organized, mediated religion necessarily non-realist?

Meanwhile, times are hard. Rieux fights his moral battle against creation. Tarrou objects, 'But your victories will never be lasting.' Rieux replies, 'Yes, I know that. But it's no reason for giving up the struggle.' 'No reason, I agree,' says Tarrou, 'Only, I now can picture what the plague must mean for you.' 'Yes. A never-ending defeat' (1, 7).

Later in the book, Tarrou tells Rieux of his childhood horror on watching his own father, a Public Prosecutor, successfully demand the death penalty for a poor wretch of a defendant in a murder case. He concludes that 'on this earth there are pestilences and there are victims, and it's up to us, so far as possible, not to join the pestilences'. Later, he adds: 'What interests me is learning how to become a saint.' 'But you don't believe in God,' objects Rieux. 'Exactly. Can one be a saint without God? That's the problem, in fact the only problem, I'm up against today.'

Rieux demurs: 'You know, I feel more fellowship with the defeated than with saints. Heroism and sanctity don't really appeal to me, I imagine. What interests me is – being a man.' 'Yes, we're both after the same thing,' says Tarrou, 'but I'm less ambitious.' The world is so tough that we may not be able to achieve 'being a man', and perhaps we will be obliged to settle for something less, namely, 'becoming a saint' who can accept unfulfilment. Tarrou has no choice but to do so, because the plague kills him shortly after this conversation (4, 6).

The philosophical novel is not an easy art-form, but in the past many Christians have greatly admired *The Plague* for the unflinching terms in which it presents the problem of evil and the plight of the morally-serious atheist in a cruel and indifferent universe. For Rieux and Tarrou the moral life has no initial rational foundation and no final reward. It is an objectively-gratuitous act of protest, and is condemned from the outset to be a never-ending defeat. The virtuous man simply sides with the victims against the pestilence and goes on doggedly doing so to the end. He fully recognizes the certainty of his own final defeat, while at the same time he holds on to his values and refuses to capitulate morally. In this one can glimpse a possibility of sanctity, and even of a religious triumph that makes a moral victory out of defeat.

The Christian reader could readily admire the book, because of the powerful influence of Christianity upon it. Even for atheists, it seems to say, the moral truth of life is still Christian. There is a vein of nostalgia for Christianity and of Modernist romantic pessimism in *The Plague* which has flattered and seduced the Christian reader into admiring the central characters while at the same time feeling a little superior to them. This, he concludes, is how tough things are for those unfortunates who know our values are right but lack the gift of faith, and so must endure life without the supernatural consolations that have been vouchsafed to us.

There is an element of sadism in this: we are always glad to hear how unpleasant life is for those outside the fold. More seriously, the response is religiously false. 'Faith' and the consolations of religion as popularly understood are egoistic and eudaemonistic. They would not at all vindicate, but rather would utterly destroy the vision of the moral life and of the possibility of sanctity that the book is attempting (falteringly) to develop. Using the word 'God' in a realist sense, Tarrou asks if one can be a saint without God: to which Rieux might well have retorted that one cannot be a saint *with* that sort of God. It is central to twentieth-century experience that human beings must extract such moral and religious dignity as they are capable of directly from a clear-eyed and illusion-free recognition of the tragic nature of the human condition, and can find it in no other way. Heidegger's *Being and Time* (1927) is the classic spelling-out of the point, but many others could be cited. Doris Lessing's *The Making of the Representative for Planet 8* (1982) is an example, and it is far more spiritually austere than Camus' novel. The Representative is a group, who are informed that it has been decided that unfortunately the entire population of their planet must suffer creeping extinction by cold. They, the Representative, are given the responsibility for persuading their people to accept this fate calmly and uncomplainingly; and they do it. The book owes its moral weight to the fact that it is in every sense as chilling

as could be imagined, and its religious weight to the fact that it is
nevertheless spiritually ennobling and not depressing.[6]

Still more important is the fact that those Christian readers who
thought they could *look down* on Tarrou and Rieux – who
thought they had special information in virtue of which the facts
of life for them were not the same as for the people in the novel –
were by no means the sole representatives of Christian truth.
Indeed, in the seventeenth century the story of *The Plague* was
acted out in miniature in a village in Derbyshire. The community
leaders at Eyam were an Anglican priest and a dissenting minister,
who found they had to play the parts of the Representative and
of Rieux. To contain the plague the village was persuaded
voluntarily to seal itself off even though many, who might have
saved their own skins by fleeing, thereby chose instead to stay and
die. For more than a year Eyam waited out the plague and buried
its dead; and were not the facts of life exactly the same for those
two clergymen as for their fictional successors? Were they granted
any special exemptions?

In the present century Christians have increasingly accepted the
truth of something like the Heideggerian vision. Our supposed
enemies – homelessness, finitude and mortality – are friends in
disguise. Death, the Great Teacher, is like God in that it is the
unthinkable that by closing our life and making it finite gives it
to us. The metaphysical evils and limitations that seemed so
threatening because they progressively unself us prove to be allies,
for in doing so they purge us, make us disinterested and give to us
our proper freedom. Of course morality is a continual unavailing
struggle, for if it were not so it would not be itself and would not
have worth. And of course the religious ideal is never actualized
in space and time, for such a material embodiment of the ideal
would be precisely an idol, something forbidden. Life gets its
worth from its finitude, and from the tenacity with which we
maintain that special combination of acceptance and striving,
contentment and discontent, now and not yet. To be human is to
be always *in via*, on the way, and never to claim one has arrived.
Moral activity is continuous production, never a completed work.
Religious objects and ideals guide the journey, but never portray
the destination. Where we eventually got to will never be said by
ourselves, but only by others – in our absence.

The new emphasis on tragic necessity and the necessity of

tragedy shows itself particularly in attitudes to Christ's death and resurrection. I have elsewhere stressed the pioneering importance of Albert Schweitzer's tragic Christianity. Like Rieux a doctor combatting suffering, Schweitzer sought to affirm life while recognizing that life is everywhere cruel and divided against itself, to moralize nature while knowing that nature cannot be moralized, and to follow as a loser the Christ whose spiritual greatness lay precisely in the fact that he was himself an heroic loser. Since God is the union of what is with what ought to be, faith in him took for Schweitzer the form of an unavailing moral struggle to achieve the impossible by uniting the two. Belief in God thus itself became a tragically absurd heroic endeavour. Rudolf Bultmann's fidelity to the Heideggerian vision shows itself everywhere in his theology, but perhaps most of all in his treatment of Christ's death as his glorification, and in his refusal to permit the resurrection to be regarded as a second, corrective occurrence. So seen, it would detract from and even annul the religious grandeur and finality of that death. If Christ was raised in the sense that most people seem to have in mind, then his death was indeed in vain, having occurred only to be promptly cancelled.[7] Dietrich Bonhoeffer also stayed close to Heidegger's view of the human condition, and to the doctrine that it is in just those respects in which we seem to ourselves to be most derelict that the seeds of our salvation lie. He followed not merely a Christ who was a loser, but even a God who was a loser, for God had allowed himself to become powerless, to be edged out of the world and to die. You will not know what God is until you have accepted the death of God. Christ's glory is revealed in his humiliation, man's in his finitude, and God's in his powerlessness and death.[8]

The powerful expressive rhetoric used by these and many similar theologians often conceals from people what is really happening, and no detailed literary analyses of their language are yet available, but in brief the point is as follows: their ways of writing derive from the New Testament, and in the greatest New Testament writings we find a deliberate and highly sophisticated deconstruction of the major distinctions entrenched in the received tradition of religious thought. God and man, the holy and the common, the righteous and the sinner, rich and poor, strength and weakness, glory and humiliation, victory and defeat, life and death, bondage and freedom – all these distinctions are teased,

ironized, reversed and dissolved, with the object of revealing to
us the nature of salvation. It is not something to be found outside
the limits of the text of life but something that lies hidden within
the text, if we will but learn to handle it in the right way. Christ's
resurrection does not annul his death, but is what his death can
mean to us: salvation is not a special dispensation exempting us
from the tragic conditions and necessities of life, but is what they
will make of us and what we can make of them, if we will but
accept them not as enemies but as friends.

The upshot of this discussion is that militant religious humanism
does indeed represent a valid form of religious expression. Guided
by religious symbols, it is marked by a bias towards the poor and
towards the future which is yet coloured by a sense of tragic
absurdity. These three features are interconnected. The poor are
the victims of present reality, and the religious humanist seeks the
actualization of a hoped-for future state of affairs in which they
will no longer be victims. However, as soon as that hoped-for
condition of things starts to become present it must itself come
under scrutiny, because the completion of human projects is never
perfect and unambiguous. Thus the moral struggle becomes
unending, and requires constant vigilance about one's motives,
methods and successes.

On the frontier between the actual and the ideal there is always
a certain tragic absurdity. The moral ambiguity of the struggle
for change is most familiar in the case of revolutionary politics,
and need not be dwelt on here. A better example – although it
should be said that policies and conditions have already begun to
change since he began to write in the 1950s – is given by Foucault.[9]
He has reminded us that the poorest of the poor are that strange
miscellany of people who are kept out of circulation because
society cannot bear to see them or because they are felt to be too
young, too old, too incapacitated, too dangerous to themselves
or to others, and so on. They inhabit a largely-unseen archipelago
of residential institutions – asylums, homes, camps, prisons,
centres, orphanages, clinics. Not so very long ago these institutions
scarcely existed: now, millions inhabit them. Why are they there?
Any plausible analysis of the reasons would be too disturbing for
society to be able to entertain it seriously, and the institutions are
therefore represented as being necessary. The religious humanist
always pricks up his ears when he hears that little word 'necessary'

being used in a social context, because it is invariably used to protect something questionable. How is he to aid these people? Here the moral ambiguity arises, for he can help them only by joining the service of the very institutions that incarcerate them, or, if not that, then at least he will find himself having to learn the language that is used to define and exclude/seclude them; and this must surely compromise him.

Now it is often objected that militant *religious* humanism is nothing but militant humanism dressed in hyperbolical religious metaphors which add nothing of real substance. The prosy philosophical distinction between what is and what ought to be, the actual and the ideal, is dramatized in terms of this world and the coming of the kingdom of God on earth, but the real issues remain just the same.

However, our analysis has suggested that the religious metaphors do after all do real work and make an important difference at a crucial point, the point where the question arises: 'How can I be confident that effective, disinterested and non-defiling moral *action* is possible, in the face of my recognition of its incurable ambiguity, gratuitousness and absurdity?' The answer suggested by religion is that these very limits themselves, rightly accepted, create in us a kind of inner emptiness, or void, the death of the ego. To stay in that emptiness is (for Christians at least: others have other representations) to be united with Christ in his death, and to become capable of fully disinterested action, action that is not debilitated by the sense of its own guiltiness and absurdity. This is eternal life: to be able to say 'We have done all we can, and we are unprofitable servants', to be both attached and detached, to say both Yes and No.

Religion makes a difference because it makes possible a wholehearted commitment to action that does not become fanatical, or lead to spiritual dissipation or break down into pessimistic inactivity. It does this by representing to us in myth those ambient conditions of life which seem at first sight to be most threatening to the possibility of virtuous action, making it appear interminable, futile, ambiguous and absurd. The myth works as myths do: conflicting representations are reconciled in narrative and the flow of life is restored. Enemies are made into friends. The conditions that threatened to destroy our confidence in the possibility of effective moral action are cunningly deflected, and redeployed to make it selfless.

The argument now completed seems to describe a final position in the religious life, that should be maintained until one's last breath. We have at last reached maturity – which perhaps creates a further paradox. Has the spirit come to rest by being reconciled to infinite restlessness? We open a chink for further development in a later chapter, by observing that so far we have not considered the relation of human action to the physical and biological world in which it is set.

13

SLIPPING AWAY

Imagine one of those crowded seventeenth-century paintings, perhaps by the younger Breughel, depicting scenes from everyday life. The centre of the painting is full of ordinary worldly folk drinking, gossiping, trading, pursuing their love-affairs and so forth, and gets its charm from the light irony with which it draws attention to their self-satisfied absorption in their own business. After a while, though, we also become aware of certain anomalous characters around the margins of the picture. Through a bedroom window can be seen a dying man; at a party a stiff, upright figure stands alone and ill-at-ease; and at the edge of the canvas a woman can be seen slipping away.

These three are minor characters, who wish to be unseen and may soon in fact be so. There is nothing especially attractive about them, and it would be artistically impossible to make them central to a popular painting of this type. Marginal they have to be, but one begins to suspect that the artist has designed the whole painting in order indirectly to say something about them, a device which in the Middle Ages was called *alieniloquium*.

I have described in visual terms what is to be found in almost all of Iris Murdoch's last dozen novels, and in particular *Nuns and Soldiers* (1980), where the woman slipping away is the spoiled nun, Anne Cavidge. She is but one of a whole gallery of minor characters who in one way or another do not fit into the comfortable everyday world of people engaged in the pursuit of pleasure and personal fulfilment, and feel they must leave it in search of goodness or holiness. The quest is lonely and austere, demanding the relinquishment as egoistic of the comforts given by bourgeois society, erotic love and a personal God. Murdoch does not make it easy for her characters. Although the reader can suppose that Brendan Craddock in *Henry and Cato* (1976) may well become a saint in Calcutta, the other seekers' prospects are more doubtful. The kind of vision of Christ that is possible for Anne Cavidge in the twentieth century is in painful contrast with that available to Julian of Norwich in the fourteenth. Anne's Christ is a young drifter, defeated and yet casual about it, who warns her, in effect, that she is on her own. Others may be led astray by the temptations of spiritual mastery, like James Arrowby in *The Sea, The Sea* (1978), or by sheer eccentricity, like Father Bernard in *The Philosopher's Pupil* (1983). All in all, they are an odd crew, their various departures unlamented, their inadequacies emphasized, and the highly questionable nature of their enterprises made very clear. Just what is it to renounce the world? After all, the poor people among whom these drop-outs will live and work at each of their various destinations – Calcutta, Greece or Chicago – will themselves constitute a society just as much as do the well-heeled Londoners they have left behind. And yet there is no question but that the author of the novels is intensely interested in these people, their decision, their project and their fate, and wishes us to be so too.[1]

To Iris Murdoch's own philosophy of the religious life we will return; meanwhile, let us ask why the project of slipping away and leaving the world has become so problematic. The difficulty is partly practical: the surveillance and the demands of the modern state have become so comprehensive that it is no longer even legally possible to elude them entirely. There has also been an historical change. In the past there was a very substantial and socially established sacred sphere of 'the religious life', as contrasted with secular life in the world. Anyone who wished to renounce the world would have had no doubt about what must be done. Today, however, that established sacred realm is drastically impoverished and reduced, and has itself become so spiritually unsatisfactory that several Murdoch characters having tried it out find they must abandon it to live alone.

The most serious difficulty of all, though, arises from the nature of cultural life in the advanced societies. It is so peculiarly flexible and all-encompassing and rich that it is aware of everything, has everything and makes everything the object of aesthetic

enjoyment. Its world is at once so complete and so cosy, familiarized and humanized that it is hard to envisage any reality outside
it. Naturally, it includes religion – and especially the pleasurably
nostalgic culture-Christianity whose most sophisticated form we
called in Chapter 10 aesthetic expressivism. We terminated that
chapter with an abrupt, and perhaps unexpected, twitch of
irritation and revulsion against it; and we have now to ask whether
that twitch of irritation can in fact develop into anything. Is it
possible to become an individual, to opt out of the world, and to
find a feasible religious alternative to immersion in the all-
comprehending modern bourgeois culture?

Kierkegaard was the first writer to diagnose the challenge here,
and correctly saw Hegel's philosophy as the supreme intellectual
expression of it. The Hegelian System was a generous all-inclusive
objective immanentism which understood everything and swal-
lowed everything in its devouring maw, including all protests
against itself. The individual, and Christianity itself, were painlessly absorbed, and no reality exterior to the System remained.

Kierkegaard had considerable problems in trying to find a way
out that would work, not least because he was of course himself
a kind of Hegelian, deeply implicated in the very phenomenon he
was combatting. Today the puzzles are even worse, because the
developing objective culture has not neglected to ingest all the
protests against itself from Kierkegaard onwards. The prophets'
tombs have been carefully whitewashed and they themselves have
been posthumously made into cultural monuments, part of the
canon. Kierkegaard, Nietzsche and others foresaw this fate and
roundly cursed it in advance, a fact which the objective culture
recalls with an ironical, self-deprecating smile. It can well afford
to be self-deprecating, when it knows that it has won so easily. It
always wins.

It is against this background that I shall suggest that post-
modernism is now emerging as a more flexible, refined, subtle and
ironized version of Hegelianism, which will be very much more
difficult to escape from even than the older version.

At first this thesis must seem paradoxical, for deconstructive
thinking presents itself as being in the highest degree marginal,
errant, subversive and anti-systematic. It declares that old-style
Modernist atheism was merely the mirror-image of the classical
theism against which it rebelled, and sets out to demolish the

deeper assumptions behind both doctrines. The aim is nothing less than to subvert the whole tradition of Western thought by undermining the long series of binary contrasts, established in the Bible and by Plato, on which our culture has hitherto rested. The God of metaphysics has been the product, the master and the guarantor of these contrasts; and when humanistic atheism rebelled and put the human subject at the centre of things instead of him, it was still relying on these same contrasts and exclusions to state its position and to order its world. But when the last implications of the death of God have been worked out, not only is God demythologized but the contrasts are also, and then the rational world-ordering human subject goes too. So the death of God leads to the end of metaphysics and also to the death of autonomous man: the dissolution of the absolute subject, perfectly rational, free and present to himself, is followed by the dissolution of the fixed cosmic order and of his creation and finite counterpart, the human subject. The same process is repeated in the world of written language, where the author-book relation has tradition-ally been modelled on the God-world relation. The book has been seen as the transparent vehicle of the mind of its author, with just one meaning, namely *his* meaning, so that through the book the reader directly and unambiguously apprehended the mind of its author. To read the Bible as the word of God was, obviously, to read it in terms of this model; but it is a model which has been thoroughly undermined, first by biblical criticism and then by literary critical theory in general. The consequences of this extend from the Bible to history at large, for history too has been seen as like a narrative and as capable of being captured in narrative: history was a purposeful, coherent drama, conceived as a whole in the mind of God, acted out by us under his direction, and epitomized in scripture. But now all ideas of history as meaningful and of a purpose in the world are lost. There is nowhere any single centred totalized coherent purposeful systematic and foun-dational meaning of things, whether the topic be a text, my life, history or the universe itself.[2]

In all this we see the post-modern completion of at least the critical part of Nietzsche's project. It seems that the Hegelian ideas that dominated nineteenth-century thought have been finally exploded and that the Western tradition is at last completely demythologized. Thought ceases to be in any way *anchored*, either in the old deified patriarchal Reason with its firmly maintained distinctions, exclusions and hierarchies, or in legitimating narratives about growing Enlightenment, moral progress, history, providence and the like. It is left . . . free-floating.

Thus far the postmodernist programme may seem to be nihilistically destructive, but this impression is mistaken, for post-modern free-floating turns out to be light, genial, ironical and playful. It is not in the least apocalyptic or despairing, for it sees such attitudes as being typical of a Modern period that has now been left behind. The Modernists were gloomy because they felt that they lived just after a great historical cataclysm, and were compelled to make an entirely fresh beginning. They could not see how to make any use of the fragments of the past that lay around them, so they sat lamenting among the ruins. Postmodernism, however, not being historicist any more, does not see itself as locked into just the present phase of the historical process. We need not feel constrained by the *Zeitgeist*. Post-modernism likes history, and ranges freely and eclectically over it. (Everyone has noticed the effect in architecture, or perhaps in Stravinsky's music.) It is as if, when the programme of deconstruction is completed and there are no coercive capital-T Truths any more to restrict us, we emerge to find the world become a boundless glittering ocean of meanings in endless play, forming, dissolving and reforming, whose dance gives endless intellectual and aesthetic pleasure. It is a surface without beginning or end, without height or depth, and we are part of this surface. Without stability, anchorage, position or direction, old-style 'seriousness' is gone and is replaced by levity, irony and incompleteness. A flux and reflux of multiple signs and messages shimmers through us unceasingly.

Just after the Second World War the student generation in Paris were deeply affected by Jean Hyppolite's powerful interpretation of Hegel's philosophy, and worried about how one could escape from a system of thought that already included everything and had allowed in advance for every argument that you could bring against it. It appeared impregnable. How could it be attacked? It had to be made to subvert itself, its own cunning turned against it so that it ate away its own Greek rationalist skeleton – the equation of the rational with the real and of both with the good, the notions of identity, contradiction and logical progression, and

above all the supremacy in the spiritual life of the philosopher's
clear intuition of rational necessity. So this subversion was
accomplished. Hegel's all-encompassing system was filletted and
spread out flat. All foundationalism and hierarchizing, all
contrasts between Appearance and Reality, all heights and depths
were abolished – and we found ourselves on the surface of the
trackless ocean of meanings.

Yet nothing is missing and there is nothing to complain about.
Post-modernist thought, like Wittgenstein's, is therapeutic and
aims to cure us of nostalgia. All possibilities flicker on the surface,
and we may follow them as and where we will. Now that there is
no Truth, everything is true and nothing is excluded. Notice the
contrast here between the Modernist who said gloomily, and with
the old seriousness, that no religion is true, and the post-moderns
who say with the new playfulness that of course all religions are
true. But notice also that although the post-moderns may have
finally managed to overthrow Hegel, logocentrism and the
tyranny of Greek reason, they seem to have shrewdly contrived
to retain Hegel's all-encompassing irrefutability.

In a word, the ghost of Hegel still hovers over the ocean. Is it
not possible to see in post-modernism a kind of anti-prison that
itself becomes the cleverest, most permissive and most ironical
prison ever un/built? It has been created by demolition. No walls
remain, and nobody need feel in the least confined. Everybody is
perfectly free to do exactly as he pleases. There is no deprivation,
but on the contrary, a superabundant provision. All possible
escape-routes have been thoughtfully provided, and they all lead
straight back in again.

Lest it be thought that I am speaking only of the ideas of a
few French thinkers, I must insist that post-modernism is the
intellectual expression of the cultural condition of the advanced
liberal societies. It is our world. In a great bookshop, or in a
week's output from a major broadcasting organization, there is
poured out an overwhelming abundance in which everything
ironizes everything else in multitudinous incongruity. More
simply, there is an image of the Sea of Meanings in what passes
before our eyes as we flick over the pages of a colour magazine:
women's faces, starving Africans, motor cars, bull-fighting,
cathedrals, fried chicken legs, glaciers, fashions, traffic accidents.
We have everything – in two dimensions: we have everything,

except what used to be thought the one thing needful, depth or seriousness.

However, is not even that also provided for us? Post-modernism claims to be the outcome of a major religious development in which we are – a little ironically, no doubt – invited to see a kind of realization of Christian eschatology. The first post-modern theologies are beginning to appear, and they find in the death of Christ the deconstruction of the great antitheses between God and man, the sacred and the profane, time and eternity. The response to that death in the earliest Christian texts is a highly post-modern play with images of loss and gain, life and death, slavery and freedom, folly and wisdom. It is not for nothing that Derrida comes from a Jewish background and knows all about the ways in which biblical exegesis is often most spiritually illuminating when it is most playful and fanciful.

So what is missing? Depth? – that is only another image, part of the surface. Seriousness? – but what could be more serious than ironical play?

Perhaps there is nothing missing, but rather something present that ought not to be present? Post-modernism establishes itself by rehearsing a series of great themes: the death of God (in Christ), the breakdown of all the walls of partition, the disappearance of the human subject who dies with God in Christ, the end of history and the closure of the book. All these themes have been developed out of Hegel, and also Hegelian is the suggestion – veiled and teasing, but still indubitably present – that a series of major themes in Christian doctrine and eschatology have at last found their proper fulfilment by being taken up into and given more general and adequate expression in the language of philosophy.

To be self-consistent, post-modernism must present this suggestion in an ironical, joking way, and it duly does so. It may be said that we are here in violation of the principle discussed in our last chapter, that we may never regard any actual state of affairs as being a full and satisfactory embodiment of our religious hopes, and must be content to be always discontented. But lest we think we have found a loophole, let us remind ourselves that the interplay between Kant and Marx, between those who think the kingdom of God cannot be built on earth and those who think it can, between futurist and realized eschatologies, itself takes place on the surface of the Sea of Meanings.

Enough has been said by now to show how it is that our culture
has become so fabulously rich and diverse, and so ironized by its
consciousness of its own infinite multiplicity and resourcefulness,
that there is no way of getting any purchase on it, nor of even so
much as formulating any escape plans.

Is the last resort, then, to fall silent, slip away and become
absent? There can of course be no explanation of this action.
There will be no farewell speech in which we denounce the state
of the culture and give reasons for our departure, for however
well-made the speech it could not weaken our foe but only enrich
him by adding to his already boundless resources. We do not even
formulate the reasons for our going to ourselves, for we fear that
the reduction of absolutely everything to a surface play of imagery
has left us no terms in which we could state them. We leave it to
others to comment on our going as they will, and slip away
unremarked to seek silence, emptiness, namelessness and waiting;
waiting for something that cannot be distinguished from death.
In the past there were many who rejected all the images and
trod the Negative Way, but our action is now inevitably more
questionable and our poverty more extreme than theirs. They
seemed to themselves to have at least *some* words in which to give
an account of what they were doing, and to what end, whereas
we have none left. All we have is gestures, which is why the
modern ascetic slips away not so much to the contemplative life
as rather to the hidden and probably ineffectual service of the
anonymous poor. Provided that it is left unexplained, this ethical
gesture may give some orientation to the act of waiting.

In the last chapter we were discussing the most thoroughgoing
form of the active, militant, world-affirming religious life, and it
was certainly discussable. Here, however, we deal with the most
extreme form of the world-renouncing religious life; and it is not
discussable, as Schopenhauer was the first to point out. The one
who goes has by that act cut the lines of communication and has
become nothing. Unless the lines of communication are cut
completely, the rejection of the world is not consistently carried
out—and so not accomplished at all. There cannot be a satisfactory
painted image of someone who has renounced the images. Nor
can his or her life be described, either in a work of fiction or in
the language of a world that has itself become nothing but a
fiction. Only a silent slipping away can be shown.

Iris Murdoch's many discussions of the possibility of the religious life today, in her novels and philosophical essays, are not set against the background of postmodernist thought. Rather, she writes in the manner of someone raised on Christianity and Plato, who first felt the full blast of atheistic humanism (Marx, Freud, Sartre) and then came to feel that its treatment of morality was wholly inadequate. Following the same path as Simone Weil, she worked her way back to a more religious view of life in which the Platonic and Christian influences are strong. However, there can be no easy optimism, for she continues to accept in broad outline the bleak modernist vision of the world, the human condition and human nature. Thus in 1969 she gave the following summary of what seemed to her to be true in Freudian theory:

> Freud takes a thoroughly pessimistic view of human nature. He sees the psyche as an egocentric system of quasi-mechanical energy, largely determined by its own individual history, whose natural attachments are sexual, ambiguous and hard for the subject to understand or control. Introspection reveals only the deep tissue of ambivalent motive, and fantasy is a stronger force than reason. Objectivity and unselfishness are not natural to human beings.[3]

Already in this statement there is a whiff of Plato's equation of the good with the real, for egoistic illusions are contrasted with moral reality. The moral task is the defeat of egoism, a powerful fantasy-generating machine which produces a continual 'proliferation of blinding self-centred aims and images', and it is a very difficult task. We need the sustained and disciplined use of techniques that will direct our attention habitually away from ourselves; and such non-egoistic attentiveness to reality is, quite simply, love.

Iris Murdoch's view of art is a little like Schopenhauer's. Much art is merely consoling fantasy, and in so far as it gives aesthetic pleasure perhaps no art is wholly free from egoism; but great art by its attention to reality has the power to draw us out of ourselves into a juster, more disinterested and compassionate vision of things. For the novels this means that the egoistic, pleasure-seeking middle class social world they depict must be treated with the utmost generosity – a generosity that misleads many readers who miss the note of irony, and fail to see the moral importance of those minor characters who slip away.

Habitual loving attention to the truth of things, such as great art may teach us, can refine our moral perceptions and gradings and give us a glimpse of the unity of virtue. We may thus come to see that the supreme guiding ideal and goal of the moral life is the Good, which (as we noticed earlier) Iris Murdoch defines in what amount to the same terms as Anselm used to define God. However, if this supremely perfect object of attention is truly to cure us of egoism it can neither be conceived of as a personal God, nor be thought of as existing in the way people used to think that God existed. Its face is blank, its nature mysterious, and its pursuit unselfs us by being entirely unconsoled. If we understand our own radical egoism and the utter lack of finality in human life, then we may be ready to accept the truth:

> The Good has nothing to do with purpose, indeed it excludes the idea of purpose. 'All is vanity' is the beginning and end of ethics. The only genuine way to be good is to be good 'for nothing' in the midst of a scene in which every natural thing, is subject to chance, that is, to necessity. That 'for nothing' is indeed the experienced correlate of the invisibility or non-representable blankness of the idea of Good itself.[4]

As the Good is invisible and non-representable, so a saint – if any such existed – must also be invisible, and therefore cannot be represented in fiction, which can deal only with the world. Those minor characters in the novels who are serious about the religious life must slip off the page and disappear. If the religious quest was primarily about suffering then of course they could be portrayed, but suffering is easy, human, gratifying and seductive. It can be a temptation. 'Plato does not say that philosophy is the study of suffering, he says it is the study of death, and these two ideas are totally dissimilar.'[5] One might add that in a church the central image is usually a cross from which Christ is simply absent or a crucifix on which he is, not suffering as some people suppose, but simply, dead. Death, rather than suffering, is the Great Teacher, and as in Schopenhauer the condition of the saint approximates to the condition of the dead. In the whole corpus of twenty-two novels to date, the only person described on good authority as a saint is Brendan Craddock's mother, of whom we learn only by hearsay, *in absentia*, because she is dead.

Iris Murdoch's most recent large-scale exposition of her views about religion has been her Gifford Lectures, which at the time of writing are unpublished. Within the novels and the essays that have been published there is a good deal of variation in the teaching. Nevertheless, I hope the account I have given is accurate so far as it goes; and it should be clear from the discussion in this chapter that although Iris Murdoch's views are formulated against a generally Modernist background, they remain equally relevant in post-modern times. Here we have the most impressive statement currently available to us of one particular line of religious response to our conditions. It is an extreme response, but then, extremes are interesting.

Critics have suggested that there is in Iris Murdoch's account some conflict between ethical Idealism and Realism, between pure contemplation of the Good and loving attention to the variety of the world and the joys and sorrows of particular human beings. Each must surely tend to exclude the other. The parable of the Good Samaritan seems to suggest that I ought to give my whole and undivided attention to the needy fellow human before me. To do this is in itself a sufficient moral and religious discipline, from which I should not allow myself to be distracted by thoughts of any distinct sacred duties over there in the Temple.[6] Alternatively, if Iris Murdoch's idea of the Good is coherent and intelligible, and if it can indeed become the object of sustained unselfing contemplative attention, then I should surely attend solely to it. If my fellow human beings are just so many egoistic fantasy-producing machines like me, then to look at them can be little better than to look in the mirror, and I should rather follow Plato himself, for whom finite affections must fall away as one approaches the vision of the Good.

The dilemma suggests (as it did long ago to St Augustine) that a doctrine of Christ is needed to link the Good with my neighbour, so that in a single act I can attend fully to both at once. Iris Murdoch has often said that Christ is very important to her, but has not I think developed a detailed account. The best comment seems to be that given by her Christ to Anne Cavidge: 'You must be the miracle-worker, little one. You must be the proof. The work is yours.' That is to say, in so far as we have been purged by the discipline of death ('One of my names', remarks Christ) and have learnt to love the Good, then we will be able to act rightly. We will be the miracle-workers, because the unity of the Good with some minute ethical particular will be established in us.

The second objection we need to consider applies not only to Iris Murdoch's teaching, but also to many other general accounts of the human condition. It is that they condemn us so sweepingly as to injure themselves, by leaving no space for the path to salvation that is to be described in the second half of the doctrine. Our state of bondage is portrayed as being so complete that we are made unable to understand the way of escape from it that is subsequently offered to us. Iris Murdoch's characters often positively rejoice in the point, declaring that to us human beings goodness is impossible, non-existent, not on the map at all and wholly beyond our reach.

As I say, this paradox is by no means peculiar to Iris Murdoch. It is very ancient. Originally, no doubt, the point was that salvation must ultimately be sought from above, and would be found only outside this life altogether, beyond death. Alternatively, we might say that when the language becomes paradoxical we are being shown that we must here go beyond language into moral action. Mere words no longer make sense, but a deed can. That is true and always was true, but moderns have to accept that the first interpretation is no longer available to us. Like Simone Weil, Iris Murdoch rejects the belief in personal immortality as being egoistic. Death is a better teacher than life after death. It warns us that the night comes when no man can work, so we must labour with all our might while the daylight remains. We must be good for nothing, in at least three distinct senses of that phrase (good-for-nothing, good . . . for Nothing, good without reward or consolation). Our radical egoism can be countered only by a religious discipline equally uncompromising, and based on a vision of our task in which the ideas of the Good, death, and absolute disinterestedness are closely inter-connected.

After all this, can such a life-project make sense? That must depend entirely on how deeply our understanding of ourselves and of the social scene makes us wish to depart.

14

SUBVERSION

We are in the midst of discussing a set of three forms of religious consciousness, each of which has some claim to be seen as expressing a fully mature religious life-view and programme of action. All three are uncompromisingly world-rejecting, saying both that human beings fall far short of what they could be and that the prevailing objective culture is an obstacle to human fulfilment: but they express their rejection of present reality in different ways. The first is like a soldier who combats the existing order of things, the second is a refugee in flight from it, and the third, as we shall see, lives in it like a fifth-columnist with a dual identity, and looks for ways of subverting it from within. To understand this third position we need to place it in relation to the other two.

Militant religious humanism (12) interprets the barriers to human fulfilment and the task of breaking them down in quasi-political terms. It is a struggle for social liberation. It brings people into association for the purpose of directly combatting present reality on its own ground and with weapons it can understand – that is, forces at present operative within it. Standard methods of political action are adopted in order to bring about social change – to secure civil rights, to vanquish poverty and so forth – the idea being that when the legal and economic framework of social life has been appropriately changed, then human beings will be able to attain a fulfilment barred to them under present conditions.

At first sight this would seem to be the least unsatisfactory form that religious action can take today. For (as we said earlier) modern civilization differs from all previous cultures in the dominance of questions of method or technique in every area of human endeavour, and in its realization that society and even the self are historically produced artefacts, open to reshaping. People used to think that technology's only function was to take materials from the natural environment and use them to construct an artificial human environment adapted to serve human needs. Now, however, techniques of reorganization and reshaping are being extended so far – to society, the self, values, the planet and beyond – that modern man is increasingly unable to recognize any reality other than that which can be viewed as raw material for technical reshaping; and, since technology as such knows no value but efficiency and no disvalue but 'snafus' (the 'snags and foul-ups' that temporarily impede its progress), its unrestrained development threatens to sweep aside all other moral and cultural values and to enslave human beings.

The problem, then, is to seize control of technology – now understood to include the technologies of social and personal change – and make it our servant, not our master. The workings of the technical system must be directed towards the attainment of ethical ends. But in an age in which unharnessed technologies have already run amok and have largely devalued the empirical world and the objective culture, where are the needed guiding values to be found? They must be sought from beyond present reality. What we need is something like the biblical hope: a powerful vision of a better state of things in which human beings live truly fulfilled lives, the kingdom of God; a vision of something future and supernatural which yet presses imminently upon us and can guide our present action. The old Judaeo-Christian language of eschatological hope may be highly metaphorical and even mythical, but it is very precisely balanced to guide action effectively and is the best language available. It supplies us with a regulative ideal which requires us continually to transcend ourselves and to direct our technical activity towards moral ends. The precise content to be achieved should not be too closely specified in advance: rather, what is needed is a continual self-transcendence towards an open future. The future is God (or God's), and will in due course deliver its own content if we but live by it in the right spirit. The now and the not-yet are both affirmed: the kingdom of God is close enough to constitute a judgment upon present reality and to be a guide to present action, while yet it always remains supernatural, transcendent and future. Faith teaches us always to maintain a critical distance from present reality and what has been achieved so far, in order that the gospel may continue to judge and inspire our action, and to make all things new.

Uncontrolled technology is demonic and destroys every value but efficiency; but the militant religious humanist does not on that account repudiate political technique. On the contrary, he seeks control of it, because he believes that right action flows from the union of technique and transcendence. A theology of hope or of liberation functions as a manifesto, a programme to guide action; hence the fashionable emphasis on orthopraxis rather than orthodoxy. But the manifesto will never be completely implemented, for as long as there are human beings their life will be a process of becoming and change, and there will continue to be the tension between the now and the not-yet, between what currently is and what must come to be.[1]

It is noticeable in this account that, in order to retain its dynamism and to avoid the 'idolatry' of supposing that any actual social order can ever be a full realization of the religious ideal, militant religious humanism must say that no actual human beings are ever perfectly fulfilled. The full renewal of humanity in Christ has to be projected forward into the future and becomes an ideal that always inspires action but is never fully realized in practice. Salvation is never completely achieved: the most that can be claimed is that in the moment of gospel-inspired action to liberate people there is an anticipatory glimpse of what human fulfilment might be.

This consequence follows from the denial of individualism. If the self is a social product and no individual human being can achieve human fulfilment on his own, then full social liberation is a universally necessary condition for the full realization of our humanity. But social liberation is never fully achieved; and in the world as it is we are bound to recognize that militant religion is in practice as often demonic as it is liberating. The militant religious activist is himself, by his own admission, only imperfectly human: the forces with which he must ally himself, and the methods he must use to be effective, together always threaten to corrupt him. Although we can indeed point to a few heroic examples, the successes that even they may hope to achieve cannot be more than local, small-scale and partial. The great centres of political, military, financial and technical power which at present control our destiny are going to remain untouched.

Thus after beginning by suggesting that militant religious humanism is *prima facie* the most concrete and potent form that religious action can take today, we have fallen back into something like the pessimism of the later Heidegger. According to Heidegger the one great opportunity for Western cultural renewal had come in the heyday of German Idealist philosophy. The manifestos for renewal issued at that time varied, some putting at their head philosophy, some art, some religious experience and action, and so on. But somewhere in the first half of the nineteenth century German Idealism collapsed. Men lacked the strength to realize spiritual ideals and chose extension and number rather than depth, the routinization of culture rather than the life of the spirit. 'All things sank to the same level, a surface'[2] – and it was with that complaint that life is becoming all surface, and religion impossible, that we turned to the spirituality of 'slipping away' (13). Fastening on one aspect of post-modernism, its post-historical eclecticism and irony and its tendency to reduce all reality to appearances on a shimmering endless surface, we tried to suggest why a few people at least might wish to make an unnoticed protest, and disappear.

It was poetically appropriate for Iris Murdoch's recent characters of the Good to vanish overseas, to the anonymous service of the anonymous poor in Calcutta or Chicago, or even to a coastal hermitage in Greece. But the message should not be misunderstood. The spiritual quest is beset with dangers. The pursuit of spirituality for its own sake leads to magic, demonism and downfall. Romantic pessimism leads to embitterment, and the peculiarly English temptation to identify spirituality with a refusal of adulthood is no less dangerous.[3] A spirituality has to be earthed. The sustained attention to what is true, just, pure and lovely needs to be embodied in some humble and ordinary way of life if it is to bear any fruit. *Mansfield Park* is not so very far away, after all. The world is vanity: goodness is to be found in the obscurity of private life, not the glare of public life, and the religious life must of necessity be completely secluded, and apolitical at least in the sense of being without an audience.

The degree of seclusion that must be sought, however, is greater than it was, for since Jane Austen's day the expansion of the objective scientific-industrial culture has been so enormous and so annihilating that it is now far more difficult than formerly to find a niche within which the good life can be lived. It is no longer sufficient merely to live in retirement in the country and avoid London, nor to choose domestic life rather than public life, nor to put one's trust in the old-style consolations of religion, nor even to live within a religious community. Tolstoy's virtuous peasants are long vanished. The situation has become so extreme that individuals must be prepared to go to great lengths in the struggle for the survival of religion – and in particular they must recognize from the very outset that in this struggle there is neither consolation nor success nor reward.

We know well enough what is meant here. We are reminded of the lengths to which certain Russians had to go in order to keep the spirit of poetry alive in the darkest post-revolutionary years. When publication was impossible they simply accumulated manuscripts; and when they could not even write down their poems, they memorized them or passed them on orally as best they could. However bad the times become, one must keep on singing whatever happens. Less dramatically, all artists and thinkers have known for generations that soul-nourishment is no longer to be found in the objective world. Instead they have learnt to seek it in a daily period of solitude, silence, emptiness and waiting. The world having become barren, it is necessary instead to make friends with Death and get life out of him. The more intimate the friendship, the better the results. Hence the move away from a personal God who expresses himself in the way things go in the world, to a darker and more spiritual theology and to an outlook that is in many ways more Buddhist.

As we have already remarked, an obvious difficulty with this typically modern view of the religious life is that by opting out of the public realm and therefore out of publicly-intelligible language it is in danger of becoming incomprehensible and contentless. It may try to get a sense of what it is about by referring back to the past, to Plato and to the mystical traditions of the West and the East; but this is not enough. Unless its concerns can somehow find expression in the living language of the present, it must be slowly squeezed out.

Schopenhauer is defiant on this point, making it quite clear that religious truth is ineffable and that the condition of the saint is indistinguishable from the condition of one who is dead. When the Will has been turned back upon itself and is extinguished, then there is no Will and therefore no representation – and therefore, so far as the world is concerned, nothing. But the consequence is that we can do nothing with, and say nothing about, Schopenhauer's conception of the religious life. It has entirely disappeared from view.[4]

Kierkegaard is less extreme and is rightly concerned about the problem of communication, but he is well aware of the difficulties. Following Kant, he makes a sharp distinction between the sphere of our theoretical and retrospective understanding and the sphere of freedom. The understanding, because it works by connecting up phenomena according to the law of cause and effect and must assume the coherence and continuity of all events, cannot recognize freedom, which is an utter mystery to it. Conversely, when I adopt the standpoint of freedom and begin to think truly subjectively about my own individual life, then reality becomes for me entirely ethical. The self is a process of becoming, and for me as an agent the leading edge of reality consists of nothing but my infinite responsibility for choosing what I must do just now; and the uniqueness of this present moment of choice can never be fully captured in language. Proper names, pronouns and demonstratives can be used to indicate the particular, but they do not describe it. We may pile on descriptive expressions in the hope of pinning down the individual at the point where they all intersect, but no finite set of descriptive terms can exactly and uniquely define the individual; and in any case the accumulation of descriptions merely leads us back towards theoretical understanding. Thus, for Kierkegaard also, the religious life presents acute linguistic problems. The age is such that people are able to understand things only in an objective, theoretical and generalizing way, whereas Kierkegaard can explain morality and religion only if he can induce us to start thinking about our own lives in an entirely different way. Our standpoint must become intensely subjective, practical and individual. Then and only then can we begin to learn what the religious life is.

There is a further difficulty. The immense prestige of the totalizing Hegelian system has led the age to believe that its objective and theoretical form of understanding is complete and leaves nothing out. People are therefore systematically resistant to what Kierkegaard is trying to say to them, and he must act like a fifth-columnist, a spy and a saboteur. He must use language strategically, in ways that will undermine people's confidence in the adequacy and completeness of their present ways of thinking. He cannot preach to the age in the language of the age, because what he is trying to communicate is as invisible to the age as Schopenhauer's saint would be. So Kierkegaard must find ways of using language indirectly, subversively and as a tool. He has to be all the more subversive because the age thinks that it is already Christian. The Hegelian system had taken care to incorporate within itself a theoretical and supposedly-complete understanding of Christianity. So Kierkegaard had the paradoxical task of smuggling Christianity into Christendom: he must undermine the false Hegelian understanding of Christianity in order to make room for the entry of the real thing.

Kierkegaard believed that he had found a way of being a Christian, or at any rate of becoming one, in a profoundly non-Christian age. The path to true selfhood in Christ involved rejecting mediation and cleaving to paradox – which meant in effect that all the great polarities and oppositions of traditional doctrine must become internal to the spiritual life of the individual. The result was a very highly stressed subjective life. Kierkegaard found himself inwardly at odds with his age, in a state of extreme loneliness and compelled to live like a spy who conforms outwardly but has a second, hidden identity. Being, unlike Schopenhauer, a Christian, he does have a language to hand that he can use in order to cross the infinite distance between himself and his age; but a systematic misreading of that language is already in place, and he must thoroughly undermine it before he can be understood. From the outset, therefore, he knows he must cast himself in the romantic and Christ-like role of the misunderstood and persecuted prophet, and that he must develop special techniques of communication.

The special techniques of communication pose no great problem, for they require no more than extraordinary ability, which Kierkegaard possessed in abundance. But the moral and psychological dangers of the project are a more serious matter. Kierkegaard had to draw all the material for his writing out of his own soul. How could he avoid morbid introspectiveness, psychological inflation and paranoia? P. L. Møller's satirical articles in *The Corsair* are usually described as frivolous and scurrilous, but they are also clever and witty.[5]. He saw Kierkegaard as using his brilliant gifts, behind a thin veil of pseudonyms and other devices, for public self-laceration on a hitherto unparalleled scale; and it cannot be denied that there is much in the 'aesthetic literature' that lends credence to the accusation.

However, a spirituality of subversion need not be based on religious individualism and self-dramatization. It can be masked, enigmatic, cold and sceptical. The extreme case is the fascinating figure of Michel Foucault (1930–1984), who is conventionally regarded as an icily malignant, gleefully nihilistic and deeply disturbing character, and as being about as radically post-Christian and non-religious as could well be imagined. Yet, though he certainly would not have thanked us for saying so, there remains something very strongly Christian about him, because he went further than any previous writer had gone in working out what is required of us if we are truly to take the side of the outcast.

He began in the right place, with madness. Studying psychology and the treatment of the mentally-ill in the years after 1948, Foucault conceived an intense hatred for the oppressively objectifying and scientific psychiatry of that period. The chief result was his *Histoire de la Folie* in 1961, with its striking analogy between the way mediaeval society had secured its sense of its own ritual purity by excluding a class of unclean persons, the lepers, and the way a later society to which reason mattered most had secured its sense of its own sanity and rationality by excluding the insane.[6] Derrida, in a 1963 lecture,[7] naturally pointed out that in attempting to get inside the madman's soul and take his side by writing the story of madness from the madman's angle, Foucault was trying to go beyond the texts to the thing in itself, and moreover was using the methods and outlook of the sane, both to do it and to write about it. The task of taking the madman's side is more difficult than it looks, for the barrier between sanity and madness is not just a contingent and historically-constructed social frontier, but also a deep and metaphysical one. In a footnote Derrida quotes Foucault himself as saying that 'the necessity of madness . . . is linked to the possibility of history', meaning that the social 'fixing' of a standard of sanity presupposes the definition and exclusion of madness, and that this can only be established and held by a continuing historical struggle. The rich have to have the poor, the law-abiding need criminals, and all insiders need outsiders, to secure their sense of themselves. Society must always strive to give itself shape, order, durability and value by acts of exclusion. That struggle is history, or rather, history is suspended between the mere *fact* of the violent repression of unreason, and the need to find metaphysical *legitimation* for that act of repression and exclusion. 'Descartes knew that, without God, finite thought never had the *right* to exclude madness'; but God, who is absolute Reason itself, can give it that right. We must have him, to exclude the *malin genie*.[8]

To turn his own language against him, Derrida's 'metaphoric' is entirely theological; for see how clear his point becomes when we apply it to religious doctrine. *The necessity of heresy is the possibility of church history.* The older orthodox church historians were quite correct in writing church history as a story of doctrinal disputes and battles against heresy. The church defined and secured itself historically by identifying a series of categories of persons-for-casting-out. Orthodox theology is a great monument on which are inscribed the names of many famous victories. Each battle successfully to define and eject some new group of unfortunates left as its residue a line of separation and exclusion, and the ensemble of all the lines is the structure of orthodox doctrine. Orthodox church historians relate the story of all the successive acts of exclusion in such a way as to legitimate them, by showing in them the overruling Providence of God protecting his church against successive assaults. That indeed is how it worked. Today there are (or rather, there ought to be) rebel church historians who take the side of the heretics, the outcasts of the history of faith. But a history of heresy as such would itself presuppose the concept of heresy; so something more radical is needed. A genuinely *Christian* church historian – if such a monster can be imagined – would need to be revolutionary. She (for a feminist would be an appropriate person) would have to demythologize or deconstruct the very concept of heresy in general, and then set out deliberately to undo every last one of the long series of particular acts of casting-out which have constituted the history of the church hitherto. If what is most distinctive in Christianity is Jesus' act of promising a place in the kingdom of God to outcasts of every description – the poor, the

wicked, the unclean, the mad and the rest of them – then a radical
Christian must declare open war on every society that has been
built by a long series of acts of casting-out. This will mean in the
first place the church, but as the analysis widens it will extend to
all existing human societies, for they are *all* constituted in that
way.

Foucault's first major project, then, of giving madness a voice
and letting it be heard, at once raised wider issues. Over the next
fifteen years he repeatedly modified his position and became more
and more committed to being a permanent transgressor. If all
constructive thought and social practice necessarily involves the
establishment of frontiers and the exiling of deviants, then every
actual order of things must be contested in perpetuity. Such is the
long-term consequence of a decision consistently to take the side
of the poor.

A radical of Foucault's type is, then, an intellectual rather than
a practical subversive because she seeks to expose and demystify
the devices by which society orders, controls and excludes. She
does not directly advocate the emptying of psychiatric hospitals,
but instead asks the more unsettling question: 'How has it come
about that we now believe such institutions to be necessary?' She
has no theory, no utopian programme for a better world, belongs
to no group and is an extreme loner. Her interpretations of all
knowledge-systems as power-devices and tools of oppression are
intended to contest existing reality directly: 'theory *is* practice'.
But even if she succeeds, she cannot do more than rotate the
individuals who occupy the categories of oppressor and oppressed.
The categories themselves will remain, and will always be filled
by somebody. Never mind: the continual transgression and
contestation of the existing state of affairs is itself a kind of
affirmation.

Foucault is quite unlike Kierkegaard in that he makes no appeal
to subjectivity whatever. On the contrary, he is a postmodern,
who progressively eliminated both the subject and the thing in
itself, and confined his attention to the uses of language. But his
post-modernism is quite different from that which we were talking
about in the last chapter. That type of post-modernism, the Sea
of Meanings, we saw as a kind of deconstructed Hegelianism:
Hegel filletted, spread out and ironized. Foucault by contrast
represents post-modernism at its most subversive. He is interested,

not so much in meaning, but in language as a tool of power that acts to control, to categorize and to exclude. Yet the two forms of post-modernism do have one key point in common: they are both of them highly demythologized, post-metaphysical and post-historicist. Legitimating myths about a Golden Age past, about progress and about a better future have all been lost, and Marxism is left far behind. Things are what they are, and if you are not willing to accept them as they are then you have two options: you may slip away, as in the last chapter, or you may adopt a stance of permanent subversion, as in this. The gospel assures us that the poor will always be with us, but for Foucault that is no reason for not taking their side.

A Christian of this type will be more explicitly atheistic than any other that we have discussed. In the tradition of Blake, Dostoyevsky and many others he likes Christ, but not God. He may make his point by saying that he is unable to see God anywhere else but in Christ. Perhaps because he has more than a touch of deviance in himself, he is drawn to everyone who is marginalized and excluded. He likes the poor, the minorities, the denizens of the hidden archipelago of residential institutions, and (most of all, if he is an artist) he likes the raffish and picturesque population which in great cities occupies the regions between theatreland and gangland. These people may be defined as all those on whom the police keep an eye, and indeed it is not good manners to enquire too closely into exactly how they manage to hustle a livelihood.

The subversive Christian likes all the people who live in these various twilight or shady worlds (and indeed many of them do tend to be somewhat nocturnal, and the optical metaphors are highly significant), and he cherishes the tradition that Jesus liked them too, having himself been a sort of subversive who casually transgressed the boundaries between the clean and the great unwashed, the unclean. But the God of respectable society is given by the whole system of invisible frontiers that it has erected between itself and the various minorities, to such an extent that each of the divine attributes, and even every smallest detail of the popular anthropomorphic imagery, functions as the ideological representation of one of these frontiers. God is thought of as masculine, in a way that makes women a bit less clean than men; old, in a way that brings the young under a little suspicion; light, in a way that makes shady characters questionable; stable and exalted, in a way that makes us eye askance all lowly drifters. He seems the very embodiment of all that is lofty, powerful, rational, in control and excluding, and it is not surprising that subversive Christians find him incompatible with Jesus.

All this having been said, however, there must be many who find it hard to imagine how a stance like Foucault's could ever be a genuinely *religious* option. He was the friend of Artaud and Bataille, had a touch of paranoia, and was a thoroughgoing sceptic and dissident. Forgetting the extent to which the prophets, Jesus and Socrates were themselves regarded as subversives, we still tend simply to equate religion with veneration for everything hallowed – beliefs, customs, traditions, institutions – and instinctively regard anyone who shows that hallowing involves partition, exclusion and oppression as being anti-religious. Imagine a devout Muslim, distressed by developments in Islam, who sets out to show the extent to which his own religion functions as a tool of cruel oppression – and must do so because of the very way the basic beliefs and social practices are set up. He does not even propose reforms: he just says, 'We need to know that this is how things are with human beings in general and with us in particular. Remember your schooldays? Bullying is bonding; every class needs a victim. Me, I side with the victim, although I know there must always be one. If I undermine your self-assurance in bullying this one you'll surely find another, and there will be equally convincing reasons for bullying him in due course. Our God is so holy he must exclude the unclean, so just that he must exclude the lawless and wicked, so true that he must exclude the infidel and the heretic, so absolutely One and sovereign that he can never abide the presence before him of anything that is genuinely other than himself – *isn't he?*' Now how is the community going to regard this dissident Muslim? Will they thank him, and regard him as having done them a service?

Yet in Christianity we have in recent decades come largely to accept precisely such a diagnosis of the way our own faith has systematically and almost from the first functioned to bring about and to legitimate the exclusion, the categorizing as unclean and the persecution of the Jews. In this instance at least we are ready to concede that the bad news is good news, for it is now religiously necessary to learn to live with the consciousness of the radical moral questionableness of religion itself and the ways it apparently needs must work. And once the point is recognized in the case of the Jews, then a critique of the same type is sure to be extended to other cases as well. It has already begun in relation to the power-functions of Christian doctrine, and in relation to Christian attitudes to other religions, to heretics, to women and so on. Maybe in time we will recognize that it is precisely the most critical, subversive and nihilistic strands in modern thought which promise to be of the greatest religious value to us.

In this chapter we have described a form of spirituality which is still dark and strange to us. Maybe it is a nil class, and there is not anyone at all who is like this. But I suggest there could be, there should be, and in time no doubt there will be.

15

LIFE EVERLASTING

For many chapters past, every spirituality under discussion has been in greater or less degree world-combatting and world-renouncing, as if we just knew that the permanent and ultimately incurable unsatisfactoriness of our worlds natural and social is now established as a fact that must simply be lived with, in one way or another.

There are many well-known historical reasons why we should have come to think this way. At the beginning of the nineteenth century Malthus in Britain and Schopenhauer in Germany introduced a new view of the natural order that was to be sealed by Darwin's theory of natural selection. The harsh struggle for existence in the biological world came to be seen as not merely a secondary and contingent corruption of nature that has entered only since the Fall, but as being integral to the way nature always has worked and always will work. In consequence all attempts to picture the ultimate unity of nature and morality, whether in a common metaphysical Ground of them both or in some hoped-for future Earthly Paradise, now look like wishful thinking. And in due course Darwinism led to the emergence of a biology-based view of human nature which has similarly banished the beliefs in our own original innocence and ultimate perfectibility.

Secondly, since the Enlightenment our conceptions of social authority and of the social order have been demythologized. Nobody now wishes to glorify the state or those persons who embody its authority in quite the old manner, nor to pretend that any particular constitution of society is or ever can be entirely morally satisfactory. On the contrary, all social authority is maintained by a mixture of force and mystification, and none can be wholly without domination, oppression and exclusion. The most we can ask is that politicians should act as humane and efficient managers who arbitrate between conflicting interests as best they can. Their task can never be performed to everyone's satisfaction, and still less will it ever be finally completed.

Thirdly, not only have nature, the self and society come to be seen in this rather disenchanted way, but morality itself in any case now looks rather different. The Enlightenment thinkers had set out to justify and systematize morality, setting it on new secular and purely rational foundations. They failed.[1] Their failure can be described in various ways. One is to say that moral theory requires a well-founded account of human nature as it is, an equally well-founded account of human nature as it would be if it were fulfilled, and a body of rules which if followed will lead us from the first state to the second. Set up the question that way, and it is obvious why they failed: the new mechanistic science had abolished the older teleological ways of thinking (i.e., that explained all processes in the light of the goals to which they were tending), leaving the Enlightenment with no possibility of a clear agreed picture of the ultimate purpose of human life. Alternatively, if they abandoned any attempt to justify morality teleologically, and sought instead to move directly from mere facts about human nature to rules of conduct, then their logic was obviously at fault. And more recently we have in any case come to see that we do not really wish to have morality fully systematized and rationally justified, for if that were done it would surely eliminate creativity and the interesting choice between a wide range of moral options to which we are now accustomed.

Finally, the recent breakdown of the old legitimating narratives that promised some sort of better future as a reward for our present efforts has completed our disenchantment. It seems that we have lost all the myths that promised to unify and harmonize in a perfect world nature and morality, the self and others, the ideal and the actual. Not even the self itself, nor morality, can be so unified. Instead, things are what they are, and plurality, conflict and general untidiness must be accepted.

We have studied the five major patterns of religious response to this new perception of our condition. It may provoke a crisis through which the individual is led to a primal creative choice of

selfhood as full responsibility for his own life and faith and values
(9,11). He may find within his own religious tradition, viewed as
a great communal work of life-art, a sufficient stock of reconciling
and guiding symbols to contemplate and to live by (10). He may
commit himself to an open-ended programme of social action to
transform present reality, arguing that religious action is just
secular action guided by an eschatological vision. The End is
always coming-to-be and always not-yet – and precisely therein
lies its religious tension and creative power (12). He may,
oppressed by the sense of universal egoism and illusion, turn
away from social life altogether and seek goodness through self-
abnegation, discipline and obscurity (13). Lastly, his vision of
society as being always a cruel system of power-relations may
lead him to attempt consistently to take the side of its victims and
become a permanent protestor, subversive and transgressor (14).

   However, as we have said, all these five responses are in varying
degrees world-renouncing or world-combatting. They all accept
much the same demythologized and pessimistic analysis of nature,
the self and society. The same image of the life-world as a theatre
of cruelty in which life is for ever divided against itself in a
perpetual struggle for power underlies them all. Religion may
give us the moral courage nevertheless to choose life and responsibility (9, 11), it may offer consoling and reconciling symbols (10),
it may inspire militant struggle (12), it may lead us to renounce
the world and vanish from view (13), or it may impel us to choose
the unclean (14) – but still the deep assumptions, derived from
half-a-dozen or so major thinkers, remain.

   This makes us uneasy, for it leads us to suspect that in spite of
everything metaphysics, that cunning old trickster who seeks to
persuade us that some deep 'necessary', 'natural' and immovable
framework surrounds human existence and cannot be altered –
has after all crept back. We thought we had finally freed ourselves
from that particular bogeyman. We thought we had learnt the
habit of being instantly suspicious of anything that tried to pass
itself off as being obvious and unalterable, because in so many
cases it has turned out that such claims are merely ideological
devices for protecting against criticism what was really no more
than a transient social creation. Yet now we are backsliding once
again, falling under the domination of a set of socially produced

beliefs that have taken shape only during the past two centuries. Why should not they in their turn *also* be called into question?

Here are two possibilities: either conflict, plurality and general untidiness are ultimate and all life remains divided against itself in a struggle that is never satisfactorily resolved, or a final resolution is attainable in a spiritual state in which we can say a wholehearted and unified ethical yes to life without reservation or dissatisfaction. How do we choose between these two possibilities, or even judge which of them is on the face of it the more plausible as the basis of our final life-view? At any rate it seems irrational to exclude one of them *a priori*. For if nowadays we really are foundationless then there are no fixed objective criteria of the validity of a particular spirituality, in the sense of a life-view and life-policy. Instead a whole spectrum of spiritualities may well lie before us as available optional forms of expression. I will find-myself-choosing, in several senses of that phrase, the one that is best for me; that is, the one through which I can best live and flourish, given my circumstances, my psychological type and my stage in the life-cycle. It will at one level be my personal choice of a particular form of selfhood-project, and at a deeper level be experienced as the life-impulse's own selected mode of self-expression in me. I find myself in and through the choice, and I find that it has chosen itself in and through me. And so it may come about that the conflict-model is appropriate to guide us in the long years of adulthood, the years of work and active ethical striving; but that when the time approaches for us to withdraw from the fray a different perspective becomes more appropriate. The struggle continues and we may still follow its progress sympathetically, but for ourselves the time has come to move into another region and live by a different vision of things.

But *is* that other and reconciling vision possible? Let us return to our hypothetical 'primitive metaphysics' of infancy.[2] I can well understand that the productive life-energy cannot achieve representation through a single subject only. There is no representation without communication, and no subject without inter-subjectivity. For there to be a private realm, there must be a public; a purely private and solipsistic language is impossible. So, rather as some physicists suggest that four-dimensional space-time with little knots of energy in it is the minimum possible configuration for a stable physical world, the primitive metaphysics emerges as the minimum requirement for the productive life-energy to be able to express itself in representation at all. The elements click into place as a coherent configuration: there is communication, and therefore there are temporally-extended chains of discrete units of signification, and therefore time, and story, and the subject of the story, and experience; communication, and therefore a plurality of communicators, and a medium of communication in which they are set, a minimal world. Physiological states, experience, and the differentiation of experience into its subjective and objective poles – all these elements cohere and yield a minimal metaphysics, the possibility-conditions for the productive life-energy's self-expression as representation. All the same, this is only a myth and a heuristic device that we use to remind ourselves that we have no intelligible starting-point other than the supposition of a plurality of subjects in communication. Then we kick it away. Subsequent objective-pole reflection may reduce the subjects to no more than so many points at which the lines of communication intersect; but still these intersections will remain.

Thus we stick to our primitive metaphysics as a heuristic device, a minimal model. The self-expression of that unknown reality which we have labelled the productive life-energy minimally requires that there be communication, a temporally-extended medium of communication, and subjects who are envisaged as being at least intersection-points along the lines of communication. That much is reasonably clear: life's self-expression must be in plurality. But does it follow that life has got to be divided against itself? Why do so many thinkers go on to say in effect that we must also include in the primitive metaphysics a series of further statements about power and conflict? Thus we are told that the communicators differ in strength; that every sending of a message is an exertion of power, an attempt by the sender to impose a certain symbolization upon the receiver; and therefore that the whole network cannot be conceived except as a power-struggle. The various expressions of the life-energy are thus necessarily in conflict with each other, a conflict in which some turn out to be winners and others to be losers.

We come here to a parting of the ways. Some thinkers see discourse primarily in terms of meaning. Ideally, it tends towards an ever more complete and satisfying reciprocal and fraternal understanding; and so communication leads to communion. Jürgen Habermas is a contemporary exponent of such a position.[3] But other thinkers, who have become very influential recently, take a less rosy view. Their observations of the way things go in the biological and social worlds lead them to analyse all social interactions in terms of power. Along broadly Foucauldian lines, we must therefore enlarge the primitive metaphysics as follows: in any group, however minimal, the strongest individual will impose his own symbolizations upon the others. There will be a leader, and there will be the led; and the led will be bonded by a line of exclusion that shows them how privileged they are in contrast with the remaining and excluded minority. Thus there are minimally two basic lines, one of domination and one of exclusion, and the latter makes the former work. Every group is formed by the same mechanism: the leader gains the allegiance of the led by making them into a *we* that has excluded a *they*. The line of exclusion, once established, operates as a very powerful sanction, making it clear to us that it is unthinkable, prohibited, intolerable that *we* should ever reject the group's norms and become transgressors, apostates, abnormal, defiled, despised, rejected and fugitive people like *them*. We feel superior to them but still more do we fear becoming like them, and this fear leads us to love our leader and to welcome every fresh extension of his power and control over us.

Foucault's own account is of course far more elaborated than this, and has many difficulties. One is that he wishes in the post-modern manner to eliminate the subject and speak only of discourses. Accordingly he writes in terms of dominant discourses which impose themselves to establish an orthodoxy or consensus that excludes deviant forms of discourse. But this move has the disadvantage of making the notion of power very obscure. What remains of the idea of power after we have repudiated any metaphysics of the subject who exercises it?[4] However, the only point we need to make for the present is that if Foucault wants to say that his view of language as a tool of power is not just an option with a limited range of application but is somehow universal and compulsory, then he needs to claim that a few theses about language, power and conflict are an integral part of the primitive metaphysics. Otherwise we could simply opt out of the world he describes, by making a personal moral resolution henceforth no longer to use language as a tool of domination and exclusion. To put it in the language of Anglo-Saxon philosophy, do the ideas of power and conflict belong analytically to the very concept of communication, in the sense that every utterance must be an attempt in some way to constrain the hearer? If so, we cannot opt out of power-relations. The alternative view is that language is not as such and necessarily a tool of power but just happens to have become so in many cases, because of the ways our knowledge-systems and our social life have developed together. There is a very familiar sense in which a knowledge-system such as theology, or medical science, or expertise in the law, is socially embodied in an élite professional group. The group's knowledge is their common possession, their mark of distinction, a means of gaining privileges and wielding power, and in general enables them to act as a conspiracy against the laity. But is this just a contingent fact, no doubt the result of the enormous and persisting influence of ancient religious ideas of knowledge, language and society; or do language and knowledge by their very nature have to work in this way?

The choice before us here is momentous. Habermas begins with meaning, and regards language as being essentially innocent. However much our actual languages may have been contingently and secondarily corrupted, language as such tends to create mutual understanding and fellowship. For Foucault, who was a Nietzschean, life is essentially a striving for power. It comes into representation as language, which is a tool of power. Power is a positive, productive and reality-creating force; and the use of language, as an expression of power, by its very nature works to create the structures he describes — structures of control, domination, exclusion and so on. Yet Foucault was also a protester and a rebel, and it is not surprising that he felt some embarrassment when giving a public lecture: how could he prevent his own discourse from falling under his description of the way all discourse works? Was he attempting to dominate his audience, or not?

The solution I suggest is as follows: it cannot be demonstrated *a priori* that Foucault is right. So far as we can see the primitive metaphysics as we described it is coherent, without the addition of the theses about power and conflict. To communicate is not necessarily to attempt to dominate. In principle it should be possible to make a fresh start, and to develop a non-conflictual use of language which would in turn lead to a non-conflictual social life, and therefore a pacific view of life in general, and a pacific view of the world. In principle, it seems possible that we should learn to love one another, and therefore to love life. At any rate the possibility is not absolutely excluded.

However, the difficulties are vast, because to make the fresh start we will have to go so far back. As we indicated in the opening pages of this chapter, power-struggle naturalism has become deeply entrenched in our whole vision of the world, and Foucault's ideas about language and society merely extend a tradition of thought already well established by Schopenhauer, Darwin, Nietzsche, Freud and others. But as we have also hinted, the issues Foucault raises go much further back than modern power-struggle naturalism, for it is obvious that his analysis in terms of power of language, truth and knowledge is especially applicable to the case of religion. Religion is the original matrix of all culture, from which everything else has been hived off. For thousands of years religious language and doctrine have functioned to bind people together in common allegiance to a central focus of transcendent sacred power and authority, making them a holy people segregated from the uncleanness and pollution outside their circle; and even in our modern secular culture we are still shaped by this long history. Religious language remains the classic model for the use of language to persuade and to bind, and religious doctrine is still the classic case of an ideology, that is, of the way knowledge systems work in their social embodiment. Religious power remains the archetypal example of power in social life, and religious conflicts are still the most absolute and intractable of all social conflicts. The mechanisms whereby religion excludes things and people that are taboo, polluted, unclean and defiling are still discernible in our more recent and secular exclusions. In this sense it can be said that the philosophy of religion is a complete fundamental education in itself, for if we fully understood what religious language, doctrine, power, conflict and exclusion are and how they work, then we would have the basis for a complete theory of how the human world as a whole works.

It is also clear that the last and greatest problem of religious thought today is religion itself, its history and the legacy that it has left us. If there is any sense in the idea that the final goal of our life is to come to rest in a comprehensive and unified ethical acceptance and affirmation of life, then to reach that goal we have to overcome the history and the legacy of religion as it has been hitherto.

Christianity itself is arguably just such a revolutionary assault on the history and the legacy of religion. Focussing around a man who was himself rejected and excluded, it seemed at first to break down all the walls of partition between God and man, the holy and the unclean, Jew and Gentile, male and female, and to promise a new fully-reconciled humanity. But then by one of the strange reversals so characteristic of religious thought, it reinstated all the lines and began, for instance, to treat the Jews as it supposed they had treated Christ; and in the ages of faith it seemed perfectly consistent to worship one heretic in the morning and burn another in the afternoon. This reinstatement is a considerable theological problem, for it lends credibility to the Foucauldian analysis of how truth-power systems must work. The lines of domination and exclusion are marked out by God's right hand and his left. With his right hand God draws the line of domination and creates the place to be occupied by the elect whom he has chosen to rejoice in worshipping him, and with his left hand God draws the line of exclusion and marks out the place of condemnation. The actions of the right hand and of the left belong inseparably together, and there cannot be the one without the other.

During the later seventeenth century people began to try to imagine a God with a right hand only, and to disclaim persecution, intolerance and Hell. But what has happened? As the action of God's left hand slowly faded away from people's consciousness, so also did that of his right. From their point of view, neo-conservative and fundamentalist movements have drawn the obvious conclusion: we must bring back the left hand of God. If we can but revive the old condemnation and exclusion, it will bring back with it the old joyful assurance of salvation. Do not blame fundamentalism: it *has* to be moralistic and vindictive, because until people see God's left hand clearly at work they will not believe in the action of his right.

To Karl Barth, as Bonhoeffer says, belongs the credit for beginning the theological critique of religion. He rightly saw in Christ's condemnation the condemnation of religion as it had been hitherto; but his analysis was too shallow, and he set in its place an authoritarian and positivist doctrine of revelation which says in effect, 'Like it or lump it'.[5] The world is still constructed by division. Everything is still seen in terms of the right hand and the left, the Yes and the No, the saved and the lost, the accepted and the excluded, the commanded and the prohibited. Indeed for Barth God himself is subject to this law, and constitutes himself by repressing his own shadowside: '*Das Nichtige* is that from which God separates himself and in face of which he asserts himself and exerts his positive will.'[6] Even God cannot affirm without excluding, and by that act bringing into being his own deadly enemy, the No-thing that lurks behind him.

The logic of division requires that one cannot say yes to this without thereby saying no to that. There is no love without hatred, no acceptance without rejection, no we without they, nothing holy unless something is unclean, no right hand without a left; and the dualism and conflict are not only external to the self, but also internal to it. While the present world-order endures, both conflicts are permanent. After it, according to Christian doctrine, they come to an end. But the sealing of Heaven and Hell, while preventing any further conflict between them, also seals for eternity the division between them. The elect will then be able to regard the fate of the damned with a satisfaction that is unalloyed by even the faintest twinge of personal anxiety.

In the light of all this we see that modern power-struggle naturalism with its vision of life as being permanently and inescapably divided against itself is only a weakened and secularized variant of far more ancient religious ways of thinking which constructed the world precisely out of oppositions and exclusions. Above all, the supreme being was One, an autonomous subject, self-possessed and sovereign, who defined himself by expelling from himself everything alien to himself, and who ordered his realm and manifested his glory by drawing great lines with his right hand and his left. He gathered a holy people around himself by describing around them a line of exclusion, and created the human subject as a finite counterpart of himself. Man must think, act and order the world in the same way as his Maker. Everything must be divided into a dominant part which is affirmed, and a subordinate part – its shadow side, the 'difference' – which must be repressed.

Here at last we see post-modernism in its most novel and

religiously-significant aspect. Highly revolutionary, it attempts to begin all over again. Like Hegel it seeks a total affirmation, but without a totalizing system. More thoroughly than structuralism, it decentres and disperses not only the Infinite and finite subjects, God and the self, but also the logical structure of all the lines of division and separation that were drawn in order to establish and secure those subjects. The result is a scattering or dissemination. God dies into Christ, and Christ into the endless interplay of meanings in the New Testament text and all the secondary writing that has grown around it. Everything is preserved but in dispersed form, as when Christ's body and blood are distributed in bread and wine. The affirmations and denials remain, but they no longer create fixed walls of partition, because they are now seen as reciprocally passing into each other. Every affirmation is also a denial and every denial also an affirmation. Everything is relativized, for the flux and reflux are without beginning or end or boundary, and everything can therefore be affirmed.

The closest parallel to this new way of thinking is to be found in certain ancient Eastern systems of meditation. What is wrong with us, they say, is that our lusts and our fears have led us to a false construction of the world in which we have become trapped. In sustained calm concentration, with our eyes open, we seek to unloose the mechanisms of falsification. When craving and anxiety are stilled the world dissolves into an endless blissful flux of experience, and the self also becomes lost in the flux. This dissolution is beatitude.

A second parallel is surely to be found in the achievements of the Paris school of painters between Manet and Matisse: Manet, who could represent light with black paint, and Matisse, who set out to make ideal bliss into a fact of present sensuous experience. In this long line of painters we repeatedly encounter a desire to overcome the traditional disjunction between the sacred and the (devalued) secular, the high and the low, and therefore an avoidance of explicitly religious, secular-excluding, themes. Instead something analogous to dissemination or dispersal occurs, as landscape, still-life and the common experience of ordinary people are invested with radiance. Common life is no longer 'low life'. By the 1890s, as the physical world is dissolved into a flux of brilliant colours laid close together in short brushstrokes, we have a visual equivalent of the Sea of Meanings. The analogy with deconstruction can be sensed again in Matisse's qualified turning towards Christianity at the end of his life. The Vence Chapel was an expression of gratitude that crowned an unusually fulfilled career, but old disjunctions such as that between divine and human creativity no longer matter: 'My only religion is the love of the work to be created, the love of creation.' 'Do you believe in God?' – 'Yes, when I'm working.'[7]

These two parallels, from Eastern meditation and from painting, may well be much easier to understand than the highly language-conscious idiom of deconstruction. Yet anyone who has struggled much with the written language must have some notion of what has happened in the post-modern era. We see how incorrigibly ambiguous individual words are: how *to cleave* is both to split asunder and to stick closely to, how *natural* and *simple* switch between wholesomeness and imbecility, how *drugs* (like Plato's *pharmakon*) are both healing remedies and poisons, how *egregious* suddenly topples from outstanding to ridiculous. Turning sentences around, we see whole vistas opening with tiny changes of word-order, as when we move *only* from one position to another. In the terrible joints between sentences, abysses yawn. Making a piece of prose comes to be like making a work of abstract art, first because it is not about anything other than itself and is only an arrangement of ambiguous signs, secondly because the maker finds that even the smallest change spreads and alters the entire composition, and thirdly because once made and delivered over to its audience it is wide open to an endless variety of interpretations. It flows straight out into the Sea of Meanings. And because every written text is in these respects like abstract art, it is not *about* anything other than itself. There is no 'transcendental signified' out there to which it is pinned down. Language does not trace an objective world-structure; rather, the nature of the world is given with, and indeed is identical with, the nature of language. The post-modern vision of the world is its vision of language. The world is in language, not language in the world.

Difficult though it is to understand, the linguistic turn has one special advantage. Painting may make a new vision of the world accessible to us with peculiar immediacy, and meditation may enable us to experience it for ourselves. But in language we can *argue* for it, even though in this particular case, because of the very odd and novel character of what is being argued for, the manoeuverings have to be intricate.

How far deconstructive thinking may succeed in making a new beginning for Western thought[8] we cannot yet tell, but at least it has correctly diagnosed the magnitude of the task. Behind our modern vision of the world (and of society, and the self) as a theatre of perennial conflict there ultimately lies a very ancient 'theological' motif: all creative activity whatever takes place according to a logic of division, opposition and repression. No creative thought or activity can be purely affirmative: there is always a remainder, a shadow, a difference, which must be excluded and held off in order to maintain the affirmation. So if we are ever to reach a purely affirmative vision of the world we have to go right back to the beginning and learn quite new ways of thinking and acting.

The way of life to which all this might lead is already visibly taking shape. It will be broadly 'green', circumventing existing power-centres by being at once more local, small-scale and cellular *and* more internationalist. It will be low on the consumption of raw materials and non-renewable energy and on general depredations on the environment, and high on electronics, communication, art, and local small-scale production and social life. We will not be so individualistic as we are now, and will instead think more in terms of networks. Life and death, joy and suffering will be seen as inseparable elements in a whole package. We will not attach so much significance to individual fates, and therefore will simply not *see* (or rather, make/make out) so much evil and conflict either in social life or in the biological realm as we do now. What matters is the humming vitality of the whole network. Thus in the biological realm we will not be so troubled as some are now by the fates of individual organisms, or even perhaps individual species, but will care deeply about habitats and about the biosphere as a whole. The biosphere and the human communications network will be so intertwined, through the incorporation of the world into language, that nature and culture will be seen as but two aspects of an inexhaustibly rich whole, the Word incarnate.

Of any vision of this type it is commonly said that it does not take evil seriously. To this it may be replied that we ourselves have by our false self-construction largely created the evils from which we suffer. Karl Barth says this expressly in the case of God, who is the supreme subject on whom the finite subject is modelled. Absolute or metaphysical evil, *das Nichtige*, is a no-thing brought into being by God because of the manner in which he has chosen to assert himself as Creator. 'There is opposition and resistance to God's world-dominion . . . This opposition and resistance, this stubborn and alien factor, may be provisionally defined as *das Nichtige* . . . The controversy with *das Nichtige*, its conquest, removal and abolition, are primarily and properly God's own affair . . . God is Lord on the left hand as well. He is the Ground and Lord of *das Nichtige* too. Consequently it is not adventitious . . . It too belongs to God.' It arises because, as we said earlier, Barth's God is subject to the logic of division, opposition and repression: 'Grounded always in election, the activity of God is invariably one of jealously, wrath and judgment. God is also holy, and this means that His being and activity take place in a definite opposition, in a real negation, both defensive and aggressive.'[9]

Barth was a Calvinist, and he goes on to celebrate the ultimate triumph of the Protestant ego in God's final conquest of *das Nichtige*. But there is another way in which God can come to terms with his own self-created enemy. He can let go of his defensive and aggressive Ego, succumb to *das Nichtige*, accept weakness and affliction, die in Christ, and suffer dispersal. And what is true for him is true also for us. While we are self-defensive, we cannot bear anything that is genuinely alien. It is perceived as a mortal threat. We become paranoiac, imagining enemies everywhere. We can tolerate only that which obligingly mirrors and confirms our own self-image, and anything that fails thus to mirror and obey us must be condemned and excluded.

In the light of all this it seems reasonable to suspect that much of the evil we do and much of the evil we complain about is directly linked to our efforts to maintain a false self-definition. God's death in Christ and our death in union with him, the decentring of both the Infinite and the finite subjects, may thus be seen as the means whereby the world can be saved: that is, through them we may be able to reach a spiritual state in which we can say a final and wholehearted yes to life.

16

GOOD NIGHT

We have considered a range of spiritualities, traditional, modern and post-modern. Now we end by asking what should be our final attitude to ourselves and our lives. The photograph, being convenient, readily available and typically of our time, offers us a starting-point for analysis.

There is something very Buddhist about a photograph. It is a relatively lasting trace and souvenir of just one moment in the flux of life, and therefore a poignant *memento mori*. Every photograph speaks of what is gone for ever. Roland Barthes says that because the photograph is produced merely mechanically, without having been transformed by passing as a whole through someone's creative imagination, it never quite becomes a true sign in the way that a painting is.[1] It remains a frozen ephemerid, lacking universality. It reminds us that without the activity of the myth-making, reality-producing imagination the world and our life is no more than a stream of vague and fleeting events that pass away from moment to moment. Hence the poignancy of the photograph, because after all it is a sort of sign, not of its subject-matter but of universal transience and insubstantiality: emptiness, the void, *Sunyata*.

Looking at old family photographs we see our own former selves as mysterious strangers, former acquaintances who have slipped away and are now beyond recall. We think how much of us has already passed away, and how soon we will be all past and no present. These many images of vanished instants fail to cohere, do not add up to anything substantial and still would not do so even if we had a thousand times as many of them. We have been and we are no more than long chains of fleeting events that cannot be disentangled from the universal flux of becoming into which they are woven. The events arise and they pass away. Of an infinitesimal fraction of them, some riddling trace is preserved awhile. The rest is fiction.

The argument can be spun finer yet, for the photograph is itself a cultural product which exists and is interpreted only within the cultural realm. My positing of it as 'real', as an image of myself, as a scrap of evidence about my past, and as being evidence for some specific hypothesis about my past life all occurs *within* the realm of language, and not outside it. A Wittgensteinian might make the point by saying that for us the world is within language and not *vice versa;* Derrida, while saying essentially the same thing, speaks not of language but of text or writing 'as the disappearance of natural presence'.[2] 'There is nothing outside the text',[3] for however far we go in chasing after some extra-textual reality which can function as an objective criterion for checking the text, we will still be operating within the realm of text. Our relation to whatever we describe as 'reality' will still be subject to the textual logic which governs all thought. We never grasp objective 'natural presence' in a clear-cut, univocal way, for the very act of grasping is itself language-shaped. Whatever we do, we are always within the logic of text, which is secondary, differential, and full of systematic ambiguities. Emerging only within the world of text, 'reality' is for us itself subject to the logic of text, so that there is no old-style monarchical objective truth of things. Truth itself is text-like.

These reflections dispel the biographical illusion, which supposes that there is an objective truth of our lives, that we can know it, that it can be captured in a definitive biography, and that we ourselves can attain personal self-realization and fulfilment in the last years of our lives by looking back on our own lives as our own nearly-completed definitive biographies. We hope, in our retirement perhaps, to be in a position to look back on a record of achievement. We assemble the story of our lives into and view it as a coherent narrative approaching its conclusion. We can then see ourselves as living through the last pages of our own biographies. And there can be no objection to any of this, in so far as reality is indeed textual and everybody does indeed generate and live by his or her own life-story. Unfortunately, we also want

our own autobiographies to be definitive, as if we were our own
recording angels. We want the whole story of our lives, as it
appears to us, to be nothing less than a definitive and final record
to all eternity of the objective truth of our lives – and that is
fantasy. We are attempting to have it both ways: we are claiming
the right to invent the story of our own lives, while yet also wishing
to suppose that the result can be a sort of absolute autobiography,
exempt from the inescapable ambiguities and the fictional
character of all such stories.

Cheered by reading the biographies of other people, we say to
ourselves that a human being's life can be made into a rounded
and completed whole. If I can one day see my own life in that
light, I shall be satisfied. If I live well, get somewhere, achieve
something or become something, then with my labour done I will
be able to review my own life as an *opus* approaching completion;
and this will be a kind of redemption. But I forget that any such
self-image that I construct in the evening of my life will be my
own fabrication, spun by me from the fragmentary memories, the
personal needs and the myths of selfhood available to me at that
stage of life. Among the best available of such autobiographical
constructs are the memoirs of people in public life, for their
accounts of themselves must at least appear to be consistent with
what is on public record. So if indeed we propose to adopt the
spirituality of the natural man, and aim at eventual redemption
by retrospection – that is, plan so to live as one day to get to a
point from which we will be able to look back with satisfaction
at our own nearly-completed lives – then I fear that our ambition
is not very lofty. We are merely living in the hope that we will one
day be able to fabricate a self-portrait of the type that is to be
found in the memoirs of a politician.

Or take a better case, perhaps the best of all, Jean-Jacques
Rousseau's *Confessions:* still, the text, just because it is a text and
text is all we can have, will be open to the deconstructive reading
that Derrida supplies. Deconstruction does not, of course, show
that a text can mean anything whatever: what it shows is that the
author's attempt to express himself unambiguously involves him
in making 'logocentric' metaphysical assumptions about meaning
and the power of language to express truth univocally. To put it
crudely, he has to write as if meanings were as clear, hard and
distinct as glass marbles; and they are not. Language is a system

of differences. The harder I try to run just one clear line of meaning, the more I will be struggling to keep other things at bay. My very act of text-making leaves a residue in the form of conflicting forces of signification within the text, which in turn means that the writer himself is systematically unable fully to command everything that is happening in the sentences he is composing. Deconstruction is a form of critical reading. Working backwards, it unmakes the text in order to bring to light all the things that the writer had to become unaware of in order to make his text.[5] This in turn means that Jean-Jacques Rousseau cannot himself have *knowingly* fixed in the text the whole truth and nothing but the truth about Jean-Jacques Rousseau, and therefore that the fully-expressed truth about any person is not accessible to that person himself. The *Confessions* is a very good book, and it might conceivably make available to the reader all there is to be known about Jean-Jacques. But the writer is not so well-placed as the reader. To the writer much must be unperceived. Therefore the kind of redemption by retrospection that we have been discussing is illusory. The whole truth about ourselves is for us a receding mirage. It is too dialectical for us ever to be able fully to catch up with it. The very act by which we try to grasp it and make a clear statement about it necessarily removes it from us.

Most lives are in fact unfulfilled, and all are utterly subject to misfortune: but even if we made a world in which everybody became a person of achievement, in a position to write a self-satisfied autobiography, the biographical illusion would still remain an illusion. No doubt some of us will eventually feel the need to spin such a justificatory story about ourselves. We will do it in order to persuade ourselves, and others, that our lives have meant something definite and lasting, that they are now being rounded off, and that we may therefore depart without regret. But the story we tell will be a fiction, our last *apologia*, and Derrida's reading of Rousseau demonstrates that in any such narrative we cannot help but betray ourselves even as we justify ourselves. In order to construct our self-justification we have had to repress the self-betrayals which deconstructive reading exposes.

I am of course not criticizing stories as such, but only the illusion that we can fully redeem or justify ourselves to ourselves by any story that we tell about ourselves. That story is nevertheless all-pervasive, that we have no alternative but at least to begin with a

story about ourselves, we recognized at the outset.[6] *Persona
dramatis persona*: there is no self without story. The self is
mythical in the straightforward sense that it emerges as the subject
of the story that it narrates. The infant is thus unavoidably at first
egoistic and eudaemonistic, the hero of his own personal myth.
Authors, being notoriously infantile characters, tend to remain
like this, and it is often said good-humouredly of them that 'he' –
for some reason it is of *men* in particular that people say this kind
of thing – 'was his own best creation'. And something similar
seems to be true of not only of fiction-writers but of all whose
lives are very well documented. The self and all our selves are
culturally-shaped imaginative productions. Guided by the myths
of selfhood and self-realization that our culture offers us, we
invent for our own purposes our personal myths of ourselves and
our own lives. We are all our own fictions – and nowadays we
know it. That, surely, is why the people who are today the most
widely admired are those who have found their highest fulfilment
by becoming all 'image', so many beautiful masks with nothing
behind them. The identity of actors and performers is entirely
fictitious – and is venerated precisely as such. Old-style 'reality'
being dead, it has been replaced by art. People dream of becoming
fictions like the stars, lost in their own myths.

The strength of post-modernism is that it has understood and
accepted these things. The rather Buddhist outlook that results
takes different forms in different philosophical traditions. In the
Anglo-Saxon tradition, which has sought objective knowledge
and has been greatly impressed by natural science, a typical result
is the cold, glittering ice-palace of W. V. Quine's late philosophy.
Reality is a vast field of minute twitches in the void, which can be
modelled in purely mathematical terms and of which we ourselves
are an integral part. The truth, and the proper subject-matter of
philosophy, is the palace of numbers. Everything else is merely
human superadded colouring, secondary to the 'hard', abstract
kind of philosophy. But the Continental tradition, which gives
priority to human philosophy, replies that physics and math-
ematics themselves constitute only one small patch in the wider
domain of human cultural activity. To be truly general, philosophy
should begin with signs and communication. The Anglo-Saxon
produces a kind of metaphysics of physics, seeing the world as a
swarm of minute events, a field of quantities. The Continental

produces a metaphysics of the sign, and sees the world as a boundless Sea of Meanings. And both visions have a somewhat Buddhist flavour. The former chastens us by its chilly mathematical austerity, and the latter by showing us that we have no 'inside'. We are entirely permeable, mere nodes or points of intersection in an endless network of communication. Our interior subjectivity is fictionally constituted out of the messages that are continually passing through us. Our subjectivity is radically relational and impermanent, and we deceive ourselves if we attempt to construct our own lives as the gradual realization of permanent and autonomous selfhood.

It is curious that Derrida, whose sustained critique of Western thought has him by implication constantly looking towards the East, never in fact takes up an Eastern book. Nevertheless, postmodern metaphysics does resemble Buddhism in that it has finally dissolved away the old 'centred' and monarchical type of subjectivity, the metaphysics of presence, in which Being constituted itself as ever-present to itself, knowing itself, willing itself, master of itself, loving itself, drawing a line around itself to protect its own integrity, and resisting and repressing every kind of 'difference'. Evaluative lines of distinction, subordination, concealment, prohibition and exclusion were drawn to separate God from the world, presence from absence, truth from error, identity from difference, eternity from time, the self from others, the righteous from the sinners, the orderly from the disorderly, society from nature, the sacred from the profane, speech from writing and male from female. These lines gave us our ontology and all our ideas of *archē* and *telos*, the beginnings and the finalizations of all ordered totalities such as the cosmos, history, the book and the self. But the lines have become insecure and have begun to wobble as we have seen, not merely that they are lines of oppression, transient cultural products and much more permeable than they ever admitted to being, but more fundamentally that they are self-subverting. Hegel first saw the ambivalence of the lines in relation to Christian doctrine, for he grasped that in the incarnation of God in Christ and the death of God in Christ the old theistic metaphysics had been decentred and dispersed. The strange post-modern condition in which negation is also affirmation and affirmation is also negation, and everything continually flows into its opposite, is a Christian product. In the

Old Testament all the lines are drawn – and in the New they are all subverted. In the Old Testament the cosmic order is established, and in the New it is dissolved away. In the Old Testament the boundaries between God and man, Lord and servant, Judge and defendant, the sacred and the profane, Israelite and Gentile, power and weakness, life and death, the holy and the unclean, freedom and bondage, the self and others, the law-abiding and the lawless are clearly laid down and fixed in rituals; and then in the New Testament Christ undoes them all. A centralized stone Temple is replaced by a new living Temple made of people in diaspora. We keep both Testaments, the Old and the New, so that the New can be understood.

Thus if the post-modern world is in some respects Buddhist in its metaphysics, it is also Christian. There is no substantial individual self; the human realm is a field of communicant intersubjectivity. Becoming incarnate in Christ, God enters this realm and is disseminated through it as bread and wine.[7] He and we both lose centred subjectivity. Thus the last story we tell of our lives ought to be, not a story of the final triumph of monarchical selfhood, but a story of *kenosis*, scattering and dispersal, a self-giving and self-loss that continue, as the hymn says, 'Till death thy endless mercies seal, and make the sacrifice complete'. If we are bold enough to call Good that Friday when darkness fell over the land because God had died in Christ on the cross, then we should be bold enough to call our own night good.

This enables us to understand our lives as end-less. The modern pagan, as we have seen, seeks redemption by retrospection. He hopes, before he dies, to be able to view his own life as a nearly-finalized project of self-realization and a record of permanent achievement. This I have made, this I have been, this is me, my contribution. His death rounds off the thing he has made, and so the book of his life has a traditional conclusion. But, we have argued, he put his trust in a fiction, for he necessarily lacked the full knowledge of the truth of his own life that he must have believed himself to possess if he was to be justifiably satisfied with his final self-image. By contrast, the Christian is progressively expropriated and dispossessed of herself, so that her life does not come to any such End or *telos*. Her selfhood is not consolidated as her lasting achievement and legacy, but is scattered and disseminated. Her biography is not rounded off but opened out

to the four winds of heaven. She passes away into life everlasting.
A psychic vagrant, a person of no established repute or fixed
identity, she leaves nothing tangible or completed behind her.
Poetically at least, we can scarcely conceive of Jesus as having left
behind him a book, a child, any property or monument, any
completed achievement, or indeed anything at all except the
difference he has made to the friends into whom he is dispersed.
The textual product of that dispersal is the New Testament. And
the difference? It is the merest collection of word-plays (which
change everything).

Loss and gain, life, death, life out of death, death in the midst
of life, a living death, a dying life, eternal life. Since life and death
are bound together and each passes into the other, there are as
many ways of death as there are ways of life. We may choose to
die fighting, 'with harness on our back', or we may prefer
the lucid acceptance of the Buddha or Socrates; but the most
characteristically Christian final attitude is one in which both life
and death are fully accepted without any attempt to repress the
one in the name of the other.

This is possible because death and life are not co-ordinate
powers at war with each other, between which we must choose.
They are one. To see this clearly, we need to think away all the
fusty trappings of death, medical and ritual, and reduce the
situation to its essentials. Imagine simply that at some moment in
the future – you do not know whether it is seconds away or years
away – your experience will without warning instantaneously
cease. You will disappear, vanish, cease to be. You do not know
just when this will occur, and you will never know that it has
occurred. You will not experience its occurrence. So this absolute
cessation is not an experience or state of yourself that can be
imagined, nor is it an event that is to be feared. Its sole content is
the knowledge that your time is limited. Thus death as such is
nothing but life's finitude, and the knowledge of it at once
precipitates us back into life with a heightened awareness of
transience. I have so long, I do not know how long, but I do know
that life is a process of continual loss.

In Christianity this immeasurably simple lesson is taught as
early as possible, for people are baptized into death not at their
funerals, nor in the last years of life, but in its very first weeks. To
live all along with life instead of fighting against it, one must

recognize its character from the very outset. When life is seen not as a process of self-consolidation but as a process of self-giving, emptying and sacrifice, then life can be loved in its transience, and disinterestedly. The continual loss which an open-eyed love of life involves adds a dash of anguish which heightens the flavour of our joy in life.

So difficult is it fully to accept transience that for many centuries religion has been read as justifying attempts to deny it. Religion has been seen as an affirmation of the hope of sovereign, ever-wakeful, invulnerable and indestructible selfhood and of incorruptible life. As a result people saw themselves as suspended in exile between a paradise lost long ago in the remote past and a paradise that was a world away in the future, and since they passed their entire lives in this state of exile their consciousness was bound to be unhappy. The fictions they lived by devalued the lives they were living. The only way to escape from the unhappy consciousness and regain paradise was by the loss of the ways of thinking that had originally led to the construction of those better worlds elsewhere. Paradise had been constructed by remotion: it had to be deconstructed in order to become present again.

Albert Schweitzer has described the whole history and task of Christianity as one of prolepsis or anticipation whereby, one after another, the things of the future eschatological world are brought forward into this present world. The very beginning of the process was the present anticipatory knowledge of the secret of Jesus' future glorious messiahship. Later, we can see the resurrection and the general outpouring of the Spirit being brought forward into the present by baptismal regeneration and the laying on of hands. Gradually, through various reverses, Christianity has over the centuries become more world-affirming:

> But it will be a mightier revolution yet when the last remaining ruins of the supersensuous other-worldly system of thought are swept away in order to clear the site for a new spiritual, purely real and present world. All the inconsistent compromises and constructions of modern theology are merely an attempt to stave off the final expulsion of eschatology from religion . . . That proleptic Messianic consciousness of Jesus (which was in reality the only possible actualization of the Messianic idea), carries these consequences with it inexorably and unfailingly.

At that last cry upon the cross the whole eschatological supersensuous world fell in upon itself in ruins, and there remained as a spiritual reality only that present spiritual world, bound as it is to sense, which Jesus by his all-powerful word had called into being within the world which he contemned. That last cry, with its despairing abandonment of the eschatological future, is his real acceptance of the world.[8]

That is to say, for Schweitzer Jesus' career itself anticipates and epitomizes the subsequent destiny of Christianity, and the path which it has so laboriously and reluctantly trodden since, of becoming wholly this-worldly. At the time when Schweitzer was writing these words (in 1905–6) it seemed to him that Christian thought was still not yet strong enough to be able to complete its task.

Eighty years later, the time for that 'mightier revolution' has come. The ages of faith can begin.

Epilogue:
The Philosophies of the Religious Life

An obvious objection to the account we have just completed is that it has been too much dominated by a variant of the old Microcosm/Macrocosm myth, namely the Romantic idea that the *Bildung* of the individual recapitulates the thought-history of the race. I warned at the outset that there would be something of this, the main reason being that for well over a century now the myth has been so popular and has so influenced children's upbringing that we have made it into a cultural fact. Individuals then find themselves faced with the task of outgrowing the pastiche-primitive representations that were implanted in them during their childhood, a struggle in which they inevitably find themselves working their way through old controversies.

As it has turned out, though, the parallelism has been disconcertingly detailed. *Mythical Realism* seemed to stand both for the thought-world of infancy and for that of tribal religion. *Doctrinal Realism* corresponded not only to the beginnings of theology among the priests and scribes who first organized the pantheon and codified religious law, but also to the period around the age of ten when children are preoccupied with rank and rules. *Ladder Realism* represented the other-worldly mysticism of Christian Platonism, and the sublimated-erotic religious yearnings of early adolescence. *Designer Realism* stood for the type of popular cosmic religion, found already in antiquity, that became especially prominent in association with early modern science, while it also reflected the impact of teenage religious thought of the ideas of physical law and the uniformity of nature. *Obedientiary Realism* was by implication linked both with classical Protestantism and with the modern individual's conversion to some form of evangelical piety in early adulthood. And so on: throughout we seem to have been correlating the personal development of the individual in some detail with the large-scale cultural history of which he or she is the product.

I have little choice but to be defiant about this, and to assert that that is how things are. We do not postulate any occult correspondence or hidden hand: we say only that since the culture is a line of texts whose later members presuppose the earlier ones, and since we are cultural products, then when we produce a text about the individual's spiritual development it cannot help but reflect the larger story in the background. Spiritual biography and autobiography on the one hand, and the history of ideas on the other, are inevitably going each to be modelled on the other and each to influence the other.

Secondly, there are also objections to the uses I have made of the idea of post-modernism. The line of great figures who have given rise to post-modernism and 'anti-philosophy' (of which more later) includes such names as Hegel, Kierkegaard, Nietzsche, the later Heidegger, Foucault and Derrida. Of these, the first two were revisionist Christians who may be interpreted either as renewers or as dissolvers of traditional Christianity, and the first four were deeply influenced by Lutheranism; while all six make extensive if sometimes veiled use of a theological metaphoric. They can indeed be seen as a line of thinkers who have between them completed the dissolution of Christianity by following out the last implications of the death of God, but their thorough knowledge of theology positively invites the ingenuity of a radical theologian who adopts their ideas but reverses the movement, translating what they have done back again into the language of the old religion. Christianity is after all notoriously protean. Itself the product of a subtle and complex transformation of its parent-faith, it already incorporates many images of death and rebirth, of scattering and reassembling. When the House of Faith becomes old and ricketty its enemies come along and dismantle it – which then enables its friends to reconstruct it from the same materials and so make it stronger than it was before.

To vary the analogy, Christianity is like an amoeba continually changing shape as it moves through time, and well able to ingest even its own death. It will be recalled that the amoeba is immortal;

and so is Christianity, for it has in its genes the capacity to draw new life out of its dissolution.

This maddens critics who hold the orthodox philosophers' belief in fixed and determinate essences. The devious manoeuverings of radical theologicans irritate them beyond measure. According to the ethical-ontological scale first established by Socrates and Plato and still devoutly believed in by modern positivists and empiricists, only clear meanings and fixed essences are good, and the protean is irrational, unfalsifiable, slippery and thoroughly *bad*. However, as every student of Wittgenstein knows, the anti-philosophers have mounted a formidable assault on the doctrine of immutable and determinate essences and meanings. To begin with, does it not represent a flight from the evident facts of historical change and linguistic usage, into a mythical ideal world? So let us simply pass back the onus of proof by retorting, 'Just what is wrong with being protean? How else can a tradition persist through time? What are your grounds for believing in your timelessly-fixed essences and meanings, and for ascribing superior virtue to them?'

A third objection to our procedure is that after first undertaking to be pluralistic and to avoid leaning too heavily on the reader, we have failed to keep our promises. Writing a linear text, we have inevitably been telling a story and therefore developing an argument. The problem of Hegelianism has returned, for have we not found ourselves compelled, first to put the restricted and exclusive perspectives earlier in the story, and then to incorporate them within the wider and more transcending perspectives that open later? The more exclusive brethren are not going to be pleased by that.

I answer that we have indeed been Hegelian in so far as we have been pluralistic, but we have not totalized. That is, insofar as Hegel was indeed the thinker who gave us the notion that there is a genuine plurality of distinct and coherent, and yet interconnected, possible forms of consciousness and ways of life, then, yes, we are indeed all of us Hegelians nowadays. But we have made no claim to absolute knowledge. We have not put forward any totalizing vision that finally swallows up all the subordinate perspectives. On the contrary, we have rested in a non-totalized plurality. That means relativism; and the objection is raised that relativism is a doctrine that destroys itself, for if the claim that 'All things are relative' is non-relativistically true, then at least one dogmatic statement is true; and if it is only relativistically true, then there is a place for dogmatism alongside it and independently of it. But I *accept* the objection, allowing that relativism is true, relativistically – and therefore that it leaves a place for dogmatism alongside it. That is, although my text was linear, the whole scheme is not. If you are a dogmatic realist, for example, then you may stay in that position, and I have no wish or right to push you out of it. I showed how one *might* move on, but not that one *must* do so. The book need not be taken as either making or justifying any claim to have transcended your position in a wider form of understanding. I really did intend to be pluralistic, in a way that would leave space both for dogmatism and relativism. The only stipulation I can make is that if your dogmatic realism is to be intelligible to others it must have a coherent logic, apparent in both your linguistic and your ethical practice. If you can do it, I envy you. I really do. Thus those who wish to travel in the opposite direction from that followed in our exposition are perfectly at liberty to do so. In fact I am even willing to accept the asymmetry which arises from the fact that, if you are a dogmatic realist, then my account makes your position licit, whereas on your (admittedly licit) account mine is illicit. I cannot say fairer than that, for I have rationalized the rules of the game as it is actually played in the world. Religious conservatives have a *locus standi* for attacking liberals, but liberals have no basis for any counter-attack.

Now, however, the ironies begin to multiply alarmingly. We have been pluralistic enough to allow dogmatism its place in the sun, but our generosity is a consequence of the fact that we have in the end adopted the standpoint of the anti-philosophers, who are as detestable to religious dogmatists as they are to mainline philosophers. I had better come clean about some of the implications of this, the fourth protest against our method.

Anti-philosophers – not their own name for themselves – are a miscellaneous group who include, as well as the half-dozen names mentioned earlier, various other American pragmatists, Continental Nietzscheans and others. They are so called because they question a number of principles which they see as having been constitutive of Western philosophy since its beginnings. Philosophy has been seen as a quest for knowledge, in the strongest

sense, of the truth in the strongest sense. In pursuit of that aim
it frames a special kind of discourse which purports to be
unambiguous and unmetaphorical, to unite the highest degrees
of precision and generality, and to conform to universal and time-
transcending standards of rationality. Knowledge consists in the
perfect conformity of thought to its object, or of the object to
thought, and this conformity is guaranteed by the concept of
form: for form is both the principle of determination which
constitutes the thing as just the thing it is, of its kind, and is *also*
the thing's abstractable intelligible content that can be fixed in
language and grasped by thought. So there is a pre-established
harmony of thought and being. It is as if state of affairs, sentence,
proposition and thought could all be lined up one behind another
like a row of dinner-plates, and seen to be all of just the same
shape. Alternatively, since that metaphor is crude, one might say
that form exists in a special intermediate or bridging realm that
is homogeneous both with the world of representation and with
the world of beings. So it is not a case of two or more things being
found to have similar shapes, but rather of the unity of a single
principle that both determines the object to be just what it is and
also makes it intelligible to thought and definable in language.

Finally, for there to be knowledge, thought and its object must
both be self-identical and reciprocally fully *present*, each to the
other.

This last requirement creates a certain demand for timelessness.
For if the object is some particular thing or state of affairs in time,
then doubts will arise. Since our vision is always perspectival,
how can the object ever be completely present to our thought? Is
it not liable to change? And as a material individual thing,
must it not (because no individual thing is ever quite a perfect
exemplification of its kind) have purely accidental characteristics
of its own which are not transparent to the understanding? As
for the subject, complex thoughts take time to complete in
consciousness and sentences take time to utter. As Hume
commented – and Kant was much troubled by this realization –
a temporal consciousness finds its act of knowing continuously
slipping away from it into the past and the uncertainties of
memory, even as it tries to perform it. Time is continual leakage
and loss of presence. Maybe real knowledge is only attained
when a timeless, fully self-present, unsleeping and non-discursive

consciousness enjoys immediate rational intuition of a timeless and transparent ideal object. If so, then philosophy must be tempted to take off into a region of pure ideality; but if not, if philosophy resolves to remain in this world, then it must hold that we can attain knowledge of the truth only in so far as our language remains rigorously subject to a whole apparatus of ideal and time-transcending standards of rationality.

This apparatus is the spirit-world of Western philosophy, a world of *a priori* and timeless truths, standards, rules, criteria, essences, necessities, ideals, axioms, principles, laws and foundations. Philosophy has ascribed to these noumenal objects the same guiding authority in the life of a fully rational person as (according to Psalm 119) the Torah has for the observant Jewish believer. They require *oratio recta*, a cool immediacy, straightness, sincerity, vigilance, probity and veracity of thought and speech in which we say exactly what we mean and mean exactly what we say, without any dissimulation, duplicity, hypocrisy (the Greek word for play-acting or feigning) or rhetorical artifice. Nor must we allow ourselves to be deflected by the passions or the imagination. This ethic of constant rational control, self-presence and univocal speech will lead us along the straight path to intellectual blessedness.

People often suppose that it was a purely religious 'puritanism' that made early Hellenistic Christianity so suspicious of the theatre, music, the arts and sexuality, and led Clement of Alexandria to declare that a Christian should not sneeze. Not so: these themes come at least as much from Plato as they do from the Jewish ideal of a life governed in every part by the Torah. And what is striking is the close resemblance between the two moralities. Their coalescence in Western monotheism, and especially in monasticism, created an immensely powerful structure, whose greatest text is undoubtedly the *Confessions* of St Augustine. For Augustine the whole of our life in this world is play-acting, a fictional realm in which language is used to rouse the passions and attach us to finite things. We are thus dragged down into self-loss and futility. The kind of integral and fully-present rational selfhood that both philosophy and religion require of us can be neither achieved nor maintained among the things of this world. Only in the relation to God can true selfhood be found. Turning to God in prayer, I am recollected: he searches my heart with an eye both exact and merciful, highlighting my defect of full selfhood and making it good by his forgiveness and grace.

In Augustine we find an almost perfect fusion of the spirit of Western philosophy with the spirit of Western monotheism. The two were very close indeed – which brings us back to the anti-philosophers. For they might be defined as a group of thinkers who consider that the same great historical and intellectual forces that have over the past few centuries been at work demytholo-gizing and changing religion require also a parallel demytholo-gizing of philosophy. The changeover to a critical point of view, the recognition of the radical historicality and the cultural diversity of the human realm, the grounding of our cognitive activities in social practice and indeed in biology, the revolution in linguistics and the loss of the old idea of a pre-established and guaranteed conformity between thought and being – all this has much the same effect in both cases. The arguments correspond, and the great names are the same. At least one philosopher who is still somewhat underrated, Ludwig Feuerbach, proceeded directly from demythologizing religion to demythologizing phil-osophy. He thought that Western philosophy was the ghost of theology, sharing with it the idea that to be kept on the rails human life and thought needed to be continually guided from above by unchanging and purely intelligible entities. Hence the phrase, 'the spirit-world of philosophy': Platonism as a kind of philosophical animism. Why do we still talk as if order, intelligibility and rationality depend upon subservience to an invisible apparatus of *a priori* standards, fixed meanings, rules and the like?

The animism arises when some manifest purposiveness of behaviour, or following of a custom, or simple regularity is explained in terms of a non-manifest entity such as an intention, rule or law, which is then thought of as transcendentally control-ling it. Of course, talk of intentions, rules and laws is fine as a shorthand *characterization* of the phenomena in question, but we are tempted to go further and to picture these intentions, rules and laws as shadowy beings whose governing activity can be invoked to *explain* the occurrence of the manifest phenomena; and the temptation needs to be resisted.

The early proponents of mechanistic science used to mock the scholastic habit of postulating final causes, hidden 'virtues' and what not, in order to explain events. And they were right: to suppose that such ideas increase understanding is like supposing that if we say that pigeons find their way home by instinct, then we have somehow explained how they do it. But the habit of seeking understanding and explanation by jumping to a higher level and picturing shadowy controlling entities is extraordinarily persistent, the central case of it being no doubt our tendency to think of the meaning of a word, an utterance or a text as a distinct but very definite and authoritative *thing*, located – where? In the dictionary, in an authoritative commentary, somewhere in logical space, in the intention of its maker, out among the things and states of affairs signified by it? We are unsure.

Anti-philosophy is post-modern in its insistence that the move to another level produces only confusion, and in its demand that we resolve to stay with the manifest, on the surface. We must seek explanation and understanding immanently, by examining how language works, what difference it contains and makes, and how people learn and follow practices.

The result of this is a certain naturalism of the sign and of practice. Coupled with the loss of the transcendental ordering of culture by fixed essences and permanent categorial boundaries, it produces the effect we earlier called 'the Sea of Meanings'. Clear lines of distinction are lost, and everything seems to dissolve into everything else. The frontiers between (to take examples from the arts) poetry and prose, painting and sculpture, and music and natural sounds, come to appear merely conventional and thoroughly questionable.

The intellectual shift required may be seen as a generalization of that which Darwin demanded in biology. To comparative anatomists and taxonomists of the old school, evolutionary theory seemed to eliminate all objective distinctions between natural kinds in the living world and to replace them by a continuous and unclassifiable flux. They really believed, for a while, that Darwinism meant the end of reason in biology. A century later we recognize that their anxiety was unfounded, but we are still struggling to allay the more general fears that anti-philosophy (so-called) is a charter for irrationalism.

Why do people think this? A political analogy will help to clarify the issue. In an absolute monarchy, all sovereignty is vested in a superperson who is exalted above society. All law and authority descend from him, all the chains of command and value-scales lead up to him. Social reality is so constituted that the king is indispensable, like God in the medieval cosmology. He is the necessary source and guarantor of order, unity and coherence. To someone who lives in such a world democracy must be incomprehensible, for he cannot see how it could work. In a democracy, sovereignty is decentralized and scattered through the whole body of the people. They establish representative institutions, of course, in which sovereignty is symbolically recen-tred; but those institutions ultimately derive their authority from no loftier source than the very people over whom it is exercised. To an absolute monarchist all this must seem bizarre. Yet in a democratic republic there still is sovereignty, even though it is now socially immanent and dispersed; and there is still a rationale for political obligation. The de-centring of sovereignty does not weaken but actually strengthens it, for at their best democratic republics have proved to be a good deal more stable, coherent, peaceful and law-abiding than the old absolute monarchies.

Now there is a close analogy between the ideas of God, of political sovereignty and of rationality; and my immediate suggestion is that the anti-philosophers' view of rationality is like the democrats' view of sovereignty. As they see it, our standards of rationality have become secularized, made immanent and dispersed, so that they are scattered through the multifarious practices within which they are operative. Orthodox philosophy thinks that to be rational our activities must be guided by a centred group of *a priori* and universal standards of rationality which are exalted above the flux of practice; but I think the anti-philosophers have shown that this is not so.

In the case of religion, the feeling that religious language and practice need to be explained and justified by reference to hidden supernatural Powers that prescribe all standards and control all events is for obvious reasons particularly deeply entrenched. People do not see how it is possible to dispense with this belief, and they will not quickly change their views. Our best recourse is gradually to build up a body of work that will show that under the new condition the religious life still make sense, is still important to us, still includes a variety of options by no means all of which are either nostalgic or quietistic, and above all still *moves*. We are at something of a disadvantage in that (as Rudolf Bultmann used to insist) we cannot elaborate an old-style system; all we have to show is a way of working and a movement, and we shall need a new vocabulary to describe it.

Now we can return to the question of the prickly and asymmetrical relationship between those who hold a realistic supernatural faith and the newer kind of post-modern believers; and I will refer to the two groups as 'they' and 'we' for convenience. The relationship may be described through two metaphors, as follows:

When they look at a painting they see it as a window upon the world; as a representation, that may be more or less successful, of something else that lies beyond itself. When we look at the same painting we see it as an evocative and symbolic ordering of paint upon a flat two-dimensional surface which, if done well enough, lodges in the memory and may permanently affect the way we see things. The two ways of looking at the painting seem very different, and certainly we will be less fulsomely descriptive than they in our interpretation of it. Nevertheless, we and they are looking at the same painting and are agreed about many features of it. They think our view impoverished, but we think it brings out a number of points that they are liable to miss. And the fact is that developments in painting this last hundred years have tended to bring about a shift from their perspective to ours.

Again, when they read a poem they read it in the 'intentionalist' manner, as a revelation of the poet's creative mind, and so as a medium through which the reader is granted intimate access to the spirit of the writer. The words of the poem have been chosen with such delicate precision that to read it is almost like listening to a gramophone record: one can hear the *ipsissima vox*, the poet's very own voice. But our way of reading a poem is different. We regard it more mundanely as a public object, an open arrangement of signs on a printed page, which is just as close and as fully available to the reader as it is to the writer himself. There is no single and uniquely authoritative personal way of appropriating it, not even the poet's; for it is not just capable of but actually requires a different creative appropriation from each other. Like a musical score, it needs a performer's personal interpretation to complete it. And again, these two ways of seeing the poem are very different from each other. They think our way of reading is depersonalized and arbitrary, but we say that it is truer to the nature of language and opens up many fresh possibilities.

In both cases, they are 'realists' who see the work of art as a window pane. They look through the sign to a thing signified lying beyond it and distinct from it. The painting or poem is regarded as portraying some state of affairs and as being a revelation of the spirit of the artist. For them it is in this way that art has depth and a determinable meaning, and they complain that our way of looking at art robs it of that particular kind of depth and reduces it to a surface play of signs. And it is true enough that for us the signifier (the sensuous mark) and the signified are, in Saussure's metaphor, as close to each other as the two sides of a sheet of paper. We reject the idea of a 'transcendental signified' distinct from the sign. The words of a poem (the marks) and the meaning of a poem are as close to each other as can be: mark and meaning, body and soul, sound and sense are inseparable. Given the one, you have the other. It is all yours.

Religion is a set of symbolic beliefs and practices to which many of the same considerations apply. Supernaturalist believers, who are 'realists', refer these beliefs and practices to a variety of religious objects and energies which they see as altogether transcending the symbols. And since they regard such an 'intentionalist' reading of religion as essential, they in effect excommunicate postmoderns. However, we post-moderns cannot reciprocate. We hear everything the supernaturalists say, and all the symbolic beliefs and practices are before us. All the evidence is available and nothing whatever is missing. Our only defect is that we do not know what the jump to a fully transcendent signified that they speak of could possibly be. Nevertheless, all that they say and do is before us, and if it hangs together at the manifest level with a tolerably coherent logic and makes sense in practice then from our standpoint their position is perfectly allowable, for we do not know what more could be asked of them. Naturally we will treat their talk about the transcendent reference of the signs as itself occurring on the surface, within the realm of signs. But that is obvious enough: transcendence is itself a metaphor, and symbols of the transcendence of symbolism are familiar to us. So they think they are jumping right out of the world of signs, whereas we see that they are not; but if their *talk* of doing so and their religious practice makes sense *within* the world of signs, then we are bound to concede the legitimacy of their position – and therefore of their condemnation of us, which follows so directly from what they say. But they for their part vehemently reject the grounds on which we are so indulgent to them. Hence the multiple ironies to which we earlier referred.

Some followers of Wittgenstein (though not Wittgenstein himself) have put forward a philosophy of religion which is unsatisfactory because it is not sufficiently conscious of these ironies. In effect, they claim that a post-modern reading of realist faith can be given which ought to be acceptable to the realists themselves. Now it is true that the entire content of realistic faith – all the language, symbols and practices – is present at the manifest level, exactly the same for the post-moderns as for the realists, and its logic can be explained immanently, at that level. But the realists retort that this post-modern reading leaves out what is most important. The post-moderns read faith like people who look at a portrait by Velasquez and interpret it brilliantly as an abstract painting. Maybe – but Velasquez *intended* to paint a representational painting, and a portrait it is. Hearing this protest – itself made at the manifest level – the Wittgensteinians try to take note of it and incorporate what it says into a more refined account which speaks of the autonomy of the religious language-game and the ultimate authority of religious categories in our lives. And this makes the realists more irritable and dissatisfied than ever. They have no way of 'getting across' what they mean, and the post-modern interpreter has no way of meeting their requirement. Communication breaks down.

In our account, therefore, we have to go a little further. The faith – every faith – is indeed a complex and rather loose-knit ensemble of signs, stories and practices which exist in the public domain, accessible to all. It can be read – that is, creatively appropriated by individuals – in many different ways. We have discussed fifteen such ways, a number of which are realistic. But since we ourselves insist that no particular reading is uniquely privileged, and since we even allow that our overall relativism relativizes itself, we hope that realists may consider themselves allowed to be realistic without feeling that they are under pressure and need therefore to counterattack. However, we do not delude ourselves into supposing that even this degree of pluralism is going to be sufficient to placate those who find pluralism as such offensive. Quite the opposite, for our pluralism has itself implied a message.

For, and here we come to the end of our windings, in effect we have said that it is only because there is no truth, and instead merely a plurality of truths, that we have been able to rehabilitate the spiritual life, as being a pilgrimage through a long series of truths. Furthermore, this pilgrimage has no great destination and is never complete, but merely passes out into scattering and endlessness. We read the New Testament as a story of the de-centring and scattering of God, of Christ, and of the people of God: a story of diaspora. And in this long pilgrimage into diaspora, which we love and in which we find joy, lies the meaning of our life.

Glossary and Definitions

This section is needed because I have introduced a number of new technical terms and phrases, and have also used some other terms which are of recent origin and may be unfamiliar. But the need is embarrassing nonetheless, for the book's main message is that it is just because our new understanding of language has shown us that there can be no one absolute and final Truth that the spiritual life can now return, in the form of a pilgrimage through many partial truths. Words are not like glass marbles, clear, hard-edged and unambiguous. Like our whole life, and like Christ, language is always secondary, mediated, differential, metaphorical, public, suspended-between, distributed, endless, plural and relative. The very nature of language precludes the univocal expression of absolute Truth. Writing – good writing – is not a manipulation of fixed essences according to logical rules, but calls for a continual unmaking and refashioning of ideas and a coining of new metaphors. It should be fluid and non-technical.

So I am being somewhat inconsistent both in using and in here defining technical terms. Still, these notes may help.

Aesthetic Expressivism A form of religious consciousness in which it is acknowledged that our religious beliefs and practices are culturally conditioned and symbolic. Claims to transcendent reference are not made: instead the religious symbol-system is regarded as a great communal work of art and as a profound expression of the human spirit. Religious objects are viewed as cultural symbols, and religious allegiance is in effect equated with allegiance to the cultural tradition of which the believer is the product.

Anti-philosophy See the Epilogue. The anti-philosophers are a miscellaneous group who are agreed only in questioning, or in actively seeking to displace, a number of central assumptions of much of Western philosophy since Plato, and especially the contrasts he made in setting up his distinction between the intellectual world above and the phenomenal world below. Many anti-philosophers are indebted to Kierkegaard's attack on Hegel, and to Darwin, whose work suggests the need for a fully-immanent account of rationality. They tend to wish to bring philosophy closer to art than to science, and many share the Buddha's mistrust of metaphysical questions and system-building. It should be added that Plato, whose books are works of art in dialogue form, and who includes in his corpus telling criticisms of his own chief doctrines, may himself be seen as a forerunner of anti-philosophy.

Deconstruction A method of literary criticism taught by Jacques Derrida (*b.* 1930), and much misunderstood in the English-speaking world. It might be described as applying to the sentences of a text something like psychoanalytical ways of thinking, for it analyses the ways in which the form of a text, or the assumptions on which it is based, or the metaphors used in it, or ambiguous words in it, may create currents of significance that run counter to the dominant and manifest line of meaning. Thus the sentence, 'We can transcend metaphor, and attain to a perspicuous and immediate rational intuition of truth' is itself saturated with metaphors. Plato uses a doubly indirect form, written dialogues, to teach an intellectual ethic of directness and immediacy.

Designer Realism A form of religious consciousness that is grounded, not in the social sphere, but in a claimed primal, natural and universal response of awe and wonder at the majesty of Nature. Where people believe that they have apprehended an underlying uniform rational order in Nature, their response to it may be formalized in an inductive argument to a cosmic Designer. The piety that results is typically lay, and logically independent of religious authority. God is seen, somewhat anthropomorphically, as a cosmic Mathematician and Engineer, and religious beliefs are seen as resembling, or simply as being, empirical hypotheses. The meaning of God's 'reality' is derived from the reality of the physical world and of the laws that govern it.

Doctrinal Realism A form of religious consciousness in which the 'reality' of God consists in the supreme power and authority of his will as the source of a systematic sacred law of belief and conduct for the community. God's power is displayed in his control of both Nature and history, and his will is revealed in language in the text of sacred writings. He may speak occasionally through the utterance of prophecy, or, less immediately but more regularly, through priestly interpreters of his revealed will.

Emotivism A theory of moral judgments which regards them as functioning principally to express the feelings or attitudes of the speaker, and to arouse similar feelings or attitudes in others. Coarsely put, moral terms are a lot of Hurrah-words and Boo-words.

Environmental Agapism In effect, 'green' Christian socialism: an attempt to extend the Christian ethic of universal love to the relations between society and nature. This movement is best understood as a reaction against the sharp disjunction between the world of natural fact and the world of moral freedom which was common in the heyday of mechanistic science. The phrase 'ecological humanism' is also sometimes used. Albert Schweitzer pioneered an ethic of this type, even though he considered that it could never be entirely successfully or consistently applied. We suggest here the possibility of a more optimistic view, on the grounds that for us language and the world are interwoven, and all images of nature are themselves social productions. Nature need not, therefore, be thought of as being permanently and intractably opposed to moralization, as Schopenhauer and Darwin led many in the past to think.

Fideism Strictly, a purely willed assent to dogmatic propositions. In the standard case the rational arguments for and against are equally balanced, and the decision to assent is influenced by the advantages to be gained by it. This type of fideism is especially associated with various French writers between Montaigne and

Pascal. Modern interpretations of faith which entirely dispense with dogma – several are discussed in this book – are also sometimes described as fideistic, but improperly so.

Foundationalism The belief that knowledge-systems resemble buildings in needing to be erected upon firm and immovable foundations at a deep, unseen level; and therefore in general the doctrine that things at the phenomenal level can only be satisfactorily explained by reference to the operation of timeless and transcendental controlling principles.

Historicality The claimed radically historical character of human life, according to which all our thoughts, beliefs, values, standards of rationality, language and other products are internal to history, conditioned by it, and not independent of it. Historicality is to be carefully distinguished from **Historicism**.

Historicism The complex belief, first in the autonomy and coherence of each historical period as a cultural totality; secondly, in an orderly, linear and quasi-logical progression in history from one period to another; and thirdly, in a special kind of necessity that constrains one to be faithful to the spirit of one's own period. Vico is popularly seen as being the founder, and Hegel and Marx as the greatest exponents, of historicism. Historicist beliefs have been under attack for at least a century, since Nietzsche; but they have proved remarkably tenacious and difficult to get rid of entirely.

Isomorphism Likeness of form or structure.

Logocentrism A term introduced by Jacques Derrida to describe a central assumption of much of Western philosophy since Plato. It is that philosophy can attain to clear knowledge of the Truth if it sticks rigorously to a special kind of discourse of the utmost generality, unambiguousness and precision, in which terms are used to designate timelessly-fixed essences, and are manipulated in accordance with *a priori* standards of rationality. To establish this ideal, many distinctions are made. In each, something is preferred and given higher rank, and something else is subordinated and excluded or repressed. Taken together, the lines of distinction generate a great ethical/ontological scale, at the summit of which stands the lucent and complete pure rational intuition of conceptual necessity, the vision of the supremely real and supremely intelligible. Derrida argues that the nature of language makes this ideal unattainable. The discourse of philosophy is inescapably haunted by everything that it has attempted to repress in order to constitute itself. He seeks to demonstrate this claim by his interpretations of classical philosophical texts. His own writing is thus secondary and differential, in line with his view of language. See also **Deconstruction**.

Metaphysical Realism (= **Ladder Realism**) A form of religious consciousness for which the 'reality' of God consists in his being necessarily at the summit of a hierarchized ontology, or ladder of degrees of existence. In himself God is regarded as being at once supremely real and supremely intelligible; but because human beings are finite and are caught up in a world of mere appearance that is far removed from him, he seems to us to be distant, mysterious and even unknowable. A human being who would approach God must therefore undertake a lengthy spiritual journey, or discipline (= ascesis, whence 'asceticism') or ascent up the ladder of degrees of being. The journey requires the soul to turn away from the things of sense and of this world, and to fix its attention on all that is unchanging, universal, and purely intelligible. Eventually it reaches fulfilment by attaining the ultimate goal of life, pure rational intuition of the divine essence, the vision of God.

Militant Religious Humanism is otherwise known as Christian Socialism and Liberation Theology. The best-known forerunners of the modern movement are certain radical sects of the Reformation period, the Society of Friends, and the French Catholic priest F. R. de Lammenais (1782–1854). Here the use of a new term indicates that we avoid historical references and instead generalize the principles involved.

Modernism The state reached when the programme of the Enlightenment was completed and culture was re-centred upon the finite subject, man, in place of the infinite Subject, God. We associate this condition especially with the period between the

1890s and the 1920s, after Nietzsche had overthrown various residually theological or 'semi-realist' ideas such as the beliefs in progress, in a permanent and objective world-order, and in timeless objective moral values. The human subject then found himself solely responsible for defining himself and his world, for positing moral values and for creating meaning. In this new situation the past could offer no guidance, and the Modern movement in the arts therefore repudiated tradition and sought to make an entirely new beginning. The Modernist temper could range from resigned pessimism or godless despair to optimistic heroic humanism.

Modernism and Post-modernism When the Modern movement lost momentum, post-modernism sought a way of escape from its assumptions. It was pointed out that Modernism was still historicist in that it saw the Modern period as the logical outcome of previous developments and regarded thinkers and artists as being in a special way constrained by the age they lived in; and that Modernism was still theological, in that the 'Man' of atheistic humanism still bore the likeness of the God whose throne he had usurped. Post-moderns have therefore sought to escape from the tyranny of the ideas of linear time and historical period, and to de-centre or demythologize man the finite subject by exposing and criticizing the beliefs that metaphysical theism and atheistic humanism had held in common.

The philosophers of post-modernism are typically the anti-philosophers who seek to cure Western thought of the domination of theory over practice, of the idea of an intellectual world-above, of all absolute beginnings and endings, and of the notion of a single sovereign world-ordering will, whether divine or human. Everything becomes secondary, plural and relative, and rationality is seen as immanent within practices. There is a certain implicit turning to the East.

Its scepticism, pluralism and historical eclecticism mean that post-modernism can shelter a great variety of distinct spiritualities; a greater variety, indeed, than was permitted by the traditional metaphysics of theism-and-atheism. Hence the possibility of the present book.

Mythical Realism A form of religious consciousness in which religious objects are apprehended through an unsystematic miscellany of stories, symbols and pictures received from tradition. These images shape perception and action in an immediate and pre-theoretical way, appearing to arise spontaneously and acting to facilitate the expressive flow of life. The 'reality' of gods and spirits therefore consists of their unquestioned and immediately-experienced potency as life-shaping powers.

Obedientiary Realism A form of religious consciousness for which the 'reality' of God consists in his being the power that makes radical religious conversion possible; for God is that by which the believer, in a moment of ultimate despair and impotence, is enabled to break with the past and receive a new and supernatural form of life.

Objective Symbolism A form of religious consciousness in which it is acknowledged that all religious beliefs and practices are culturally conditioned and symbolic, but in which it is nevertheless believed that through the symbols believers have a mediated apprehension of, and genuine dealings with, the eternal and transcendent God. This position is **Semi-Realist** in that although it is believed that the symbolism has objective reference, it is acknowledged that there can be no standpoint from which the relation of the sign to the transcendent signified can be viewed, and that there can be no non-symbolic language in which it can be explained. Thus God's 'reality' is necessarily wholly mysterious to us.

Prescriptivism A theory of moral judgments that assimilates them to commands; or (more exactly) holds that they are in a strong and distinctive sense action-guiding, and that this is part of their very meaning. It is associated especially with R. M. Hare.

The Productive Life-energy The philosopher Schopenhauer made a basic distinction between the world as Will and the world as Representation. The Will was an everlasting impersonal and irrational energy striving ceaselessly to express itself, and coming into Representation through us as the world of our experience. This scheme provides a useful model for the philosophy of life, for it suggests that 'life' may be defined as a continual coming of the Will into symbolic representation. The resulting philosophical perspective is broadly idealistic: the mind is seen as dynamic, its primary activity being the generation of metaphors, symbols and fantasies. Great importance is attached to the creative artist, and to language – and indeed the whole of culture – as a system of signs. Language and the objective world are seen as being inseparably linked with each other.

Nietzsche, Freud and the many modern thinkers who have been influenced by them make much use of such a model, and I adopt it in this book. But the claim is minimal: I use the formula, 'The productive life-energy seeks maximal expression in representation' as a heuristic device for generating interpretations – but that is *all*, for I do not intend to revert to **Foundationalism**.

Protestant Ethical Idealism A primarily ethical form of religious consciousness, for which the chief objects of religious veneration and practical obedience are a group of timeless and intrinsically-authoritative ethical ideals, standards or values. Christ is seen as their historical teacher, although they may also be acknowledged in other religions and philosophies and by people of good will generally. God is seen as incorporating them all within himself, so that his nature is their unity. God is also seen as the Creator, at least in the sense that through the course of history these values are becoming ever more widely diffused and realized, so that God and the world, what ought to be and what is, are moving steadily into coincidence.

Realism and Anti-realism In mediaeval times, realism was belief in the real existence of universals (the Platonic Forms), apart from the individuals which exemplify them. This was a realism about noumenal or intellectual objects and standards of thought. In modern times 'realism' is more often used to mean belief in the reality of the external world. Idealists think that the world-order is constituted by the mind; realists believe that there is a permanent and mind-independent objective and orderly world. Kant claimed to be a realist, by way of attempting to distinguish his view from that of George Berkeley, whom he regarded as a subjective idealist; but nowadays Kant, like modern constructivists, is regarded as holding a view intermediate between idealism and realism.

The term **Anti-realism** was introduced by Nietzsche and has recently come to be widely used. The American Nelson Goodman has also used the term 'irrealism'. The basic idea is that, rather as there are several geometries and ways of constructing space, so the world may be construed differently under different languages and systems of thought, several of which may be entirely workable; and we have no way of taking up an absolute standpoint for assessment from which we can judge that one way of world-making is correct and the others are incorrect. Thus anti-realism is equivalent to perspectivism: there are many perspectival viewpoints, but there is no absolute and perspectiveless vision of things.

Spirituality In later classical times to belong to one of the major philosophical schools was to be committed, not only to a set of teachings and a view of life, but also to a discipline and a life-path that would lead to blessedness. Something of this ancient meaning of philosophy survives in popular usage, but after Descartes (for reasons discussed in the Prologue) Western philosophy tended to become chiefly concerned with the theory of human knowledge and to contract in scope. Philosophy gradually dissociated itself from religion, and became secularized. So we use the term 'a spirituality', or sometimes 'a form of religious consciousness', to mean a complete practical philosophy of life in the older sense. A religion may be seen as a social institution and set of symbolic practices which makes one or more spiritualities widely available to people.

Synergism The doctrine that the human will may co-operate with God in bringing about our regeneration. High orthodoxy teaches the sole agency of God, and regards synergism as a version of the Pelagian heresy.

Theological Realism The theory that religious objects such as God and spirits are distinct, objectively-existing quasi-personal beings independent of the believer's consciousness, and experienced as sources of energy, or powers. Religious beliefs are therefore understood as describing or at least as referring to objective beings, states of affairs and supernaturally-caused occurrences; and the truth of such beliefs is seen as lying in their correspondence with what is the case. Theological realism takes many and very varied forms.

Voluntarism A system of thought, often associated with political theories of absolute sovereignty, which maintains in a thorough-going way the primacy and creative freedom of the will. The quest for an ultimate ground or explanation of things therefore terminates in a fiat, choice or decision of the will, and not in necessitating reasons. This brings voluntarism close to positivism, for the regress of why-questions is in both cases forcibly halted, in the one case by brute facts and in the other by the inscrutable decree of a competent will. **Theological Voluntarism** of the kind associated with William of Ockham and Calvin considers that it would be unduly anthropomorphic, and would detract from God's omnipotence, to picture the decision of his will as being in any way influenced by anything antecedent to it or independent of it. It therefore asserts that the world, the moral order, the destinies of human souls, and even the laws of logic are constituted by the eternal and unconditional decree of God's will. When, as a result of the Enlightenment, Western thought was reconstructed around man, and many of the attributes of God were transferred to man, a number of thinkers (including Kant, Fichte, Stirner, Feuerbach, Nietzsche and Sartre) began to develop a voluntarism of the finite subject. This attributes to the individual human being, or, more plausibly, to the whole human realm of language and social practice, much of the legislative, world-ordering and value-positing power that had in the past been ascribed to God. **Pure Religious Voluntarism,** in response to this, asserts that modern nihilism is now so extreme (and it includes the self) that there is no escape from it except by spontaneous, groundless upsurge of creative faith. This event is represented around the world in myths of creation, rebirth and resurrection, but it cannot strictly be ascribed either to God or to the self, because it is prior to the arising of any distinction between them. Thus pure religious voluntarism is an extreme form of religious existentialism, asserting the gratuitousness and the inexplicability of both exist-ence and faith.

Notes

Prologue

1. Robert Nozick, *Philosophical Explanations*, Clarendon Press 1981, pp.571ff.
2. William James, *The Varieties of Religious Experience*, Longmans 1902; Fontana edition 1960.
3. Andrew Louth, *The Origins of the Christian Mystical Tradition*, Clarendon Press 1981, p.xv.

Chapter 1

The argument of this Chapter is new, but related material may be found, for example, in Jean Piaget's many books on these topics, and in Ian D. Suttie, *The Origins of Love and Hate*, Routledge 1935; John Macmurray, *Persons in Relation*, Faber and Faber 1961; and for something completely different, Gilles Deleuze and Felix Guattari, *Anti-Oedipus*, Editions de Minuit 1972; English trans., University of Minnesota 1983 and Athlone Press 1984.

Chapter 4

1. All this is very clearly explained in A. H. Armstrong and R. A. Markus, *Christian Faith and Greek Philosophy*, Darton, Longman and Todd 1960.
2. The interpretation of Plotinus' precise meaning here is controversial. See Armstrong and Markus, op. cit., pp.11–12; J. M. Rist, *Plotinus: The Road to Reality*, Cambridge University Press 1967, ch.3.
3. As for example in the contrast between 'religiousness A' and 'religiousness B' in the *Concluding Unscientific Postscript*, 1846.

Chapter 5

1. Iris Murdoch, *The Sovereignty of Good*, Routledge and Kegan Paul 1970, p.55.

2. Ibid. Iris Murdoch's views are further discussed in Chapter 14, below.

3. Richard Swinburne, *The Coherence of Theism*, Clarendon Press 1977, p.1.

4. The English-language literature on all this is well-known. For an interesting French view of the crisis of representation, the end of realism, and its consequences, see J.-F. Lyotard, *The Postmodern Condition: A Report on Knowledge*, Les Editions de Minuit 1979; English trans., University of Minnesota 1984 and Manchester University Press 1984.

5. James Thomson, 'Ode to the Memory of Sir Isaac Newton', 1727; cited in Gerd Buchdahl, *The Image of Newton and Locke in the Age of Reason*, Sheed and Ward 1961, p.56.

6. Ibid., p.62.

7. Ibid., p.59.

8. In the USA Dr Darrell J. Fasching particularly stresses these themes. See, for example, his *The Thought of Jacques Ellul: A Systematic Exposition*, Edwin Mellen Press 1981.

Chapter 6

1. Jacques Le Goff, *The Birth of Purgatory*, Gallimard 1981; English trans., University of Chicago 1984, and Scolar Press 1984.

Chapter 7

1. Leo Tolstoy, *A Confession, and What I Believe*, Oxford University Press (World's Classics series) n.d., p.222.

2. Ibid., pp.231ff.

3. See Leo Tolstoy, *The Kingdom of God and Peace Essays*, Oxford University Press (World's Classics series), n.d., p.ix.

4. Leo Tolstoy, *Essays and Letters*, Oxford University Press (World's Classics series), 1903, p.154.

5. Tolstoy, *A Confession, and What I Believe*, p.76.

6. Ibid.

7. Ibid., p.77.

8. Ibid.

9. Matthew Arnold, *Literature and Dogma*, 1873, XII.

10. Tolstoy, *Essays and Letters*, pp.149ff.

11. Ibid., p.150.

12. Ibid., pp.292, 312.

13. Ibid., p.328.

14. For example in Albert Schweitzer, *My Life and Thought*, Allen & Unwin 1933, passages in Chs XIII, XVI, XVII, XXI; and *The Philosophy of Civilisation*, University Presses of Florida edition, 1981, esp. chs. 22–27.

Chapter 8

1. See D. E. Nineham, *Explorations in Theology 1*, SCM Press 1977, p.66.

2. Ibid., p.4.

3. Nineham's fullest statement is to be found in *The Use and Abuse of the Bible*, Macmillan 1976.

4. H.-G. Gadamer, *Truth and Method*, Sheed & Ward, and Continuum, New York 1975, p.263.

5. Aquinas, *Summa Theologiae*, 1a, 13.

Chapter 9

1. R. Rubinstein, *After Auschwitz*, Bobbs-Merrill Co., Inc. 1966.

2. Naguib Mahfouz, *Children of Gebelawi*, Cairo 1959, Heinemann 1981.

3. A. K. Ramanujan, *Speaking of Siva*, Penguin Books 1973.

4. Margaret Smith, *The Way of the Mystics*, Sheldon Press 1976.

5. Søren Kierkegaard, *Works of Love*, 1847, English trans., Collins 1962, p.247.

6. Martin Heidegger, *Being and Time* 1927, English trans., Blackwell 1962.

Chapter 10

1. Immanuel Kant, *Critique of Judgment*, 1790, esp. §§57–59.

2. Allen Megill, *Prophets of Extremity*, University of California 1985, Introduction.

3. Martin Heidegger, *An Introduction to Metaphysics*, 1953, English trans., Anchor Books 1961, p.31. Cited by Megill, op. cit., p.140.

4. Cited by Megill, p.136.

5. See J. Wesley Robbins, 'In defence of Attitudinal Christianity', *Religious Studies*, 18 (1982), pp.11–27. Two of Hare's lectures were reprinted in Gene Outka and John P. Reeder Jr. (eds), *Religion and Morality*, Anchor Books 1973.

Chapter 11

1. Rowan Williams, 'Religious Realism: On not Quite Agreeing with Don Cupitt', *Modern Theology*, Vol. 1, No. 1, October 1984, pp.3–24.

2. There is a useful collection of creation-myths in Mircea Eliade, *From Primitives to Zen*, Collins 1979, ch.II.

3. See Nietzsche's critique of Socrates, the prototype of 'theoretical man', beginning with *The Birth of Tragedy*, XIIIff.; Heidegger, *Being and Time*, Blackwell 1972, pp.409f.; Foucault and Derrida in Megill, op. cit. (though I think Megill may misunderstand Foucault), pp.215–18; Rorty, *Philosophy and the Mirror of Nature*, passim. Megill also cites Levinas' attack on the dominance of the metaphoric of light in Husserl.

Chapter 12

1. F. H. Bradley, *Ethical Studies*, second edition, Clarendon Press 1927, p.313.

2. Ibid., p.319.

3. Ibid., pp.320ff.

4. Bradley, *Appearance and Reality* 1893, chs.xxvf.

5. Citations from the translation published by Penguin Books.

6. At the time of writing, Philip Glass is reported to be composing an opera based on Lessing's novel.

7. Rudolf Bultmann, 'New Testament and Mythology', in *Kerygma and Myth*, ed. H. W. Bartsch, SPCK 1972, pp.38ff; and Bultmann's replies to his critics in the same volume.

8. The case for an 'atheistic' interpretation of Bonhoeffer is briefly and well stated, with documentation, in Jean Milet, *God or Christ?*, Paris 1980; English trans., SCM Press 1981, pp.190ff.

9. Foucault's concern for deviants and outsiders was constant. See, for example *Madness and Civilisation*, Librarie Plon 1961; English trans., Tavistock Publications 1967; and *Discipline and Punish*, Gallimard 1975; English trans., Penguin Books 1977.

Chapter 13

1. See Elizabeth Dipple, *Iris Murdoch: Work for the Spirit*, Methuen 1982.

2. Mark C. Taylor, *Erring: A postmodern A/theology*, University of Chicago 1984, is a particularly useful work. See also Vincent Descombes, *Modern French Philosophy*, Cambridge University Press 1980; and Roland Barthes, *Image-Music-Text*, Fontana Paperbacks 1977. Five or six of Derrida's books are now available in translation, and the works of Lyotard and Deleuze are also strongly recommended. Megill's book, cited in ch.10, n.2, is good on Derrida but less so on Foucault.

3. Iris Murdoch, *The Sovereignty of Good*, Routledge and Kegan Paul 1970, p.51.

4. Ibid., p.71.

5. Ibid., p.68.

6. Stewart R. Sutherland, *God, Jesus and Belief*, Blackwell 1984, pp.95ff.

Chapter 14

1. I assume in this account the position of those liberation theologians who recognize that the church's task cannot be completed within the historical order. Thus in Nicaragua many Christians identified themselves wholeheartedly with the struggle that led to the coming to power of the Sandinista régime. But they cannot completely identify themselves with the new government once it is in power. The end is not yet. See Leonardo Boff, *Jesus Christ Liberator*, SPCK 1979.

2. *Introduction to Metaphysics*, as cited in ch.10, n.3, p.37.

3. See the treatment of Hilary Burde and the *Peter Pan* theme in Iris Murdoch, *A Word Child*, Chatto 1975.

4. Arthur Schopenhauer, *The World as Will and as Representation*, §71; Dover Books edition 1969, Vol. 1, pp.408ff.

5. Møller's articles are reprinted in *The Corsair Affair (Kierkegaard's Writings*, Vol. XIII), Princeton University Press 1982.

6. *Madness and Civilisation*, as cited in ch.12, n.9; ch.1.

7. Jacques Derrida, *Writing and Difference*, Seuil 1966; English trans. University of Chicago 1978 and Routledge and Kegan Paul 1978, ch.2, 'Cogito and the History of Madness', pp.31–63.

8. Ibid., p.310 n.28.

Chapter 15

1. See, for example, Alasdair MacIntyre, *After Virtue*, Duckworth 1981, ch.5.

2. Chapter 1, above.

3. E.g. Jürgen Habermas and Niklas Luhmann, *Theorie der Gesellschaft oder Sozialtechnologie – Was Leistet die Systemforschung?*, Frankfurt 1971; Raymond Geuss, *The Idea of a Critical Theory: Habermas and the Frankfurt School*, Cambridge University Press 1981, pp.65–81.

4. Allen Megill, *Prophets of Extremity* (cited above, ch.10, n.2), pp.247–52.

5. Dietrich Bonhoeffer, letter of 5 May 1944, in *Letters and Papers from Prison*, Enlarged Edition, SCM Press 1971, p.286.

6. Karl Barth, *Church Dogmatics* III/3, 50. Citations here and in the remainder of this chapter are from the standard English translation (T. & T. Clark 1961). John Hick discusses exactly the same material, but from an entirely different perspective, in *Evil and the God of Love*, Macmillan 1966, ch.6, 4–9.

7. See, for example, Nicholas Watkins, *Matisse*, Phaidon Press 1977, p.13.

8. In its favour, notice the interesting convergences between Derrida and the later Wittgenstein, very well discussed in Henry Staten, *Wittgenstein and Derrida*, Blackwell 1985.

9. By way of making the point that the same well-written text is open to entirely different readings, I have cited the same passages from Barth that John Hick cites. In the Barth English translation, they are to be found on pp.289, 351, 354.

Chapter 16

1. See Roland Barthes, *Camera Lucida*, Jonathan Cape 1982.

2. Jacques Derrida, *Of Grammatology*, Paris 1967; English trans., Johns Hopkins University Press 1974, pp.158–9.

3. Ibid.

4. Ibid.; and see the comments by Barbara Johnson on this in her introduction to Jacques Derrida, *Dissemination*, Paris 1972, English trans., University of Chicago 1981, pp.x-xvi.

5. Ibid., p.xv.

6. See ch.1, above.

7. I am here again much in debt to Mark C. Taylor's *Erring*, cited above, ch.13, n.2.

8. Albert Schweitzer, *Von Reimarus de Wrede*, 1906; English trans., *The Quest of the Historical Jesus*, third edition, A. and C. Black 1954, reissued SCM Press 1981, p.284. Translation slightly amended.

Index of Names

d'Alembert, J. le R., 65
Andersen, H., 24
Anselm, 162
Aquinas, Thomas, 97f., 227
Aristotle, 5, 48
Armstrong, A. H., 225
Arnold, M., 85, 226
Artaud, A., 176
Augustine, 39, 163, 207
Austen, J., 168f.

Barth, K., 94, 99, 186f., 191, 229
Barthes, R., 192, 228f.
Bartsch, H.-W., 228
Bataille, G., 176
Beckett, S., 125
Bellarmine, R., 4
Bergson, H., 24
Berkeley, G., 62, 222
Blake, W., 175
Boff, L., 228
Bonaventure, 4
Bonhoeffer, D., 149, 186, 228f.
Bradley, F. H., 143ff., 227f.
Breughel, P., the Younger, 153
Bruno, G., 50
Buchdahl, G., 226
Buddha, Buddhism, 3, 24, 90, 123,
   130, 192, 197ff., 216
Bultmann, R., 94, 99, 113, 149,
   211, 228

Calvin, J., 44, 224
Camus, A., 1, 70, 145–7

Carroll, L., 24
Chateaubriand, F. R., 120
Chomsky, N., 20
Cicero, 66
Clement of Alexandria, 207
Cousin, V., 120

Darwin, C., 10, 21, 86, 90, 179,
   185, 209, 216f.
Deleuze, G., 225, 228
Derrida, J., 116, 137, 159, 172f.,
   193ff., 197, 203, 216, 218f.,
   227ff.
Descartes, R., 6, 8, 50, 117, 136,
   173, 223
Descombes, V., 228
Dipple, E., 228
Dostoyevsky, F., 175

Einstein, A., 58
Eliade, M., 227

Fasching, D. J., 226
Feuerbach, L. A., 208, 224
Fichte, J. G., 120, 224
Foucault, M., 137, 142, 145, 150,
   172–6, 183ff., 203, 227f.
Freud, S., 10, 24, 33, 35, 38, 75,
   137, 161, 185, 222

Gadamer, H.-G., 96, 227
Geuss, R., 229
Gioberti, V., 50
Glass, P., 228

Goodman, N., 223
Grimm, the Brothers, 24
Guattari, E., 225

Habermas, J., 183f., 229
Hare, R. M., 126, 221, 227
Harnack, A. von, 81
Hegel, G. W. E., 3f., 9ff., 24, 114,
   125f., 136, 155, 157ff., 170f.,
   174, 188, 197, 203f., 216, 218
Heidegger, M., 11, 37, 67, 99,
   112f., 121f., 125, 137, 147f.,
   168, 203, 227
Hick, J. H., 229
Hodgson, L., 94f., 101
Hume, D., 61, 65, 206
Husserl, E., 227
Huxley, T. H., 88
Hyppolite, J., 157

Inge, W. R., 92

James, W., 4, 225
John, Evangelist, 47
John of the Cross, 4
Johnson, B., 229
Julian of Norwich, 154
Jung, C. G., 28, 121f.

Kant, I., 61, 65, 70, 73, 83, 86, 93,
   101, 114, 116, 118ff., 159, 206,
   222, 224, 227
Kierkegaard, S., 9ff., 49, 72ff., 93,
   110f., 129, 137, 139, 155,
   170ff., 174, 203, 216, 227f.
Küng, H., 85

Lammenais, F. R. de, 219
Laplace, M. de, 65
Le Goff, J., 71, 226
Lessing, D., 147, 228
Levinas, E., 227
Louth, A., 4, 225
Luhmann, N., 229
Luther, M., 41
Lyotard, J. E., 226, 228

MacIntyre, A., 229

Macmurray, J., 225
Mahfouz, N., 107f., 227
Malebranche, N., 50
Malthus, T. R., 179
Manet, E., 188
Maréchal, J., 11
Markus, R. A., 225
Marx, K., 10, 35, 114, 137, 159,
   161, 175, 218
Matisse, H., 188f., 229
Megill, A., 227ff.
Milet, J., 228
Møller, P. L., 172, 228
Montaigne, M. de, 217
Murdoch, I., 54f., 161–4, 168,
   225f., 228

Newton, I., 9, 58, 64f., 117f.
Nietzsche, F. W., 3, 10, 24, 35ff.,
   87f., 90f., 114, 116, 119, 126,
   137, 139, 155ff., 185, 203, 218,
   220, 222, 224, 227
Nineham, D. E., 94ff., 100, 226f.
Nozick, R., 225

Outka, G., 227

Paine, T., 106
Pascal, B., 218
Paul, 47, 76, 97
Piaget, J., 225
Plato, Platonism, 4f., 47f., 50ff.,
   54f., 57, 81f., 84, 86, 137, 156,
   161ff., 169, 189, 204, 207, 216,
   218
Plotinus, 47, 205
Pope, A., 58
Popper, K. R., 17
Potter, B., 24

Quine, W. V. O., 196

Ramanujan, A. K., 227
Reeder, J. P., Jr, 227
Rist, J. M., 225
Robbins, J. W., 227
Rorty, R., 137, 227
Rousseau, J.-J., 194ff.

Rosmini-Serbati, A., 50
Rubinstein, R., 107

Sartre, J.-P., 1, 61, 70, 161, 224
Saussure, F. de, 212
Schelling, F. W. J. von, 119f., 125
Schiller, F. von, 119
Schleiermacher, F. D. E., 120
Schopenhauer, A., 24, 86, 90f.,
   160ff., 169f., 179, 185, 217,
   221, 228
Schweitzer, A., 81, 90, 149, 200f.,
   217, 226, 229
Sheridan, R. B., 133
Simmel, G., 13
Smith, M., 227
Spinoza, B., 6, 24, 50
Stirner, M., 130, 224
Staten, H., 229
Strauss, D. F., 114

Stravinsky, I., 157
Sutherland, S. R., 228
Suttie, I. D., 225
Swinburne, R. G., 59, 226

Taylor, M. C., 228f.
Thompson, J., 65, 226
Tolstoy, L., 81–91, 169, 226

Velasquez, D. de, 213
Victoria, 108
Voltaire, 38

Watkins, N., 229
Weil, S., 125, 161, 164
Whitehead, A. N., 11
William of Ockham, 224
Williams, R. D., 227
Wittgenstein, L., 61, 158, 193,
   204, 213, 229